Archibald Milne Hamilton was Born in 1898 in New Zealand. An early interest in all things scientific would endure throughout his life. After graduating from university with a Bachelor of Engineering, Hamilton worked on several projects in New Zealand and in 1926 joined the British Admiralty team involved in designing the new Singapore Naval Base. In 1927 he became engineer in charge of Diwaniyah in Iraq and later transferred to Kurdistan, where he would spend the next four years of his life. He died, aged 74, in 1972.

David McDowall is a specialist on Middle Eastern affairs and is the author *of A Modern History of the Kurds* and *Palestine and Israel* (both I.B.Tauris).

D0878640

SYSTEM

Tauris Parke Paperbacks is an imprint of I.B.Tauris. It is dedicated to publishing books in accessible paperback editions for the serious general reader within a wide range of categories, including biography, history, travel, art and the ancient world. The list includes select, critically acclaimed works of top quality writing by distinguished authors that continue to challenge, to inform and to inspire. These are books that possess those subtle but intrinsic elements that mark them out as something exceptional.

The colophon of Tauris Parke Paperbacks is a representation of the ancient Egyptian ibis, sacred to the god Thoth, who was himself often depicted in the form of this most elegant of birds. Thoth was credited in antiquity as the scribe of the ancient Egyptian gods and as the inventor of writing and was associated with many aspects of wisdom and learning.

ROAD THROUGH KURDISTAN:

Travels in Northern Iraq

A. M. HAMILTON

Introduction by David McDowall

TPP

TAURIS PARKE
PAPERBACKS

Published in 2004 by Tauris Parke Paperbacks
I.B. Tauris & Co Ltd
6 Salem Road, London W2 4BU
175 Fifth Avenue, New York NY 10010
www.ibtauris.com

In the United States of America and Canada distributed by
Palgrave Macmillan a division of St. Martin's Press
175 Fifth Avenue, New York NY 10010

First published in 1937 by Faber and Faber Limited
Second impression 1958
Copyright © 1937, 1958, 2004 by Archibald Milne Hamilton
New material © 2004 by David McDowall

ISBN 1 85043 637 1
EAN 978 1 85043 637 9

A full CIP record for this book is available from the British Library
A full CIP record is available from the Library of Congress

Library of Congress Catalog Card Number: available

Typeset in Monotype Times
Printed and bound in Great Britain by MPG Books Ltd, Bodmin

Cover image reproduced with kind permission by Corbis © Ed Kashi/Corbis

Acknowledgement

I have to thank all those who have so kindly lent me photographs and I wish especially to thank Miss Ella Sykes for her invaluable help in the preparation of this book.

A. M. H.

Contents

Illustrations

9

Illustrations

Maps

═════════

Introduction

My own copy of Archibald Hamilton's *Road Through Kurdistan: The Narrative of an Engineer in Iraq* has been sitting on a family bookshelf since its publication. My father was a young R.A.F. officer stationed in Iraq shortly after Hamilton had completed the road to Rowanduz in 1932, after four years' arduous and perilous struggle. Like many officers and civil servants of the British imperial presence in Iraq in those days, my father sought respite from the stifling summer heat in the hills of Kurdistan, where he very quickly fell for the tough, dignified and self-possessed people of the mountains. Like many of his peers, my father must have rushed out to buy Hamilton's book on publication. I first read it almost forty years ago, when I knew virtually nothing about the Kurds and still less about Iraq. But I do remember being entranced. Shortly after, I had the good fortune to drive along Hamilton's road through the fabled gorge of Gali Ali Beg. Even in 1971, forty years after its construction, the road still seemed breathtaking in its daring. It was impossible not to wonder how Hamilton and his team had ever managed to establish a foothold on the sheer cliff face, let alone cut a road into it. Until then no wheeled traffic had ever reached Rowanduz from the Mesopotamian Plain. Everything had travelled on mule or horseback. It was not difficult to see why, for the approaches to Rowanduz were impeded by sheer cliffs and raging torrents. As one young political officer, unembarrassed by his own purple prose, wrote, 'Never have I seen Nature so terrible as she is here. With what fearful stroke can she have cloven these mountain masses, or with what years of labour delved these mighty chasms.'

The principal claim of Hamilton's work on our attention, then, is as the account of a great engineering feat carried out in an extremely wild place and with a workforce of mainly tribal people. It is full of colour, humour and excitement, straight out of *Boys' Own*. When it was first reviewed on publication, Vladimir Minorsky, a scholar with a deep knowledge of the region, wrote that while the book had no pretence of learning, it was nevertheless:

> 'a very humane and understanding account of all people whom he came across in Kurdistan: rival chieftains, warring tribes, and the motley crowd of Kurds, Arabs, Assyrians, Armenians and Turks employed on the road . . . a book which conquers the reader by its freshness, warm sympathy to men and a keen gift for observation.'

And there, indeed, one could leave it without further discussion, for the book is perfect bathtub reading.

Readers with a scholarly interest, however, should be a little cautious. Some names are deliberately fictitious, for example John Glubb, who defeated the Wahhabi threat in southern Iraq in the 1920s, appears as 'Captain Glover'. Other British officers are likewise disguised, recognisable probably to themselves and their colleagues but not to the then public. (Their true identity is revealed in an epilogue to the 1958 edition). Moreover, Hamilton knew little about the Kurdish political world other than what he heard either directly or from British colleagues. What he was told by Kurds was sometimes highly coloured either by tribal pride or dislike, while what he learnt from British officers had been perceived through the prism of British imperial interests. Inasmuch as we now understand better some of the political characteristics of tribal life, we are indebted to the painstaking studies of Martin van Bruinessen and others.

What Hamilton does superbly well, however, is to describe his own life and encounters during this remarkable experience. He was not alone in recording his adventures in Kurdistan. Three political and administrative officers: Rupert Hay, C.J. Edmonds and Wallace Lyon all wrote about their time in Kurdistan in this brief period of Iraqi history. Each casts his own particular light on the lonely life led by imperial servants. One cannot but have regard for the quality, integrity and courage of men such as these, and for their evident respect for the people over whom they were given authority.

Hamilton's book is markedly different in tone from the books of these men. Unlike them, he had no political authority and no need to read the political landscape except inasmuch as it affected his task. But he had to build a road and this required not only great engineering skill but also the co-operation of local people, both those who worked for him and also the local chiefs. Hamilton was engaged in a creative and heroic enterprise. To succeed he needed to forge a 'band of brothers', albeit from varied cultural and linguistic origins. That he was able to do so was evidence of his personal qualities of leadership. Whatever hair-raising task he asked of his men, he was also willing to do himself.

Hamilton was a New Zealander, born in 1898 and brought up in a much more democratic and egalitarian society than prevailed in class-ridden Britain at this time. It was a far better grounding for the task in hand, one that depended as much on consent as on obedience. Hamilton saw in his Kurdish and Assyrian tribesmen the same virtues and, doubtless, vices as in his own Scots forebears and this romantic sense of affinity must have communicated itself to them. He evidently enjoyed the highest regard of all who came into contact with him. But with his British colleagues he shared the quality of self-effacement. And, typically for a New Zealander, he was evidently very direct in his dealings, something which stood him in good stead when sorting out misunderstandings with local leaders and the innumerable quarrels and tensions within his workforce.

Hamilton died in 1972 after a distinguished career. In the late 1930s he designed a bridge for military use ten times stronger than its predecessors and also faster to erect. It stemmed directly from the challenges he faced in Kurdistan. His work thus gave Britain a technical lead in this field on the eve of war. In later life he and his wife acquired a reputation for the encouragement and help they gave young aspiring engineers. In 1936 a son, William, had been born to the Hamiltons in Cairo, a boy who grew up imbued with his mother's love of nature and natural shyness but his father's spirit of adventure. It was perhaps typical that Bill Hamilton should have lost three finger-tips, tinkering with explosives as a teenager; that he should have leapt off a boat in the Amazon as a young man to plug the leak, dismissing the ferocity of piranhas as greatly exaggerated. But he was destined for great things. In 1964 he published the first scientifically-argued recognition of the self-ish gene and proved to be one of the great evolutionary biologists of the twentieth century. He died relatively young, in 2000. We may not know what or how much he owed to his mother, but to get some idea of his father's legacy, you can do no better than read this wonderful book.

David McDowall
Richmond, 2004

1. Arbil

CHAPTER I

Land of Eternal Conflict

From whatever quarter the city is approached no one can forget his first sight of Baghdad as it appears on the flat horizon—tall minarets and even taller factory chimneys thrusting above the date palms and the domes of mosques. Often above the venerable town there hangs a pall of smoke. Factory chimneys and minarets! A strange combination: all of them leaning a little this way or that.

When the hot sun beats on the desert the mirage makes the whole silhouette stand clear of the earth, and it shimmers and waves above the skyline. Like the floating island of Laputa it seems to move over the land from place to place. Even today, half-modernized, half-antiquated, Baghdad can yet look a magic city as of old.

As one comes closer this visionary effect diminishes till in the outskirts of the town the romance of the place is lost in squalid streets. Baghdad has only two main thoroughfares; the rest of the city is for the most part a rabbit-warren of flat-roofed houses built haphazard beside the Tigris River. The incoming road from the west crosses a railway-line which is actually a part of the famous Berlin-Baghdad railway planned by Germany for the conquest of India—a dream of the Kaiser's that never materialized.

During my years of service in Iraq I visited Baghdad many times. I came to it from the deserts of the south and from the mountains of the north—often enough sick and fever-ridden seeking the healing treatment of its well-run hospital. And just as with travellers of old who rode in on their camels from the dusty desert, Baghdad never failed to make its impression on me. It has a gaudy yet dreary grandeur in keeping with the barren plains around, and to the Arab mind Baghdad is Paradise itself.

The angels in this heaven, however, are of a very motley variety. The jostling, wrangling crowd of shopkeepers in the bazaars crying their wares vie with the louts and mannerless street urchins who pounce upon the newly-arrived visitor like vultures, and make him wish he had stayed in the silent and empty desert. If he can escape these birds of prey while they fight each other for the right to accompany him as guides, interpreters and whatnot, and board a horse-

19

drawn 'arabana' with its decrepit steeds and noisy bell, he may at last find some quiet lane where a sleepy carpet vendor who speaks no English will let him sit and smoke amongst the rugs and junk of his incense-scented den. Quietness is to be found in this garish town if one knows where to seek it, for Baghdad's ancient name is Dar-es-Salaam —the House of Peace.

The wide river, too, is peaceful enough except when the 'shemal' or north wind blows, and the floating Maude Bridge rocks and tears at its anchorage. In a way that even the smoking factory-chimneys cannot efface, Baghdad at night, seen from the verandas high above the river where 'Baghdadis' love to sit and gossip, is a wonderful sight. Lights gleam in the rippling water, and the round 'ghuffas', loaded to the gunwale with melons from Samarrah, steal silently to the landing-stages, while the 'sofinas' with their burden of dates from the south go sailing by. A steamboat whistles and stirs up the river-mud with its paddle-wheel, rousing curses from the fisherman who stands, his naked body shining like a bronze statue, patiently casting his net from the high nose of his anchored boat.

Women come and go over the bridge. There are batches of tribal women who fetch their produce for the morrow's market; Armenian women with white 'abbas' over their heads; women well-dressed and ill-dressed, some in western clothes, some in eastern robes, some veiled, some unveiled; women with voices harsh and querulous, or beneath lifted veil caressingly seductive to the men who pass; but most are silent, soft-footed creatures gliding swiftly by like veiled spirits, bent on their own mysterious affairs.

Here and there on the river's banks are cabarets with strings of coloured lights, and raucous saxophone bands, the quavering singing of the 'artistes' punctuated by the deep throbbing of large engines in the ice-factory nearby. Over the water comes the weird music of the Bedouin emanating from the 'chaikhanas' or tea-shops, red with the glow of cooking braziers.

From the street that ends at the bridge one hears the dismal cries of cigarette and sweet vendors chanting their wares in Arabic, 'Cigarettes, three for a "fils", three for a "fils".'[1] Sometimes yells and altercations arise, followed by the blowing of police-whistles, but the jingle of horse and donkey bells, the grunting of camels, and the calls of bargees and fishermen soon join together to drown this discord.

Now dimly, now clearly against the reflections of a myriad lamps on the opposite bank one sees moving figures, the working women who come down to the water's edge, fill their 'mesakhin' or water-gourds, wash themselves and their children in the sluggish current by the bridge and under cover of the darkness steal off to their homes again. As the hour advances the streets, the bridge, the cabarets

---

[1] A 'fils' is about a farthing.

20

and the coffee-shops grow still in sleep and only the ancient river flows on unceasing.

To this city of Baghdad I came, in January 1928, to join the Iraq Public Works Department. My first station was as Engineer-in-Charge of the district or 'liwa' of Diwaniyah, some hundred and twenty miles south on the Euphrates river, and my orders were to start at once, taking with me the wherewithal to establish a household.

In Baghdad I bought a Chevrolet car and was introduced to Hassan. Hassan was brought to me by his friend Charlie, who was boy-about-the-house or 'bearer' to my first host in Iraq, the Director of my new Department. Hassan spoke English of a sort, wore dilapidated European clothes and had an expansive smile that displayed a prominent gold tooth in which he took great pride. He produced a document of military origin which gave his photograph on the first page (an elegant young man with a black moustache strangely belying his present seedy appearance), and stated that he had served as bearer to several officers of His Majesty's Forces. He seemed from his certificates to be possessed of the most surprising virtues, and his previous employers had apparently parted from him with the greatest reluctance. Why they had eventually found it necessary to discharge such a paragon at all was veiled in mystery.

Hassan was a Kurd from Bitlis in the far north and said he wished to accompany me on my travels. He told me I must not gather the impression that he required any wages for this; but in order that he might do full justice to my honourable position in the country he felt that some money was needed to keep up his appearance as my language tutor, interpreter and ambassador. He added that he would always regard my life and property as his own. With regard to the latter assertion, at least, he spoke the truth!

I ascertained that forty rupees a month was considered fair wages for a bearer, so I gave him fifty to keep him honest and engaged him, and he served me well for many a day on the desert plains of Diwaniyah.

In the buying of my household gear and in the packing of it on the new car Hassan excelled himself. Western owners of motor cars cannot have the faintest idea of what a car's carrying capacity really is. To the Eastern mind a car doesn't *look* a car unless it has boxes piled to the hood on the back seat, bedding roped between the mudguards and the bonnet, petrol tins strapped on the running-boards, and spare tyres, an iron bedstead or two, and a few chairs loaded on the carrier. The main idea is to get as much gear sticking out sideways as possible, because this will obstruct other cars that pass and help to make pleasant repartee between drivers—especially if a wind-screen should get broken by hitting the end of a bedstead projecting from the car in front. As the vehicles are always crammed to capacity, I found that Arab passengers often choose to stand or sit on the running-boards, and now and then are bowled off by the overhanging gear on a passing car. Such incidents, together with a few highway robberies, make the roads of Iraq most interesting, just as the perpetual use of old-fashioned tooters and loud klaxons make them melodious.

When I bought my car in Baghdad I decided to enter thoroughly into the Eastern spirit of things. We loaded the Chevrolet to Hassan's entire satisfaction. The boxes of crockery and glass and bottles occupied the safest places on the back seat, for I was assured that any loss of beverages or tonics was a serious matter to a household 'out in the blue'. Then we packed the little car till it bulged on every side, and to every bulge and every bracket we hitched something or other till the vehicle looked like a Christmas tree on wheels.

After a last checking of petrol and water I climbed in over the rope-bound doors beside Hassan, who sat in lordly state wearing his best red fez. I let in the clutch of our brand new car, and we slithered out on to the strip of mud that was called the road to Diwaniyah—and so my adventures began.

This was in winter, the time of year when the roads of Iraq can be really muddy, and it so happened that when I set forth it had been raining hard for two days. The hundred and twenty mile 'road' to Diwaniyah was nothing more than a deeply-rutted track with an earth surface—no road-formation, no metalling—and after the rain it proved to be a squelching morass. Very few cars were attempting the journey, but with the aid of skid-chains, we bravely ploughed and splashed and bumped along.

We passed through several Arab villages, where children shouted at us in derision, pitched clods at us and grabbed at the back of the car to try to steal a ride, as children will do the world over: Hassan had to get out at times to chase them away.

A little over half-way betwen Diwaniyah and Baghdad we came to Babylon. The bad roads had made us late and we still had fifty miles to run, so I decided I must come back some other time to explore these ruins as they deserved. The fabulous old city looked as ancient as the desert itself as I drove by. Its walls, half-excavated, still showing traces of once beautiful frescoes, stood out like the bones of some skeleton that had been better left buried in peace under the mound of silt that covered them. The hanging gardens of Babylon and the palace of Nebuchadnezzar are now just dreary heaps of crumbling brickwork amid excavated earth. I hope that sooner or later, when archaeologists have learned all they need to know, kindly nature will bury these ruins once again. It seems more than likely: the dust of the desert blows eternally.

Just beyond Babylon lies Hillah, one of the large towns situated on the branch of the Euphrates that is controlled by the Hindiyah Barrage, a high dam with sluice-gates built by British contractors under the Turkish régime before the war. Hillah is picturesque as Arab towns go, for it is in the midst of date gardens. Above the palms rise a few of those massive and imposing, yet woefully cracked and unsafe Turkish buildings, largely composed of bricks purloined from Babylon. The Babylonian bricks, be it remarked, are among the best ever made, and are superior to those burned in Iraq today, both in their hardness and in their freedom from salt, which is so detrimental to durability. As one walks in the 'serai' or Government offices at Hillah one steps on paving from which the cuneiform characters are still not worn off. Perhaps some of the tiles record the laws of Khammurabi, not so different from those administered by the judges who walk there now, four thousand years after the original code was given to the Sumerian people.

Beyond Hillah the road became worse than I had dreamed a road could be. But this was the last lap to Diwaniyah—or so I thought—and with the skid-chains swirling mud in all directions and the engine labouring in first gear we forged slowly ahead, sometimes sliding helplessly into side-drains, sometimes stuck completely in puddles of glutinous mud a foot or more in depth. On these occasions Hassan climbed out, trod delicately through the slush to the rear of the car, made grunts as though he were pushing hard, and yelled encouragement as the wheels spun and the tyres grew hot. It says much for American cars that they stand up to the buffeting they get on such journeys. Moreover, American business methods see to it that spares can be purchased in any bazaar in the country. The servicing of English cars did not, at that time at least, come near the American standard of efficiency.

Somehow or other we got twenty miles along that road, cheered by the thought that with every yard we were getting nearer home.

But then we came to the culvert.

It looked like an ordinary culvert built of date-palm logs covered with earth and forming the usual hog-back rising four feet above the road surface. Up we ran. Crash! We were through. There was a large hole in the crown of the culvert and our back wheels were spinning uselessly in space.

We crawled out over the baggage and took stock of our position. There seemed no possibility of a move either backwards or forwards. In the distance on the right we could see the dome of a mosque, but there was no vestige of the railway or of Diwaniyah. Even if we unloaded it would take much time and great luck to jack our car out unaided. It was getting dusk and the district had an evil reputation. Hassan assured me it was more than likely we should be attacked by robbers, and described with lurid details what would happen if we were. But he was a true Eastern philosopher, and ended his terrifying anticipations by remarking, 'Allah Karim—God is good.'

If attacked we really should be in a serious predicament with all these stores to lose; and almost as Hassan spoke four Arabs appeared, coming towards us over the fields.

'Salaam alekum,' they greeted us.

Hassan replied, 'Alekum es Salaam.'

In the gathering darkness we looked at one another. Over their heads they wore long 'abbas' which fell loosely to their knees and under which any manner of weapons might be concealed. Their feet were bare and their gaunt features seen between the folds of their cloaks were as inscrutable as the desert itself.

When we asked their business they said they were tribal Arabs from the village, the mosque of which we could see in the distance. They in their turn inquired if we were thinking of staying the night here or merely resting, or, if neither, where we supposed we were making for. Somehow I began to like these chaps and felt that if they were robbers at all they could perhaps be persuaded to leave us our boots (for it was the usual custom to strip your victims naked). Hassan said that we were on our way to Diwaniyah, but added that we were now stuck —as if this was not already obvious enough.

'Do you think you are going to Diwaniyah?' said the first sour-looking Arab and began to laugh. The second laughed, the third laughed, and then the fourth joined in.

Hassan looked green, but repeated, 'Yes, Diwaniyah.'

The Arabs continued to laugh.

'This isn't the road to *Diwaniyah*, it goes to *Kufah*. You should have turned left at Hillah. You are on the *wrong road*!' they said, and they laughed once more.

In some consternation I got out the map. If, as the Arabs asserted, that was Kifl we could see about five miles away on the right, we were certainly on the wrong road, well on the way to Kufah. We were only about forty miles wrong. There seemed nothing else to do now, so I laughed too. The Arabs thought this was the best joke they had heard for weeks and were so pleased about it that they helped us lift and drag the car out of the hole in the culvert then and there. I turned her round and pointed her nose for Hillah once again.

How we drove back after dark along that morass of a road I cannot tell. Perhaps our own wheel-ruts helped us, as they sometimes do in heavy mud. Later I became a past master in this sort of driving and got to know just which kind of mud would break transmission shafts and which kind would not. That night, however, I was lucky in more ways than one, and the new car somehow churned and floundered back to Hillah without a breakage.

In all the larger towns of Iraq Government Rest-Houses had been built for the use of officials on tour in their districts, for it was in-advisable that officers of the state should have to thrust themselves upon local hospitality—though sometimes there was no alternative to this. These rest-houses were usually just unfurnished buildings that gave shelter to those who might have occasion to use them tempor-arily.

As we searched through Hillah in the darkness for the local rest-house the prospect of spending a night there seemed none too joyful, yet better that than to sleep in the open by the muddy roadside. When after following and returning from many wrong streets and alleys I at last drove up to the rest-house, I was most pleasantly surprised to see lights and the flicker of a fire within and to be greeted cheerily by two other wayfarers who seemed already quite at home.

'Come right in out of the mud,' they said, and I required no further pressing, for never had a dingy, smoky room lit by one hurricane lamp and a wax candle looked so attractive. A meal was being got ready in an annexe and the smell of frying meat was most alluring to a man dog-tired and hungry.

I introduced myself and discovered who my companions were. One was the civil surgeon of the district, the other an officer of the local levy troops. They were 'old campaigners' and men whom I was to get to know well, as they were on outstation duty like myself. Let us call them respectively Captains McNish and McTavish,[1] for they both originated north of the Tweed. The first was a bronzed, wiry man of the R.A.M.C., famed for his skill with a shot-gun and his amusing tales of a doctor's life among the Arabs. He spoke Arabic with the most perfect fluency and was revered among the tribes as a great healer. The other, a taciturn little soldier from Glasgow with a merry red face, baked hard as nails by many a long summer under desert sun, was a man obviously quick-witted and capable in time of danger.

As the dinner cooked we sat by the crackling fire of dry camelthorn and date fronds and I told them the story of my day's misadventures. They laughed heartily at the account of my long and unfortunate trip down the road to Kufah, and rather blamed Hassan, now busy helping with the dinner. He was certainly my interpreter, but I felt guiltily that it was I who had the map.

'Of course,' I concluded, 'those four chaps were perfectly harmless labourers and I don't suppose there has been any lawlessness to speak of in this country since we took it out of Turkish hands; nor likely to be.'

'We've both seen too much of Iraq to be able to share that optim-ism,' said McNish. 'Those Arabs you met happened to be good fellows. Some are, but many aren't. However, dinner is served, so let's

---

[1] When referring in this book to people still connected with Iraq, fictitious names have been freely used.

go and encourage the cook, and for your very necessary education as newcomer we'll tell you some stories of the district later on.'

Half an hour later with pipes filled and a pleasant sense of comfort within, we returned to the fire, and the world seemed as if it had always been full of peace and contentment. Yet I knew I had better listen carefully to what these men had to say, as I noticed now for the first time that as we sat and talked there were rifles and pistols within easy reach and a sentry could be heard tramping outside the door.

'You have today by mistake visited a most notable place,' said McNish. 'Probably the heaviest, and in my opinion, the most unnecessary loss of British life in this country since the fall of Kut-el-Amarah, occurred on that Kufah road. Like to hear about it?'

'I certainly should,' I replied eagerly.

'Well, this is what happened,' said McNish. 'During the Arab revolt against the British in 1920 a battalion of the Manchester Regiment was overwhelmed near Kifl. They had been sent out to relieve the garrison at Kufah which was besieged by the Arabs, but before they reached the beleaguered town, and owing to the failure to find drinking-water where expected, the order was given for the column to retire to Hillah in the darkness. The rebel tribesmen, hovering on the flanks, hadn't dared to attack in the daytime, but a night march over that broken country gave them just the chance for which they had waited.

'In summer the desert between Hillah and Kufah is a maze of dry watercourses and ditches, over which field-guns and wheeled transport could be dragged only with the greatest difficulty even in daylight. The previous day had been long and scorching and there had been only brackish water to drink, which even the camels had refused. Thus the troops were certainly in no condition for the march they had to undertake. Had they stayed where they were all might have been well, for they could probably have reached the Euphrates next morning.

'In many ways the Arabs resemble the "pi" dogs of their villages that never attack or even show hostility until they know their prey is already in difficulties. So the tribesmen came out to await their chance and knew just when to swoop.

'After nightfall, from the perfect cover of the ditches, they opened fire on the struggling horse-teams. The column was thrown into confusion and became scattered in the darkness. An heroic effort was made to counter-attack and win through to Hillah, but the remnant that survived the retreat was less than half the battalion that had set out to the relief of Kufah. There were heavy British casualties and many of the men got lost in the night and were taken prisoners by the tribesmen.

'A field-gun had to be abandoned by the Manchesters after they had removed the breech-block to render the weapon useless; but that was by no means the last we heard of that particular eighteen-pounder.

'Speaking of field-guns,' the civil surgeon continued. 'While all this was happening near Kifl, I was myself with another column about thirty miles away accompanying the train that was evacuating Diwaniyah and coming northward. We made slow progress, for the rebels had destroyed the whole length of the railway, and our engineers, protected by machine-gun pickets, had to repair almost every foot of the line. Meanwhile, as close behind as they dared approach, the Arabs pulled it up again. Fortunately we were able to keep them at a respectful distance by shelling them with shrapnel, but some of the empty shrapnel-cases happened to fall among our own Indian rearguard and one man was wounded severely.

' "Why didn't you chaps keep out of the way of those falling shrapnel-cases?" I asked him when I was dressing his wound.

' "Oh," said the casualty, "we didn't think anyone could get hurt by those things because they had gone off already."

'That railway line was a cursed thing to try to defend and there were some desperate fights along it. The most heroic of all was at Samawah, ninety miles south of here. The evacuating train went off the rails and couldn't be got on again. There were only two or three men in charge, but they refused to surrender to the rebels and with their pistols held several hundred Arabs in check. At last the train was set on fire and the defenders had to abandon it; then they fought on in the open and sold their lives dearly. The Arabs still speak with wonder of those mad "Englises" who refused to surrender.

'But you make McTavish here tell you how the garrison at Kufah got on after the Manchesters failed to turn up to relieve them,' concluded the doctor as he reached for the matches to relight his pipe. 'He was one of the lads who has good reason to know.'

McTavish demurred when it came to talking about his own exploits, but finally agreed to do his bit towards the evening's entertainment and my education.

'Well, we had plenty of ammunition', he began, 'and a strongly fortified position in the heart of the city only about a mile from the great mosque of Ali. Kufah, you know, is one of the most holy places in the whole Mohammedan world for the Shiahs, as it was there that Ali who founded their sect was said to have been murdered about the seventh century.

'On several occasions we were attacked and at one stage the Arabs even attempted to tunnel under our defences. But we had good walls round the barracks and enough machine-guns mounted on them to beat off any direct assault.

'The guns, too, commanded the Euphrates which ran right past the barracks beside the quay-wall or landing-place. Here as an extra help in our defence we had the little river gunboat *Firefly*. She was moored at our front door, so to speak, and the gangway which ran on to her was so well protected by sandbags that you could get in reasonable safety from the barracks to the gunboat without being potted at. We were quite proud of our gunboat and she was very useful in such a position, much more use than if she were cruising on the river, where she'd probably have stranded on a sandbank as the *Greenfly* did at Samawah. In that event it's a pretty hopeless position if the banks of the river are high and the Arabs command the boat with rifle-fire. In the case of the *Greenfly* it's not certain whether the Indian crew mutinied or not—at the time it seemed a pretty suspicious business— but anyway she was lost near Samawah. The *Firefly*, however, seemed safe enough at Kufah because our guns had command of the position —or so we reckoned.

'Our aeroplanes sometimes flew over and dropped messages and even food. We heard how the Manchesters had come out to relieve us and had retired, but that headquarters wanted us to hold on in spite of this reverse. Even cases of ammunition were being dropped by parachute into the various besieged forts—for we weren't the only garrison cut off at that time. If the cases didn't fall as they were meant to within the defences a party had to go out and fight to recover them. There were several stout efforts of this sort in May, 1920, usually successful in spite of the heavy odds against the sortie party.

'One morning at dawn some time after we'd heard about the Manchesters, there was a flash and a tremendous report from the date garden on the opposite bank of the river, and to our surprise and dis- may we saw that the *Firefly* was ablaze. She had been hit by a shell. We didn't know that the enemy possessed artillery, and in any case it was a most unexpected disaster that the boat should have been set alight by the very first shot.

'The machine-gunners had noted the flash in the date garden and now spotted the field-gun, and the enemy gun-crew was quickly dealt with. There was no more heard from the field-gun that day: neverthe- less the *Firefly* had to be sunk by Lewis-gun fire from the barracks as she couldn't be saved and her magazine might explode.

'Elated with their success, the Arabs moved the gun during the night to a new position, and at dawn aimed and fired again, this time at the defences. But the wall of the barracks was solid and the shell did little damage, and once again the crew of the gun was caught in a hail of machine-gun bullets. So for many mornings this went on, a few shots being fired from the gun at considerable expense of life to the enemy, till at last they gave it up. But that first shot was an un- lucky one for us when we lost the *Firefly*.

'We held on at Kufah. Bread and flour ran out, so we had to kill a cavalry horse or two and eat them. But meat alone is poor food and we got very sick and came out all over in boils. After three months of this we were at last relieved, but it took us a long time to get fit again after that horse-flesh diet.

'There were a few loyal Arabs who stuck by us during the siege. One told us afterwards how the field-gun had been aimed at the *Firefly* by the Arabs who didn't know a thing about the sights. They simply looked through the barrel before they loaded. As to where the missing breech-block came from, that's still a mystery to us. The story goes that the rebels indented on the British Ordnance Department at Baghdad, and were supplied! It sounds highly probable to me,' and the Scotch officer laughed as he finished his modest story of the historic defence of Kufah.

CHAPTER II

Diwaniyah

Diwaniyah is only a small Arab town situated on a canal, yet it is the centre of a wide tribal district which embraces all the branches of the Euphrates thereabouts and extends southward to the fringe of the great Arabian Desert.

The town has the inevitable bazaar with narrow, smelly, roofed-in streets, a railway station and a serai or block of Government offices built of poor bricks in the crude Turkish style. Within the serai are to be found the rooms of the officials of the departments of Irrigation, Administration, Customs and Revenue, and of the Law Courts, the Treasury and the Jail, not to mention those of the Public Works Department to which I belonged. We were accommodated in two rooms with domed roofs, in one of which Jewish clerks dealt with accounts and typed letters and reports with that business ability which distinguishes this race the world over. In the other were drawing tables and cupboards full of plans and mathematical instruments which make the engineer feel at home wherever he may be.

Outside in the general courtyard there rose a perpetual babble of voices speaking Arabic—a language I was already beginning to learn. Petitioners in law cases argued in tones of high altercation, stilled periodically by the melancholy cadences of the court-crier from the balcony above announcing judgments and calling the new cases. A rattle of chains and a clatter of rifles and many loud, sharp orders told me when a bevy of prisoners in their grey-white convict clothes were being escorted from their cells for labour duties, usually chained hand or foot.

The Diwaniyah serai was a building typical of the old Turkish administration. It had been condemned by my department as rotten and unsafe, but was still in use for want of funds to build a new one. No doubt the Turks would have given the same reason for their neglect of it, so one must not criticize too severely.

There was indeed one survival of the Turkish régime that I thoroughly approved of. Copious trays of tea and coffee were provided every hour or so, brought in by old men called 'chaichis', to all the offices in turn and offered to everyone who might chance to be there.

Diwaniyah

The tea was served in very small, narrow-waisted glasses with much sugar but no milk; and coffee was drunk as a thick fluid from a thimble-like cup. I found that both tea and coffee had a very desirable tranquillizing effect upon the troubled stream of humanity that flowed in past the sentry at the serai doorway from the turbulent desert around.

Across the road the hospital, also a relic of Turkish times, was an offence not to be condoned. The walls were cracked, the rough poplar beams of the roof were broken and sagging and patched between with 'scrim' to keep scorpions, ants and dirt from dropping on the patients as they lay on the earth floor groaning in the noisy way Arabs have when sick. To give the place the proper medical odour, or perhaps to obscure worse smells, cans of disinfectant were poured over the floor by the one-eyed Arab orderly. Next door was the operating theatre, a room much like the others, but a little smaller and having a slab table in the centre. There was wire gauze over the window openings to keep out the flies, though this seemed to be mainly for the sake of appearances, as the insects could and did enter as freely as they wished through the broken door, which would never more than half shut. The floor sloped to a sump in the middle leading to the usual cesspool beneath, into which refuse from the operating table or from the collapsing roof could be conveniently swilled. There was the same drainage in the courtyard outside; but, as these sumps led nowhere, they were usually, in the winter-time at least, in an overflowing condition and the smell of disinfectant was not always the predominant one. In the women's ward there were even a few iron bedsteads, though they were seldom used; Arab women prefer to lie on the hard ground. Accurate diagnosis and treatment was almost impossible, as these women refused to take off their veils, let alone their abbas, so they lay and wailed on the floor believing that the magical influence of the noble 'Khasta-Khana' or hospital building (they had probably never seen a better) would cure them of all ills as surely as the wonderful apple of Prince Ahmad was said to do in the Arabian Nights stories. One of my first jobs was to inspect and report on the condition of this building. I did this in such a way that even the serious-minded Jewish clerk grinned as he typed the report. There is a new hospital in Diwaniyah now!

I found myself in charge of a very mixed staff at Diwaniyah. In addition to the Jewish clerks there was a huge Indian Sikh named Natha Singh, who acted as senior supervisor. He had a cheery smile and good manners, but his greatest asset was that he never complained, no matter where he was sent or what job he was given. Further, I had a Baghdad Christian, a Kurd, and a Turkish carpenter, all of them willing enough but none possessing the technical ability of the Sikh. They were scattered here and there in charge of various jobs then in progress. The Indian was driving piles for a long bridge over one of the branches of the Euphrates, the others were building block-houses or making roads. Curiously enough, the Christian was busy erecting a fine new school in the Holy City of Najaf, where the gold-plated dome of the huge mosque of Ali gleams afar over desert and marsh, and to which corpses are brought for burial from the ends of the Shiah Mohammedan world. Formerly Christians entering Najaf were murdered, but here was Jacques Teresa building a school!

The strangest man of all my staff was Fattah Bey. One day an old man came into my office with a letter from my Director at Baghdad asking me to find him a job, if possible. He could speak little Arabic and no English, but addressed me in fluent German, a language I can't even pretend to understand. The Jewish clerk came to my help with his knowledge of Turkish and we heard some part of the story of Fattah Bey, ex-Colonel of Turkish engineers, ex-custodian of British prisoners-of-war in Turkey, and one-time opponent of Mustafa Kemal Pasha. As his testimonials a strange collection of documents was laid on the table before me, curiosities indeed. There were diplomas in engineering from the important German university where Fattah Bey had been educated, press cuttings telling of the daring feats he had performed in the Turco-Grecian wars and letters from certain cele-brated British admirals and soldiers thanking him for his kindly treat-ment of prisoners who had been under his charge. When I asked why he had left Turkey he confessed that he had been banished from his native land because of his political activities, and that he would be put to death immediately should he return. I took the old man on my staff, and he proved a willing worker and seemed satisfied with his humble job. Perhaps he had once aspired to be the leader of all Turkey, but I hesitated to question him, and he for his part remained silent concerning the mystery surrounding his banishment.

The greatest engineering difficulties I experienced in the Diwaniyah liwa were caused by floods on the Euphrates River. Floods occur annually and have done so for thousands of years. Roads are washed out and bridges, buildings, and even whole towns, may be endangered if not destroyed. The chief reason for such wide inundation is that the river by its own deltaic action in depositing silt has gradually built its bed higher than the level of the surrounding country. The Arabs attempt to confine the river in its channel by keeping the banks in repair, but in flood-time it usually breaks through somewhere, the breach quickly widens and the whole surrounding country is sub-merged. When the flood-waters recede it is sometimes found that the river has chosen a completely new course, but usually the breach can be repaired and made safe for another year.

Even in ordinary years the quantity of water carried down by these rivers at flood-time is ten times the flow in the low-water season; and

2. Diwaniyah

3. Nairn Desert Transport crossing Falluja Floating Bridge, 1927

4. The Blind Beggar on the Kirkuk Road

5. An Altun Keupri Fish

when the rainfall on the plains has been specially heavy and synchronizes with a rapid melting of the snow on the high mountains of the north where the rivers rise, there may be sudden and tremendous floods on the Tigris and Euphrates.

The flood of 1928 was a most serious one, and more than half the arable land of the district was inundated. Leagues of flat country were literally converted into rippling oceans, and often as far as the eye could see there was no land in sight. Tents, animals and even men were whisked off on the rising waters, and nearly all travelling had to be done by boat. In Iraq many of the roads are formed on bunds or high embankments, which are supposed to raise them above flood level. These were cut through in many places, and the floating bridges over rivers and canals had to be temporarily dismantled to save them from being washed away. In my shallow-draught 'bellum' I sailed for miles over vast newly-formed lakes, only a few date-palms appearing here and there above the water where the gardens and villages had once been.

All the Semitic religions, Hebrew, Christian, and Mahommedan, have stories of vast floods that covered the whole earth. Sir Leonard Woolley tells us that the Flood mentioned in the seventh chapter of the Book of Genesis undoubtedly occurred in Mesopotamia, when 'the waters prevailed exceedingly upon the earth; and all the high hills, that were under the whole heaven, were covered'. As I sailed my unwieldy craft, caulked with native bitumen just as was the Ark of Noah, over the flooded plains, looking for landmarks that were once our roads and bridges, and brought the workmen to safety with some at least of their belongings, I realized that this story of the first flood originated in very real experiences.

The Rebellion of 1920 had flared first and worst in this district, and many Arab as well as British lives had been lost here. The majority of the Arabs of Diwaniyah however were not now openly hostile to the British officers who remained. In fact, the tribesmen and the poorer folk were usually trusting and friendly; but the leading townspeople seemed jealous and inclined to resent the influence of the English, and perhaps this was only natural.

Among the Arabs were some who realized the advantage they had gained and who remained consistently loyal, often at considerable loss to themselves. One tribal chieftain at Diwaniyah who had lent a helping hand to several Englishmen in those times of trouble, extended his hospitality to me when I arrived. Well do I remember the Arab banquet at which I was the guest of honour. My digestion found it difficult to cope with the extensive and unusual menu and I took days to recover completely; but that does not lessen my gratitude for an old man's kindness to a lonely engineer.

We sat round a large tray on the ground with our legs crossed under us—the soles of the feet must never be turned towards anyone, for that is extremely bad manners. Arab servants brought in the carefully prepared meal on many smaller trays and set them before us. We began with Dutch beer and lettuce. Then came a lamb roasted whole and stuffed with raisins, almonds and spices. According to the custom of the land the meat was torn in pieces by our host and passed round together with the stuffing in large handfuls. The eye, which is considered the most delicate titbit of all, was offered to me, but I politely refused it, and instead was given a portion of the tail which, from these fat-tailed desert sheep, is really delicious. Meat, together with handfuls of rice, was laid on flat thin sheets of 'khubz' or unleavened bread, which was then folded over to form a package that could be conveyed to the mouth (etiquette demanded that the right hand only should be used) and nibbled or gulped according to one's skill. The more audible the mastication the better, as this showed how much the food was being enjoyed. Following the meat and rice, or rather simultaneously with it, for all the dishes lay on the tray together, we were given a kind of chutney and rice wrapped in vine leaves, some sweet confections that I cannot name, and finally large Basrah dates dipped in the 'liban' or buffalo butter-milk which makes such an amazingly fine drink in these hot climates. For the dates it was provided thick, like junket, but there was also a bowl of milk-like consistency which was passed round for all to drink from in turn. At the end of the banquet came Turkish coffee and cigarettes.

In Iraq the eating of meals together is considered a very important matter and is usually regarded as a pledge of friendship; but it is necessary to learn the correct etiquette or the host and his party will feel most uncomfortable. Fortunately I had been told about the various customs, and since this notable Arab continued my good friend while I was in Diwaniyah, and often visited my house, my mistakes cannot have been so flagrant that they could not be overlooked.

There were two British officers attached to the 'liwa' when I arrived, one the Inspecting Officer of Police, the other the Administrative Inspector. Both were men who knew their business well or they would not have been put in charge of this turbulent area.

There were about eight hundred mounted police in the Diwaniyah district, with a striking force of three hundred quartered in the large barracks in the town, behind which was the landing ground for aeroplanes. It was a stirring sight to see the mounted police on parade. The Arabs are fine riders, and so also are the Kurds who formed a large portion of this 'gendarmerie'. The police officer, Captain Bentley, came from a British cavalry regiment, and therefore the equipment and smartness of the force were well-nigh perfect, and the drilling and manœuvring always splendidly executed, in spite of the fact that every horse was an Arab stallion. Magnificent beasts they were too, not nearly as big as an English hunter, but hardier for the kind of work they had to perform—long journeys over desert lands with little food or water. The example of the British officers in Iraq has eradicated much of that neglect and abuse of animals that unfortunately characterizes the East. A policeman might be excused duty for some minor or even imaginary sickness without much question, but let his horse get a sore back or let him leave some slight injury uncared for, then woe betide him. The result was that every horse on the parade-ground shone with well-groomed fitness. A finer sight I have never seen than the charge of the long line of stallions thundering and snorting across the desert aerodrome, led by their officer on his tall thoroughbred.

When, as often happened, I had to do investigation work for roads or bridges in distant spots to which no car could take me, I had to borrow a horse from the local police post wherever I happened to be 'out in the blue'. The Arabs seemed to have the idea that all Englishmen were as good horsemen as Bentley, for I was usually given the wildest animal they could produce. I had done very little riding since I was a boy, so when on the first of these occasions I found that the horse chosen for me bucked, I promptly dismounted and exchanged it for another that bolted straightway. The track led along a railway line, and only by a miracle was I able to keep the creature out of the sleepers till at length I managed to pull him up. Fortunately my riding gradually improved, for these horses can be wicked and difficult beasts to control; and often I found it almost impossible to manage a strange Arab stallion that had not been ridden for some weeks. On one occasion the moment I was mounted my steed was off like a rocket. As we were on open desert with very few ditches, I decided to let him go till he was tired and more controllable, but soon realized that the beast had no intention of giving in. For six miles we fairly flew over the plains and my companions were left far behind. I pulled at the reins until my hands were blistered and raw, and eventually stopped the brute against a water-course. But even at the end of that terrific effort, he was quite prepared to start off as wildly as ever, and the Arabs assert that a good thoroughbred in this mood will never give in owing to fatigue, but will dash on till he drops dead.

Often half the trouble with these horses arises from the use of the English instead of the Arab bridle they are accustomed to. The proper Arab gear for a horse's head has no bit, nothing whatever in the mouth. Instead there is a curious little chain which goes round the nose like a halter and to the end of this is attached a single rein by which the horse is guided by pulling to left or right, and the animal readily gallops if the rein is let a little loose: the horses seem happier with this single rein and are actually much easier to control. If such bridles are better for these steeds, nothing can be said in favour of the rest of the Arab equipment. The police had English saddles, but the native saddles that I often had to use were a curse. The stirrups, made of sheet-iron, were so wide and had such sharp corners that they could be used as spurs if necessary. They hung directly under the seat, and not forward, as on the English saddle, and were always too short, one almost invariably shorter than the other, and they could not be adjusted. The seat was narrow and uncomfortable and to keep the feet in the stirrups required an agonizing contortion of the knees, while to let them dangle free allowed the swinging stirrups to hit the horse's ribs and drove him crazy. Many were the miserable hours that I spent in those native saddles on long wearisome journeys before I became accustomed to them. They were made of coloured leather with gaudy tassels and hangings; the wooden pommel was usually adorned with brass, or, on the saddles of the important sheikhs, even with gold.

Yet there were many compensations. To go for a good gallop in a company of these Arab horses, their heads high in the air, their long manes and tails flying in the breeze, was ample reward for the discomfort of the saddle. The Arabs themselves with their coloured abbas and kefiyahs streaming behind them as they leaned forward on their horses' necks looked magnificent careering over the desert; and how the horses loved the exhilaration of the race!

Let me return to the police and their work in Diwaniyah. The worries caused to me by floods and horses were temporary and insignificant matters compared to the troubles and responsibilities of my companions of the administrative branches of the liwa.

Practically every Arab tribesman had a rifle hidden somewhere which could be produced at short notice, though the law forbade them to carry firearms. The police therefore often met with determined opposition when they set out to arrest murderers and robbers. Nevertheless wrong-doers were usually caught on the deserts or in the marshes, though often at great sacrifice to the police, and murderers were actually hanged in the main street of Diwaniyah as a grim warning to others.

The Public Works Department to which I belonged contributed its share towards securing order. No less than five large brick-fortresses had been constructed and still more were to be built in inaccessible places where hostility was feared. These forts, situated so that there was a clear field of view all round them, were usually square in plan and had bastion towers at each corner. Both bastions and walls were loopholed for rifle-fire, and one side of the fort was formed by the government offices of the serai which was usually incorporated in these large police posts. Behind these offices, within a massive brick wall with a strong steel door, was a courtyard for the camels and horses of the police, and always a well of good water. The workmanship and architecture were of a high standard and these buildings should last for centuries. We often experienced great difficulty in constructing such forts, both in transporting materials and in per-suading men to work far from the coffee-shops and bazaars of the towns in hostile territory.

Let us take the story of the building of the block-houses in the Southern Desert which borders Diwaniyah to the south-west, and of the Englishman who was known as 'Abu Hunaich', who broke the power of the notorious raider, Faisal Ad-Dawish, and averted war with Arabia.

Arabia was at that time believed to be hostile to the kingdom of Iraq. The reason lay in the fact that the Wahabi or Puritan leader of the Arabs, King Ibn Saud, had displaced King Faisal's father, King Hussein, as ruler of the Hejaz. The dream of that United Arabia, comprised of all the Arab-speaking peoples of the old Turkish Empire, had fallen through owing to this disputed question of leadership; and the historic work of Lawrence, Newcome and others in uniting the Arabs during the war had been largely undone by the Arabs them-selves, as seems inevitable while Arab character remains unchanged.

There had been no boundary between Arabia and Iraq when these were both part of the old Ottoman Empire, and the southern tribes migrated freely from Arabia up the Euphrates. Hence when it was proclaimed by Britain that a boundary must be observed one hundred miles south-west from the Euphrates, there was grave danger of war. The Arab tribes near this border were accustomed to move about continually in search of fresh pastures, and they took no notice of the injunctions that they should not cross into Iraq territory. The Bedouin love to go where they wish, free as the desert air they breathe, raiding their rivals if the chance comes their way. Some friction was expected, but nothing of a serious nature. Unfortunately, however, there arose a veritable fanatic by the name of Faisal Ad-Dawish, Chief of the Ilwah Mutair, and leader of the Ikhwan, who raided over the frontier descending upon, looting and killing those tribes that preferred to accept the jurisdiction of Britain and the Government of Iraq. It was no mere boast that this raider had killed eighty-nine men with his own hand.

The Ikhwan (or 'brothers') were extremely fanatical Mahommedan Puritans. They neither smoked nor touched alcohol as do less strict Mussulmen; they worshipped only the Prophet Mohammed allowing no place to his various relatives whom the Shiahs hold in reverence. Thus they looked upon all others, whether Mahommedan, Christian or Jew as libertines and idolaters fit only for death: moreover they put these sentiments into practice, and it would have gone hard with the Euphrates towns had the Ikhwan tribesmen attacked them in force. They loved war and murder and in battle it was said they would charge recklessly against machine-gun fire, plastering their faces with the blood of their fallen comrades.

37

Diwaniyah

The seriousness of the situation became evident when several raids were made by Faisal Ad-Dawish, and he not only carried off flocks and herds but ruthlessly murdered all the tribes-people he conquered. This happened far out in the desert, so that by the time the news reached Baghdad the raiders were well away with their spoils.

As Britain was still the Mandatory Power in Iraq, aeroplanes were brought into use; but it was found that news of the raids always came too late—the raiders had vanished. Even if the Ikhwan were discovered, the airmen had no easy task when operating hundreds of miles from their nearest base. The planes were liable to be shot down when flying low in order to be able to distinguish the raiders from peaceful tribesmen; at times pilots were lost in the terrible dust storms of the desert and had to make a forced landing, when they were in grave danger from thirst or from a rifle bullet of the enemy.

In such circumstances it was decided to build block-houses in the vicinity of the frontier. At a spot, Basaiyah, there were wells of rather brackish water, and here in the heart of the desert a party of Arab workmen sent out by the Public Works Department under an Indian Supervisor, began to build. A small police guard was provided.

Determined to challenge the claim of the Iraq Government that its sovereignty extended so far into the desert, a raiding party of Faisal Ad-Dawish came over the border on fast-trotting camels and arrived outside the walls of the unfinished block-house one dark night. Camels move silently with their large soft feet and the desert Arabs can silence these grunting brutes in a wonderful way when they wish. Armed to the teeth and quite unnoticed the raiders crept to the doorway, where the sentry on guard dozed as he leaned upon the barrel of his rifle. No police picket had been placed outside and no signalling system had been arranged to give the alarm, for when the sun had set that evening over the stony desert there had been no sign of Bedouin on the far horizon, no hint of danger; yet not one of those who lay so wearily on the ground after their hard day's toil was ever to see the sun rise again.

At a signal there was a crashing volley and the guard at the gate fell dead; with fierce fanaticism in every eye the raiders surged through the doorway to massacre the sleeping inmates with pistol, rifle and dagger. When day broke there was silence at Basaiyah. There was no living soul within the fort, and the camelmen were far out of sight of their bloody deed.

Thus do the Ikhwan know how to strike their blow and how to vanish into the desert again.

When a fresh squadron of police came out to relieve their companions they entered a fort that seemed asleep. Against the wall leaned a man wide-eyed and grinning. They shouted a welcome, but he made no reply; so they poked the silent mirthful one and a stiff corpse fell sideways and bumped to the ground. Such was the welcome at Basaiyah.

The challenge to Britain and to the Iraq Government was a serious one, and Ibn Saud, King of Arabia, was warned accordingly. He promptly denied all knowledge and responsibility for the doings of Faisal Ad-Dawish, and though at the time it was thought that the King secretly favoured the raids, later events proved him innocent of any connection with them.

Meanwhile something had to be done to prevent repetition of such a disaster. So Captain Glover, the Administrative Inspector of Diwaniyah, known to the Arabs as Abu Hunaich, was sent to deal with the situation. No man could have been better fitted for the task, for this quiet reserved officer of the Royal Engineers knew the mind of the desert Arab as few men knew it. He was held in the highest regard among the Bedouin tribes for his fairness and for his understanding of their peculiar tribal laws. Moreover, he had that indefinable quality of leadership of the tribes which comes only from years of self-sacrifice and labour amongst them.

In the conventional garb of an Arab, Glover set out for the deserts of the South where Faisal Ad-Dawish raided across the border. His only guard was a powerful Nubian of great ugliness who for ever fingered a long old-fashioned Turkish rifle with which his marksmanship was famed. This strange pair wandered many a mile together by camel and horse, and wherever Abu Hunaich of the desert went, tribes came to tender their respects. Under his influence their confidences were never long withheld, for their visitor had a 'name' in the desert, a reputation that was widespread. Glover quickly sifted the truth from the falsehood, for he knew all the tricks of talk of these Eastern people. At first they are just cordial and speak on every subject under the sun except the matter they have come to discuss. Eventually they do come to their story, and then usually exaggerate and even lie if they have secret reasons for giving false information, as, for instance, when they wish to cast suspicion upon an innocent tribe with whom they are at feud. But knowing their ways, Glover soon determined the identity of the guilty Ikhwan.

The next question to decide was whether or not armoured cars could be used. Their speed would be invaluable in getting in touch with the enemy and for pursuing him. Their fire-power in an engagement was overwhelming; and their range enabled them to travel a hundred miles to the nearest telegraph station to give the Air Force information on which it might operate without delay. The Southern Desert was known to be rocky (quite different from the silty desert of most of Iraq) and tyres would be cut to ribbons in no time. Yet the extensive, rapid and daring survey that Captain Glover made of this desert in less than a month in conjunction with a fellow Royal Engineer showed that some few tracks, more especially those beyond the first rocky belt, were at least passable for cars. He collected his information with the help of the tribes, who loved him, and he noted carefully the position of wells of water, good, bad or indifferent, which they showed him near these usable routes. And this was the scheme he matured.

Armoured cars and Ford trucks mounting machine-guns, fitted with field wireless and carrying ample provisions and fuel, should be based at certain of the good wells, and their drivers provided with maps of the newly discovered routes which ran more or less along the frontier. A British squadron of armoured cars was to be the nucleus of the scheme until such time as native drivers could be trained. Accordingly, these tracks which lay beyond the line of the proposed block-houses were patrolled, and it was possible to recommence work at Basaiyah and to begin the building of two further forts at Salman and Shabicha in exactly the same way.

This was the end of the peril of the Ikhwan. No sooner was a raiding party reported or sighted than wireless news of it was flashed over the desert to the R.A.F. Squadron at Shuaibah, and before the enemy could retreat even into their own territory they were being punished from the air.

So Faisal Ad-Dawish gave up his raids and retired southward, where his personal ambitions and lawless defiance of King Ibn Saud eventually brought attack on him from that quarter also. He was driven into the neutral territory of Kuwait, his final move on the great desert chess-board where he had played so desperately throughout his life, and there, checkmated, he gave himself up to the British and was handed over as a prisoner to King Ibn Saud, only to die shortly afterwards in captivity.

Thus ended the stormy career of Faisal Ad-Dawish, a wild desert chieftain better fitted for the romantic days of Harun al Raschid than for an unequal combat against the deadly weapons of this modern age.

CHAPTER III

Northward to the Mountains

By early summer the floods were over and for the first time since I arrived I could feel that the sub-division was no longer a constant anxiety. As the months wore on, I was pleased to find that in spite of the terrific heat of the dry summer I was able to stand the climate without undue distress.

I was now busy with some difficult surveys necessary for the planning of new roads and other works. This entailed a lonely life, as most of my time was spent moving about the vast district with car and camp-gear accompanied only by an overseer of my staff. In order to avoid having to work in the heat of the day, we were usually up before dawn and, in the first light, ate a breakfast of unleavened native bread and dates. Sustained by this and a cup of tea, we would set off, perhaps to make the tour of a proposed road line leading across the desert. It was usually necessary to go much of the way on horseback, which meant swimming, ferrying or jumping the animals across the innumerable irrigation channels, large and small, that barred our way. We had to dismount often to take measurements, levels and observations, and to interrogate the tribesmen at work in the rice-fields as to the ownership of the lands we were traversing. Thus we covered many miles of country till the midday heat—often 120° F. in the shade—drove us to the shelter of a date-grove or the tent of some hospitable Arab. Here we ate our lunch, which was usually supplemented by the kindly people with welcome bowls of 'liban'.

If possible, I had a talk with the village headman or with the local Government 'mudir' (the Iraqi superintendent of the district), with whom I discussed my plans and explained the benefit their people would derive from my work. I inquired also about the local labour available and was as friendly as possible, so that there should be no antagonism to the project when it was begun.

The afternoon was usually spent much as the morning had been, following the narrow Arab paths through date gardens or riding across the trackless desert, till darkness finally sent us back to our temporary quarters in the local serai and the hot meal of rice, meat and cucumber that Hassan was busy preparing—or

41

which with skilful laziness he had persuaded someone else to get ready.

Even then the day's work was not ended, for in the evenings the overseer's pay-sheets and cash-balance had to be checked, the observations and measurements made during the day worked out and tabulated, and perhaps a report or sketch made concerning suitable bridges and culverts for the road under consideration. I might also have to prepare an estimate of the cost of the complete job to send off to my Diwaniyah office to be typed and despatched to Baghdad. I had found that it was customary to keep other departments informed of what was taking place, so I had to send copies of the reports to Captain Glover, mentioning the names of any dissatisfied landowners; and possibly to the district irrigation engineer asking for ratification of the proposed bridge-spans over the water channels. Bentley, the police officer, might also have to be notified if the people seemed hostile or unfriendly, though fortunately this was rarely necessary.

At last, when my office duties were over, I could extinguish the hurricane lantern and mount to the flat roof of the serai, where I was soon stretched out on my squeaky and insecure camp-bed under the cloudless and brilliant starlit sky. For a few waking moments, I might lie and listen to the sounds of the village beneath hidden under the long fronds of the graceful date palms, which were laden with huge clusters of unripe fruit almost on a level with my high sleeping place. The sound of stringed instruments playing tunes in the melancholy Eastern scale of quarter-tones came up from below, and sometimes lights and banners passing by showed me that a religious procession was in progress.

The more important of these Shiah festivals, such as the Muharram, are usually gruesome affairs, for they are led by fanatical men who beat themselves over the head with swords till the blood pours down over their bodies. To the booming of drums, the brilliantly lit procession of devotees marches with a slow rhythmical step, some crying the names of their Shiah saints, Hassan, Hussein and Ali, in long-sustained accents steadily rising in fervour, while others chant a dirge of a few bars endlessly repeated. Hassan! Hussein! Hassan! Hussein!

My servant, Hassan, was of the more orthodox Sunni Mohammedans and therefore despised such goings-on, but he dared not show his face outside the building when the rival Shiah rites were in progress. Leaning over the parapet of the roof he would call me, however, in high glee, crying: 'Come and see, sir, he is beating 'isself, he is beating 'isself.'

Interesting as a Muharram procession might be, it held nothing that could intrigue me when I was really tired, and the mournful requiems of Hussein and his family served but to lull me to sleep, while Hassan gazed down on the passing throng alone.

Our work was sometimes interrupted by raging dust storms, which, in Iraq, may blow for days at a time and extinguish the sunlight as effectively as a London fog. When such storms are at their worst, cars cannot move on the roads. The wind is often hot as the blast from a furnace. Hands and face are stung by a sharp hail of grit. Lights have to be lit in all houses and offices, and a fine dust pours in through every chink in the closed doors and windows till it covers every article in the room and the air is thick with it. Master and servants alike cough and sneeze and wipe the dirt from their eyes. On such days as these I was forced to stay indoors and seize the chance of bringing my office-work up to date, but it was a discouraging business when every plan and report was smudged by the fine silt of the storm.

My time at Diwaniyah was not all spent in hard work and discomfort. After a few months of isolation, I welcomed a short holiday which I had been invited to spend with the Divisional Engineer in Basrah (the 'Balsorah' from which Sinbad started on his remarkable voyages). After my little Arab town this seemed to me a large city, though, apart from its hospital, it had few up-to-date buildings. There I met again white women-folk and shared in the typical club life of the merchant and civil servant of the East. What a change after my life at Diwaniyah, a change that I fully appreciated for the week I spent amid the comforts of electric fans, filtered water, telephones, well-built houses and kind hospitality. At first I envied the life that was regulated by office hours and week-ends of rest, but I had grown to be so interested in my work and in the Arab tribes of the deserts that after a few days I realized that I actually preferred Diwaniyah with its mud-houses, its narrow, smelly bazaars and its veiled women washing their clothes in the canal with their little dirty-nosed children upon their shoulders.

My work there was unlimited in extent and most absorbing. I felt pleased to be on a job with real possibilities, for Diwaniyah, though set among wild people, was generally regarded as one of the wealthiest liwas in Iraq on account of the vast date gardens and rice-fields within the ramifications of the Euphrates. Moreover, the money spent on public works there was not only producing more revenue, but it was also making the district more peaceful. I had been appointed to accelerate the work of development, and many schemes were now in hand for new roads, bridges, buildings and water supplies, some in Diwaniyah town itself. I hoped soon to have half a dozen buildings under way, including an electric power station, a school and a hospital. Unfortunately, however, much money had been spent that year in checking the Ikhwan raiders in the Southern Desert, and the Public Work's budget for Diwaniyah had to be curtailed in consequence.

For this reason, about midsummer, I was notified that I was to be transferred to Kurdistan, where the need for the pacification of the Kurdish tribes-people and for the introduction of Government influence urgently demanded road-building. There, among the mountains of the north-east frontier, I was to take part in the construction of a new highway called the Rowanduz Road which would eventually lead from Iraq to the plateau of North Persia and the Caspian Sea, passing through rugged inaccessible highlands said to be inhabited by brigands and rebels, who had been a constant source of trouble to the Administration.

It sounded very exciting, though at first I felt disappointed that I was to be sent away from the plains. I had found Diwaniyah a fascinating place in spite of its dust-storms and Ikhwan raids and the wild yet responsive tribes-folk. When my transfer to the north was ordered the 'Ikhwan' problem was practically at an end. Two of the most important block-houses in the proposed chain on the Southern frontier had been completed and a third begun. Armoured cars patrolled between them, and the claws of the raiders had been cut at last.

Yet on the very day I left, ten dead Arabs and twelve wounded were brought in from the desert, and the Administration had one of their usual domestic problems to deal with. This was one of those blood-feuds customary since the remotest times among people with wild, unforgiving laws of their own. Blood-feuds and the curious unwritten code known as 'tribal law' have proved to be, and will long continue to be, among the most difficult problems to be dealt with by any Administration in Iraq. 'An eye for an eye and a tooth for a tooth' is still the tribal watchword, and a man who is a man is bound to vindicate the 'honour of his tribe' whatever princes and powers may say to the contrary. I was soon to find that this code was held throughout the land from the Persian Gulf even to the farthest mountains of Kurdistan.

Only a few hundred years ago, I suppose my own ancestors in Scotland were little different in their customs and their rules of honour from these men whom I was sent to try and civilize, and I could not feel unsympathetic towards a people in whom genuine kindness and the primitive traditions of violence were so strangely mixed. Tribesmen are in some ways almost like children in their savage simplicity.

Hassan's eyes sparkled when he heard of my transfer to Rowanduz, and he began at once to tell me of the wonders of the mountains of his beloved homeland, Kurdistan. There, he assured me, I should find a mild and delightful climate. He spoke of vineyards and of beautiful trees which bore all manner of luscious fruits by the side of the rocky streams. Rain fell plentifully for more than half the year, quite unlike these barren deserts farther south, where the rainy season lasted only a week or two. As for Rowanduz, with its gushing springs, its mountain torrents and its gorges, that was the most wonderful place of all. His vocabulary failed him. I must wait till I could see it. Nevertheless, he told several tales of grim horrors that had occurred there during his time in the Turkish Army that made me think that demons as well as saints must dwell in this paradise of Kurdistan.

My Director had wired for me to join him at once, for he was just at that time touring the proposed road-line near Rowanduz, so I stored my car and went north by train as the quickest way. Besides, the car would at first be useless in the roadless country in which I should be working.

On the night journey from Baghdad to Kirkuk, which is the northern terminus of the Iraq Railway, the train trundled slowly along, stopping at every station. At each halt the railway police got off and patrolled up and down to protect the sleeping travellers from attack and robbery, though in recent years trains in Iraq have only very occasionally been raided.

The line ran through oil-bearing country and in the moonlight I saw many drilling rigs standing out against the skyline. We were passing through the Jebel Hamrin, the first of the foothills of Kurdistan, and came to a stand for some minutes at Sulaiman Beg, where there is a huge workshop belonging to the Iraq Petroleum Company. The sidings were packed with pipes and gear ready to be sent to Baba Gurgur, near Kirkuk, where a valuable new oil-field had been discovered as a result of the extensive trial-boring and prospecting the Company had carried out. I heard the story of the striking of the Baba Gurgur oil-bed from a fellow-passenger on the train—a young employee of the Company returning from leave. When they struck oil it burst forth with such terrific force that the string of drilling tools was blown out of the well, the oil and gas spurting high above the tall steel rig in a black cloud and descending upon the drillers with its deadly fumes. It poured into the wadis and hollows in the vicinity. Fortunately, this 'gusher' did not ignite, but several men lost their lives from asphyxiation while others performed heroic acts of rescue to save their comrades.

This oil-field has proved to be one of the greatest in the world and has since warranted the construction of the pipe-line, in itself a fine engineering achievement, across the many hundreds of miles of barren country between Kirkuk and the Mediterranean, where merchant vessels are now supplied with crude oil and refineries distil the petrol for the motor-cars and aeroplanes of Europe.

In the early morning I arrived at Kirkuk. It is an ancient place. Successive cities, built one upon the other, have raised a mound which stands well above the surrounding plain. Round it runs a wall which makes it a 'qala'—a fort or defendable town; but only the main residential quarter is today contained within the wall upon the mound, for the straggling bazaar has long ago overflowed on to the flat land by the river where it is at times threatened by widespread floods. In spite of the bombardment of flood-waters, the bridge, of a series of short-span masonry arches, is one of the few built during the Turkish régime that still stands. Usually bridges of this type, where they cross the deeper parts of the rivers, have been undermined and washed away, and in many cases the gaps have been filled by adding steel spans, giving a curious combination of old and new types of construction.

Near Kirkuk, a fire has been blazing for countless centuries where the natural gases rise up through the earth from some hidden lake of oil: the tradition of the district says that this is the ancient fiery furnace of the Book of Daniel.

That day I had to travel ninety miles farther by car to Shaqlawah, the Kurdish village which was then the road head camp of the new Rowanduz road, so I had no time to do more in Kirkuk than introduce myself to the Divisional Engineer, Major Perry. He was just going on leave, but later I was to know him well and come to admire him as perhaps the finest of the many tireless and unassuming servants of the British Mandatory Administration, who with such self-sacrifice and labour built up the Kingdom of Iraq. Of light build, with lean and determined face deeply lined from endurance of great labours and hardships, he sat in immaculate white in an office that spoke clearly of order and discipline, wild and primitive though the field of his work might be.

I have not forgotten the words he spoke to his new subordinate before I left Kirkuk.

'Remember that in this Division our labourers must get as good living conditions and as fair a deal as we can possibly give them. Don't expect your men to do more than you would be willing to do yourself. This country is still in the Dark Ages as far as labour conditions go, and we have to fight against the old state of affairs that was little better than slavery.

'I had to struggle hard to get our men paid as much as eighteen-pence a day, which is just enough for their food and cigarettes in most districts, provided the prices in the canteens are not inflated by the scheming merchants of the towns near by, and that the professional gamblers who prey upon the men after pay-day are kept at a distance.

'I am still trying to get the Government to agree to a scheme of compensation for injured men and medical attendance for the sick and provision for the wives and children of those who are killed on the work, but it is an uphill fight.

'As far as our Public Works Department goes, we give the best value we can for the money allotted to us. We pay what to these men is a good day's wage and we expect good work in return. Here in the North we labour under great difficulties, but that only makes our job the more interesting and our accomplishments the more creditable. You will be living by yourself in our farthest out-station, and I hope you won't find it too lonely a life. No club, no tennis, no amateur theatricals at Rowanduz,' he said with a laugh. I had already found that 'amateur theatricals' was the stock joke of all out-station men against their fellow-officials who led a more comfortable existence in Baghdad. Of course they in their turn joked about us and our ways!

'Finally,' he said, 'remember always to be strictly a man of your word. Be fair to your men and to your staff and to the Kurds you will be working among; don't cheat them and you will find they won't cheat you. Administrators who should know better, sometimes overlook the fact that in this respect the Kurds are exactly the same as any other people and are not difficult to get on with if one keeps faith with them.

'I shall be back from leave in six months' time and will come up and see how your work is getting on; I haven't had leave for six years, and don't want it now, but the Department insists that I must take it. Good luck in the meantime.'

As I drove away from the old town on the last hundred-mile stage of my journey, I came upon a lonely blind beggar by the roadside, hands extended for alms. He was squatting upon the bare stony ground, and there was neither fellow man nor sign of village for miles around. He looked a pathetic figure so I stopped to give him a rupee; whereupon in the Kurdish tongue he called down the blessings of Allah upon my head. As we journeyed on I thought of some of the reports I had heard of the country to which I was going, and felt that the goodwill of Allah might well be needed by any who came to live and work in Kurdistan.

From Kirkuk, my route led across an upland plain to the Lesser Zab River and the town of Altun Keupri, which in Turkish means the 'Bridge of Gold'. Perhaps there may once have been a bridge of gold, but today a steel military bridge of the 'Inglis' type has replaced the structure blown up by the Turks when they retreated in 1918. The town is for the most part built on an island in the Lesser Zab and is famed especially for the huge fish, up to two yards in length, which the natives capture by throwing in drugged bait which stupefies the fish so that they can be netted and dragged ashore—a most unusual method of angling!

A farther thirty miles, and we came to Arbil. Rising above the plain to the height of 120 feet like the truncated cone of some extinct volcano and topped with great brick walls, there stood the most ancient of all the inhabited cities on the face of the earth.

Mark Twain speaks eloquently of Damascus as being an old city even in a land of old cities, but Damascus is a fledgling compared to Arbil. Ur of the Chaldees may be as old, so also may Babylon, but neither of these have been inhabited continuously for thousands on thousands of years from before the dawn of history to the present day.

Yet such a record can Arbil claim with certainty. Who built the great mound on which the modern city stands? There is no tradition of its having been the work of one or other of the kings or conquerors who ruled there. It merely grew. City upon city decayed into the mound which slowly rose through countless ages till today it stands about twice as high as any other such mound in the world.

It is recorded in the Scriptures that the city of Arbela (Araba Ilu— the Four Gods) was one of the group of four cities of ancient Assur, namely, Assur, Nineveh, Nimrod and Arbela. Arbela was the religious shrine of this early pre-Assyrian civilization, probably because it was the oldest of those towns. Even then, three thousand years ago, it was a very old city that had held the temples of gods and goddesses since Sumerian times. As to what records, perhaps even of the neolithic period, might be found at the bottom of the mound, none can tell, for as it is still inhabited no archaeologist has dug there, and in any case it would take batteries of steam shovels to move the many millions of cubic yards of earth that form the mound of Arbil.

One of the reasons for its continuous habitation down through the ages is that Arbil has its own water-supply, rising from deep tunnels called 'Karez' dug long ages ago. They cannot be destroyed by vandal conquerors as could the irrigation channels of Babylon and Ur and the cities of the South. But the gods would seem to have had a special care for Arbil and to have protected and kept her alive long after her far greater rivals had decayed, for neither Khorsabad nor Nineveh were at the mercy of artificial water-supplies, yet for thousands of years they have been dead and obliterated, while Arbil has flourished serenely.

It was to Arbil that Darius fled after his historic defeat by Alexander the Great, the first European conqueror in Asia. The great battle was fought in 331 B.C. only a few miles away near the banks of the Greater Zab. Alexander then penetrated the mountains of Kurdistan and his name, Iskander, is revered in the East today and survives in many legends and place-names.

'The vitality', writes Soane, 'that kept Arbil in existence since those early days has not deserted it at any period, for it has been worthy of mention at least once during the supremacy of every one of the nations that successively ruled it, Assyrian, Mede, Persian, Greek, Parthian, Roman, Armenian, Roman again, Persian and Arab.'

For a time it is said to have been the seat of the famous Saladin who repelled the Crusaders in the twelfth century. The Mongols, who destroyed nearly all other cities of Mesopotamia, sacked but could not exterminate the immortal town, and the Turks, whose indifference let so much fall into decay, were outlived by Arbil. They abandoned it days before the British walked in, and never a shot was fired by British arms and never a bomb was dropped on Arbil.

6. Arbil from the Air

7. A Kurdish Ploughman

Northward to the Mountains

Arbil by day towers as a mountain and a landmark, by night its lights shine as a beacon for many miles. It was fitting that this historic city should mark the beginning of the new road that was to pierce the age-old mountain barrier of Kurdistan.

CHAPTER IV

The Road

As we drove from Arbil towards the mountains we passed fields where crop-cutting was in full swing. The Kurdish people, whom I now saw for the first time on their native soil, wore clothes quite unlike the long flowing robes of the Arabs among whom I had lived for the last four months. They had wide baggy trousers and loose tunics made of woven goats' hair, a coarse cloth, grey in colour, but dyed in stripes of deep blue and purple and embroidered with more brilliant greens and whites. Round their waists were knotted wide cotton waist-bands which I afterwards discovered might be six or seven yards of full-width material, the selvedge edges hemmed together so that valuables could be kept inside the band and the whole length then wound and twisted many times round its owner's body. On their feet were hard leather shoes, rather boat-shaped with their pointed tips turned up; and on their heads wide-brimmed hats that Hassan told me were only used during the harvesting, in place of the usual grey silk turban. There were women, too, among the harvesters, clothed in a single dark-blue garment, shapeless above and ending below in loose trousers rolled up round the ankles; their heads were uncovered and their straggling hair, in many cases dyed red with henna, fell loose upon their shoulders.

Arbil is an ancient city, but it is no more ancient than the agricultural methods I saw in use in the unfenced fields through which we were now driving. In this district there is quite a fair rainfall during the winter months and the plains have been famous for their fertility since the earliest times. The land is still ploughed with the same style of plough that the patriarchs used—the fork of a tree cut with one limb long and the other short to form a wooden hook that is dragged through the ground by a pair of oxen. The ploughman manipulates the implement with a wooden lever attached to it and prods the oxen into activity with a spiked stick. Sometimes, though by no means always, there is an iron ploughshare attached to the point of the hook to increase its efficiency.

The grain is sown broadcast by hand as it was in Biblical days. A better method was known four thousand years ago, for an engraving

50

on a stone seal of the Sumerian period has been found that shows a plough of exactly the type I have described, but with a seed-sowing tube attached which fed the grain into the newly-formed furrow, much as an agricultural drill sows grain on the up-to-date farm of modern times.

Harvesting the grain, which ripens quickly once the spring rains cease, is done with a sickle, wisp by wisp. Here on my first visit to the Arbil district I came across one of the most curious customs of the Kurdish people. Hassan told me that as the first handful of wheat was cut down in a field it must straightway be gathered up and brought to any stranger who may be passing; he must accept the gift and offer in return a silver or a golden coin to the harvester. In no sense is this a means of begging, but just an old custom of rejoicing with the traveller in the first fruit of the land.

From a field of standing grain, at one corner of which a small company of Kurds was gathered, sickle in hand, a labourer came running towards us with a wisp of corn. Having been told what this meant I took the grain and gave the harvester some silver pieces. The superstitious Hassan smiled with delight.

'You will have good fortune in Kurdistan for giving to the harvest field, as well as to the blind beggar of Kirkuk,' he said—and so indeed it proved to be, though I think Hassan had personal reasons for praising my occasional generosity.

The Kurds may be backward in their method of ploughing and reaping, but in the matter of threshing their harvest they have an invention that is, I should think, entirely their own. The cut wheat or barley is laid on the ground in the form of a flat stack twenty yards across and some two feet high. Round and round on top of this stack walks an ox or a mule drawing a curious carriage which, instead of wheels, has a wooden roller from which project iron blades. As the roller rotates these blades cut or crush the straw into short lengths and the grain falls out of the ear. Winnowing is carried out by throwing the cut heaps of grain into the air with fine-meshed wooden forks on a suitably windy day, so that the straw and grain are blown into separate heaps. The grain is gathered up into bags and stored, possibly under the dry ground near the village from which the harvesters have come, or perhaps in the granary of the rich and pious Mulla Effendi who owns large tracts of land round Arbil and whom I always heard spoken of as a wise and kindly man.

The whole system of cropping sounds primitive enough, yet many hundreds of tons of grain are gathered in good years from the historic plains of Arbil—always provided the locusts do not arrive before the harvest is ripe. If they do there is famine in the land, for no blade of grass, no leaf of tree, escapes them.

We had been following a narrow earth track between the harvest

The Road

fields and now climbed steeply over stony ground till we reached the Khanzad Pass, said to have been once the boundary of the territory of the great Kurdish princess, Zad. Here at last was the beginning of the new road-formation which I had come to carry through the mountains to the Persian frontier. I carefully studied the pioneer road-line below me winding in a steep gradient to the river-bed of the Bastura Chai which was now dry, but which in the winter could be a swirling torrent not to be forded by car or man or beast.

My hired car drove me over the Bastura for the first time, and we climbed again steadily past an old bastioned fort to the village of Banaman where a spring wells up in a pool by the side of the road. We drank from the slightly sulphurous water and rested in the shade of a mulberry tree, laden with white mulberries, which passers-by could eat to their heart's content. Then on again up an endless zigzag road with an unfinished surface of sharp rocks till we arrived at the top of a high limestone mountain range on which grew a few scattered and stunted oak trees. We had risen a thousand feet in the last six miles and were met by a cool, refreshing breeze coming from the peaks beyond.

This at last was the real Kurdistan, and what a panorama was unfolded! North-eastward before me lay range upon range of mountains—higher and still higher in the distance as far as the eye could see, the farthest topped with snow still unmelted from the winter storms. My map showed that many of the peaks were over ten thousand feet high and that the most distant of them rose somewhere near the Persian frontier about a hundred miles away.

To the right were the Safin Mountains, on the far side of which lay Shaqlawah village, which I must reach that evening. Beneath me the road zigzagged down a steep thousand feet to the bed of the stream that flows past the village of Kora. In the clear mountain air the great valley seemed not a stone's-throw across.

Some forty miles away upon a mountain range in the middle distance Hassan pointed out a dark cleft. Beneath that cleft, said he, lay the Rowanduz Gorge, the wildest spot in Kurdistan. I had been told at Kirkuk that Indian sappers and miners—the 63rd Field Company—had begun the task of hewing a roadway from the side of the ten-mile canyon and had been at work there these six weeks past.

As I looked out over the silent mountains I wondered what fortune lay before me and whether I should ever see the road reach the wilderness of rugged peaks on the far skyline, through a land said to be inhabited by people little better than savages. With a last backward glance at the plains, stretching away to Arbil and the deserts of the South whence I had come, I jumped into the car and, with a secret exhilaration I have rarely felt, entered the land that was to be my new home for four long years.

The Road

The road-gangs were working near Shaqlawah when I arrived to report to my Director who, together with a senior officer of Royal Engineers, had just returned from Rowanduz. That day there had been a desperate fight with stones, sticks and knives between several of the coolie road-gangs during payment of the fortnightly wages, several hundred men having been involved. By the time I reached the road camp in the evening the trouble had subsided and the injured had been taken to a local Turkish 'doctor' for treatment. All was peace again, but such was my first introduction to Persian coolies and their ways.

Shaqlawah is perhaps the most highly endowed village in Kurdistan for, from the base of the towering Safin Mountains, burst forth springs of ice-cold water in such profusion that they irrigate a sloping hillside several square miles in area where forests of poplar and walnut trees grow, and where gardens produce pears, apples, plums, apricots and grapes of the largest size and the most delicious flavour. Above the springs on the higher slopes of the valley are extensive vineyards of the low-growing black grapes which seem to be one of the hardiest of plants, for they lie buried under the deep snow in the winter and are exposed to the hot dry summer without any watering whatever; yet they bear masses of fruit.

I learned that Shaqlawah had been a troublesome spot for some years as far as administration was concerned. The headman, Kadir Beg, was known as 'Henry the Eighth', not so much from his impulsive character as because of the striking resemblance he bore to Holbein's well-known portrait. I managed later to get on very good terms with him and found him not a bad fellow. His village was of course mainly Mahommedan, but there were a few Christian houses within it. Though the Kurds had such a bad name, it was not uncommon for Jews and Christians to be living thus peaceably in Kurdish communities. There were also many entirely Christian villages in Kurdistan, one of the largest being Ankawa, near Arbil. I had come across no Christian villages in the Diwaniyah area, and it appeared that the fanatical Shiahs of the south resented other religions more strongly than did the Kurds who are Sunni Mohammedans.

The engineers' camp was pitched in the corner of the vast garden of Shaqlawah; there were two tents for living quarters and one for an office. Our beds were set up in the open air, draped in mosquito nets, though mosquitoes were fortunately few, probably because they cannot breed in the running water. The Director called for a large map and began to explain the task that the department had undertaken, and I heard for the first time the full story of the Rowanduz road-project.

Speaking of the district from which I had just come, he pointed out that we now had a fairly complete network of roads in the south and that there were few districts along the Tigris and the Euphrates which

The Road

floating bridges and roads had not opened'up, though lack of funds and the immense mileage of these tracks meant that the surface, especially during the winter rains, was not all that might be desired. Nevertheless it might be said that cars could now travel to almost any spot on the plains of Iraq by means of the large number of bridges and culverts that the Department had constructed over the rivers and irrigation channels. Except for the trouble caused by occasional wash-outs in the flood season, there was really little difficulty in making roads there. Surfacing them so that they should be fit for use in wet weather was a very different matter. Rock or gravel or the natural bitumen of the country had all to be brought from any distance up to three hundred miles, and only the roads near Baghdad were paved with these materials. For the rest, the earth surfaces had to be re-formed every year after the rains.

'You'll find', said the Director, 'that road construction up here in Kurdistan is on an entirely different basis. In many places it will mean cutting a track out of the solid rock of the mountain-side and you'll need steel bridges of fairly long span to cross the rivers. The work will take longer and cost a great deal more, but once done it should be of lasting and permanent benefit to the people.'

When I asked why this road was being constructed, he replied: 'There are two reasons, trade and administration. You know that all great nations, past and present, have found roads essential for main-taining law and order. Once highways have penetrated a region the wildest people are pretty sure to become peaceful simply by copying civilized modes of life. Moreover, empires that rely purely on military conquest usually fail to hold their people together for long.

'Of course it remains to be seen whether roads will be appreciated out here as they are in the West. A few have already been built in these mountainous regions, notably near Kirkuk and Mosul, and have already begun to show something of their pacifying influence. So now an extensive road programme has been laid out, the chief of the pro-posed schemes being the building of this Rowanduz road which incidentally should bring much more commerce to Iraq. It is planned to reach eventually right through the Zagros Mountains to the Persian plateau beyond: but the first objective is to carry it as far as the town of Rowanduz.'

Making use of his map to emphasize his points, the Director ex-plained that the large Persian cities of Tabriz and Teheran were not readily accessible from the Persian Gulf and their only railway connec-tion with the outside world was through Russia. Tabriz lies to the east of Lake Urmia in the Azerbaijan province, which is said to be the most fertile part of all Persia, this district being not more than two hundred miles as the crow flies from Shaqlawah, where we sat. For centuries a caravan trail had led through Rowanduz to North Persia

The Road

and had always been an important trade route. So it was anticipated that a steadily increasing trade would come down the new road once it was completed and made safe from robbers, and thence pass either westward to the Mediterranean, or by rail from Kirkuk to the Persian Gulf.

From the point of view of the time that might be saved in travelling from Europe to the Persian capital there could be no question of the advantage of the route. Using European and Turkish railways as far as Nisibin in Southern Turkey and motoring onward through Mosul and Rowanduz, travellers need take no more than ten days from London to Teheran, whereas by the Persian Gulf this is a journey of some weeks.

The matter had been discussed with the Shah of Persia who had been convinced eventually that the road had no motive other than trade and the tranquillization of the Kurdish tribes—a problem of as much importance to the Persians as to the Arabs, for Kurdistan lies partly in each of the three countries, Persia, Turkey and Iraq. The Shah had agreed to construct the connecting link on the Persian side and the two roads were to meet on the frontier pass of Zini-i-Sheikh near the village of Rayat. The prospect of a new outlet to the Mediterranean seemed on the whole to be welcomed by the Persians, possibly because they considered that, as matters then stood, Russia had too great a control over the trade and affairs of the Northern Province. Also it was soon apparent that nearly all the engineering difficulties of the proposed road lay in Iraq and that the construction of the Persian section would be easy in comparison. So it was agreed that the work should begin in both countries.

The first plan had been to construct a narrow-gauge railway rather than a road, so it happened that the first survey party had been under the leadership of a railway engineer.[1] He had, a year previously, laid out the section of the road, now partially completed, between Arbil and Shaqlawah over which I had driven that day. But the idea of the railway was given up and the project handed over to the Public Works Department, who had undertaken to build a road with reasonable gradients to the high pass on the Persian Frontier. Whether this was possible remained to be seen, for Kurdistan was unquestionably a land of unknown dangers and difficulties.

The line of the proposed road rose steadily from Arbil and crossed no less than five mountain ranges before it reached the Persian frontier at a height of six thousand feet. The summer months had proved to be much cooler in these northern mountains than on the plains of the south, but as to the Kurdish winter very little was known. It was believed to be bitterly cold and it was doubtful whether work would be possible between November and February. Also it was unlikely that the road already formed could be kept open during the deep snows

[1] W. J. Moffatt, C.B.E.

55

and the widespread mud that followed, mud so deep and sticky that a mule could scarcely wade through it. Therefore it seemed probable that the engineer-in-charge would be completely cut off from the south and isolated in this rocky wilderness for months at a time.

The work had been started as a co-operative affair between various Departments, but the Public Works Department had now been given complete control, and I was told that in the autumn I must be prepared to take over the whole job.

It was a thrilling prospect from every point of view. The road would be a romantic one, for it would pass through mountains where road-building had never before been attempted by any of the past civilizations, owing partly to technical difficulties, but mainly to the intractable character of the inhabitants.

Soane, who knew the Kurds better than any European of the century, had recently used this description of them:

'Shedders of blood, raisers of strife, seekers after turmoil and uproar, robbers and brigands; a people all malignant, and evil-doers of depraved habits, scorning the garment of wisdom; but a brave race and fearless, of a hospitality grateful to the soul, in truth and in honour unequalled, of pleasing countenance and fair cheek, boasting all the goods of beauty and grace.'

What a wealth of paradox is here, yet these were words hardly calculated to reassure the new engineer!

Certainly the Company of well-trained Indian Sappers and Miners at work in the Rowanduz Gorge had been unmolested during its few months in the district. It was, however, a fully-armed force, and the Kurds had considerable respect for Indian troops since they had encountered the Gurkhas during the 1920 rebellion. It remained to be seen whether or not, when they were withdrawn (for the Sapper Company was to be repatriated to India), the tribes would then show themselves to be hostile or not. This was really the main problem.

From a scenic point of view the road was likely to be unique. Even the section of it over which I had already come was of singular interest, while ahead there lay the wonder of the gorges: first the Rowanduz —said to be perhaps the finest of its kind in Asia—where a tributary of the Greater Zab had cut its way through the Kurrek Mountain which rises to a height of seven thousand feet. Beyond this was the Berserini, a place so rugged as to be well-nigh impassable, the ancient caravan route to Persia avoiding it by surmounting a pass nearly five thousand feet in height rather than penetrate between its sombre crags.

The engineering difficulties presented by these gorges would not however be considered out of the way in any civilized part of the world where skilled workmen and proper machinery are always available. But here the men employed on the road were Persian and Arab coolies accustomed only to hand tools and entirely ignorant of the working of machinery. Possibly they could be taught, but there were bound to be many breakdowns before they had learned to use pneumatic rock-drills and heavy steam-rollers with any skill, and there were no repair workshops nearer than Baghdad, three hundred miles to the south.

The gangs at present working on the road were carrying on the job with picks, shovels and crow-bars. Machinery had been ordered, but it would be many months before it could be delivered. It had to be sent from England to the port of Basrah on the Persian Gulf, six hundred miles away, thence by rail to Kirkuk, and by lorry to Shaqlawah. Beyond that it was a question of mule or camel caravan.

Sir William Willcocks, the famous irrigation engineer, once said:

'With the power of steam and electricity at our disposal, with blasting powders and dynamite, and above all with labour-saving machinery, we shall be able in our day to accomplish in a score of years as much as a whole dynasty of the ancient kings working with hundreds of thousands of prisoners.'

Quite true, provided that the machinery can somehow be transported to the work and that men can be taught to use it when it gets there.

Yet we were fortunate in having in London the services of the Crown Agents for the Colonies who, among their varied activities, supply engineering and other equipment to the British Protectorates. We knew that their great experience would enable them to select the kind of bridges, sheds, winches, steam-rollers and stone crushers that we needed. They are accustomed to supply anything from a needle to a battleship; they know just what an engineer requires in the jungles of Burma or the deserts of the Sudan and always send something well suited to the job in hand.

It was a pity that the uncertainties of finance promised to add greatly to our difficulties. Definite annual allotments for the expenses of road construction could not be settled beforehand as they depended on the general state of security of the country—always an unknown quantity.

In spite of all the worries such a job was sure to entail, the adventure of this great scheme could not fail to grip me, just as it later stirred the imagination and brought me the co-operation of the very people whom I had thought to find my worst enemies—the Kurdish tribesmen themselves.

I was to begin work on that portion of the road that led over the Spilik Pass, a lonely spot with an unsavoury reputation for robbery and murder, about twenty miles beyond Shaqlawah. Beyond this pass lay the Rowanduz Gorge, and my orders were to go to Spilik, collect my own gangs from such labour as presented itself and get to work.

The Road

A few days later, with my little caravan of tents and stores guarded by two Kurdish policemen, I set forth accompanied by a native clerk and by Hassan and an Assyrian called Guerges, whom I had engaged to cook my meals and help Hassan in the affairs of the camp.

Over the Mirowa Pass and down the Batas Valley we trekked steadily towards Spilik, and I had ample time to look around me as my mule jogged slowly on. On my right rose a steep mountain range, the Harir Dagh, just bare rock and scant vegetation. Upon it, high up on a prominent spur, stood the ruins of an old castle, the fortress of the famous Princess Zad, and farther on, near Batas village, I was told there was a rock carving of great antiquity to be seen near by on the hillside. My eyes, however, became fixed on the zigzag trail leading from the beautiful valley we were traversing, up and up to the summit afar off—the celebrated Spilik Pass. There was enough and more than enough for an engineer to think about besides rock carvings.

CHAPTER V

I Camp on Spilik

If you look at the map of the Rowanduz district you will see that this pass is the only one that leads over the Harir Dagh and that it commands the way to Turkey and Persia. The caravan track winds up beside a deep abyss on the steep mountain-side, among great boulders higher than a standing man, and as we climbed up it I was reminded of Kipling's lines:

There is rock to the left, and rock to the right, and low lean thorn between,
And ye may hear a breech-bolt snick where never a man is seen.

Spilik Pass had always been the home of robbers and brigands.

That day when I arrived to begin work on the pass I knew little about the country or the people and I could speak no Kurdish at all, but I revelled in the mountain scenery and the invigorating air. As I looked back from the top of the long zigzag, I could see an old Kurdish road, or 'raiga' as they call it, winding through 'wadis' and over low ridges to the blue foothills of Babachichek on the far skyline towards Arbil. This was a shorter route from Arbil than the one I had followed through Shaqlawah. Away to the north-west lay the silver thread of the River Zab where it pours from the narrow inaccessible gorge by which it pierces the high mountains of the Harir Dagh. Like a portcullis the range shuts the highlands of Rowanduz off from the lowlands, and only at Spilik where the ridge drops below four thousand feet could the merchant traffic find a way. For many centuries travellers had come and gone by this road, and in consequence the brigand chieftains had flourished merrily, as became Kurdish gentlemen.

But I was thinking more of engineering problems than of possible brigands and looked around for a spot to make my camp. My tent was finally pitched near a spring not far from a deep rift in the rocky hill-side, and near a Kurdish village which I was told was called Kala Chin. A clump of oak and wild-pear trees gave a little shelter from the sun and wind, and I could see no better camping place.

A Kurdish overseer, Ramze Effendi, had been appointed to assist me, but he had no knowledge of road-making and could speak no

English. A year earlier he had been a rebel, but had capitulated and been taken prisoner with the famous Sheikh Mahmud after that leader's third great effort to form a Kurdish State independent of the new Kingdom of Iraq. Ramze had won repute as an able leader of the rebel tribesmen and had harried the Iraq Army and the British Levy Troops from the hill-tops round Sulaimaniyah. A man with his knowledge and his reputation among the people would be likely to prove invaluable, so I determined to do my best to gain his loyalty and to teach him his job thoroughly.

There also came an Assyrian overseer called Benyamin Yonin. As the Assyrians are Christians and the Kurds Mohammedans, these mountain folk had often been enemies—as indeed they were during the rebellion of Sheikh Mahmud in which Ramze Effendi took so important a part. It was the Assyrian Levies in conjunction with the R.A.F. who brought the trouble to an end, so I wondered how my two overseers would get on together.

The surveyor was a Hindu, and my clerk a Chaldean Christian. Yet with the help of this strangely assorted staff, I managed to get together some hundred workmen, offering them the magnificent remuneration of one rupee a day (about one and sixpence), or a little more for masons or craftsmen. The men who joined up were chiefly Arabs and Persians, though we also conscripted a few tribal Kurds by authoritatively ordering them to come and work—a bit of pure bluff, for we had no force except two policemen with which to back up our commands. It was a relief when later they came readily of their own accord.

With an Armenian as our expert in blasting (he said he had learnt the job in the Turkish Army), this party of different races and religions set to work with a will to clear the huge boulders and use them to form a wide well-graded road, partly cut out of the solid rock of the hillside. Fortunately we all seemed blessed with enough sense of humour to laugh at our racial differences, and the work forged ahead without trouble.

It was hot on Spilik in the summer of 1928. The blazing sun fell full on the rocky face at midday, and the temperature usually reached 110 degrees in the shade. This was my first experience of road-making in tropical heat, and I found it trying, for we worked hard for seven days in the week. In the towns of Iraq the Mohammedans must not work on Friday, the Jews close down on Saturday and the Christians rest on Sunday. To simplify the holiday problem we compromised by having no holiday at all. I had yet to learn that it pays to have one day's rest in the week and to give up two or three hours to the midday siesta during the summer, making up the time in the early morning or late evening when it is cooler; but during that first onslaught upon the new road we stopped work only when darkness compelled us to, and took no more than an hour's rest at midday.

I Camp on Spilik

The waters of the spring above which my tent was pitched oozed down the hillside in small puddles and perhaps it was here that the mosquitoes bred. In the evening they appeared in millions and attacked mercilessly. The district was malarial and as it seemed impossible to escape being bitten I had to live more or less on quinine. Eventually I found a way of defeating most of the swarm when they came out at dusk athirst for my blood, for I adopted the dodge of lighting a very smoky fire of horse-manure in my tent. When the acrid smoke had driven my tormentors away I ate my meal in a thick fog and crawled under my mosquito net before the fire went out. They returned only to find themselves baulked of their prey. It is perhaps questionable whether the mosquitoes were much worse than the smoke, but in this way I was usually able to get a night's sleep. Nowhere else in Kurdistan did I find the mosquitoes quite so bad; perhaps I got used to them later, and also I made use of those excellent insecticides that are sprayed into the air, and thus made life much more bearable.

There were scorpions too which had a habit of climbing leisurely up the inside of the tent (to get a better view of their victims, I suppose) and then dropping down on to the table and waving their deadly tails in the air ready to strike if they should see the chance! Snakes of many colours and all sizes were also in abundance in the summer months. Sometimes they visited my tent, but more often I saw them wriggling off into hollow trees or under rocks as I walked along the hillside.

Then there was Guerges—his name is Assyrian for George—whom I had engaged to cook for me. He produced strange varieties of indigestible Turkish dishes and while I writhed and swore, he made voluble excuses saying he had no proper fireplace and no 'mudbukh',[1] but just two stones and a petrol tin. Now Guerges was a character, a man of rather mixed antecedents, and certainly of many experiences. He had been with the Russian army which had sacked Rowanduz and, like most Assyrians,[2] was more accustomed to the use of firearms than of cooking utensils. He was feared in the camp because he never moved even at his cooking without his pistol, and never seemed to sleep. He spoke a jargon of Persian, Kurdish, Turkish and Arabic dialects and could make himself understood in any of them. I conversed with him in my bad Arabic, though his grammar was, if possible, worse than my own. His linguistic versatility however made him invaluable to me where so many languages were in common use. But as a 'chef' Guerges was, I must repeat, a failure. Except during the fruit season, which lasted about three months (and fortunately was just beginning), I lived almost entirely on the highly flavoured dishes to which he gave Turkish names, or else on hard-boiled eggs and the

[1] Cookhouse.
[2] Guerges was really a Persian Christian, and not a true Assyrian.

61

unleavened bread of the country. The latter is a mixture of barley and wheat-flour (and grit) moistened with water and baked in ovens which are merely holes in the ground lined with mud, well dried, and fired with glowing charcoal. The thin sheet of dough is plastered on to the hot interior of the oven and left there a few minutes to cook. It either falls off into the charcoal or else brings away with it some of the hot earthy surface on which it is baked. There was of course no butter available to eat with it, but I found that the native cheese made from goat's milk had a pleasant though rather aromatic flavour and was most sustaining.

No Indian cook could be made to stay in these wild mountains for love or money so I had to be thankful for Guerges. And let me be just to him. Out on the mountain-side he was a splendid scout, and no trek was so hot or so long, so cold or so difficult, that he could not provide some sort of a meal, bought, borrowed, or stolen at a halting place. He had a rough, unpolished exterior and fairly broad ideas as to where my property began and his ended, but, later on, I was much better able to judge both his good and his bad qualities, as you shall hear. I paid him well and never checked his local purchasing account very closely, so he decided that I was worth keeping alive lest worst masters should befall him; and in time his cooking actually did improve a little.

Neither the heat nor the mosquitoes nor even Guerges could hinder the progress of the road as could the lawless tribesmen of the district if they chose. My overseers delighted to tell me of the battles which had occurred on Spilik. It had been a favourite spot not only for brigandage and fights between the settled tribes and the nomads, but also for the more serious encounters of military forces of different nations.

Long ago on the east side of Spilik, where the road drops to the Rowanduz Gorge, the Turks established the fort of Kani Uthman to try to control the depredations of the brigands who made the pass their headquarters. It seems more than likely that the Turkish gendarmes shared in the spoils of the robbers, for the lonely outpost seems to have done little good from this point of view. It played its part, however, in checking the Russian Army which in 1915 tried to pass through Kurdistan from Persia to Mesopotamia, where they hoped to join the British in capturing Baghdad. The Russians by a marvellous march reached Rowanduz. They failed, however, to win the exits of the Gorge past the Turks and had to retire to Persia. But before doing so, they destroyed more than half the town and behaved with unnecessary barbarity.

Again, in 1920, when open rebellion against the British spread up to Kurdistan from Diwaniyah and the south, many of the tribes proved tough customers to subdue. Elusive as the mountain ibex, they know every track and hiding-place in their wild fastnesses, and their grey-blue clothes match the grey-blue rocks to perfection. They are born huntsmen and splendid riflemen, seldom missing their man. Conspicuous amongst the Kurdish rebels of that period were the brigands of Spilik, whose activities continued unchecked until there appeared a certain Captain Lymington.

Lymington was at that time an officer of the Levies, a man untiring and without fear, the equal of any Kurd in hill-craft. He fought his way right through this country in revolt, with no assistance other than a good horse, a ·45 calibre Colt pistol and a mere handful of followers. On lightning raids he captured several of the rebel leaders and brought them to Arbil as prisoners. Sometimes he made secret marches by night to capture these men, often lighting fires as he went to guide pilots of the R.A.F. who could thus co-operate by night-bombing if there was any resistance. The 'coups' had to be timed to the minute if they were to be successful, and their sheer audacity had a great effect in bringing the troublesome tribes to heel. Lymington himself could never be ambushed or caught napping. He had a curious defect in the control of one eye that somehow caused the Kurds to attribute supernatural powers to him. By night or by day they felt they were never safe from the man whose roving eye hypnotized his enemies and who could surely see through the night like the mountain leopard.

Spilik was the scene of important military operations as late as 1923. After the withdrawal of British administration from Rowanduz in 1920 the town was occupied for a time by a small Turkish force under the military adventurer, Euz Demir; and though the British fought several small actions against the Kurds in the Batas Valley they made no effort to dislodge these Turks from Rowanduz until the intrigues of the latter with Sheikh Mahmud and other Kurdish leaders—notably one Nuri Bawil of Rowanduz—made such action imperative.

Probably because they still feared retribution for their active part in the rebellion of 1920 and their still later resistance to British authority, Euz Demir had been able to persuade a fairly strong force of Kurds (mainly consisting of Nuri Bawil's followers and the local Surchi tribe), to hold Spilik Pass against the expected advance of the Levies from the Batas Valley. The Kurds were supported by a considerable number of Euz Demir's men from Rowanduz.

Spilik Pass was difficult to take by frontal attack and presented a perplexing problem for the Air Vice-Marshal, Sir John Salmond, who commanded the ground as well as the air forces of Iraq at that time. He dealt with the situation by brilliant strategy. In order to mask the real plan a fairly large force of the Levies was mustered on the Batas plain as if in readiness for attack, while airmen bombed the defenders of the pass. Meantime a second British column had set out from Koi Sanjaq far to the south of Spilik and was steadily advancing through the mountains to reach such a position that they would be able to attack the enemy in the rear and thus cut them off from their base at Rowanduz. The Turks discovered the manœuvre too late to arrange any strong defence against it, though they contested the British advance in one sharp action at the head of the Alana Su Valley.

When this action failed they wisely considered that their position on Spilik was untenable. It is often said that though Turkish soldiers can make a determined stand against a frontal attack, they dislike the unexpected in warfare and to be thus taken in the rear on Spilik was not at all to their taste. Moreover their alliance with the Kurds who were assisting them was always a frail one, so the enemy took to their heels and sped back through the Rowanduz Gorge before they could be intercepted. They even evacuated Rowanduz town and the two British columns occupied it unopposed.

The Levies then established a camp at Diana some four miles from Rowanduz, where there is a fair landing ground for aeroplanes, and this remained their base in the district until they were disbanded in 1932. During these nine years Diana became the chief village of the Assyrians in Iraq, and many of them proved of great assistance in my work as they were excellent stone-masons, clerks, storekeepers and guards.

I had been advised to secure a reliable man to protect my possessions on Spilik and I employed one of these Assyrians, an ex-Levy corporal, as night-sentry for my tent. At first I considered this almost an unnecessary precaution and was apt to be annoyed at his excess of zeal when I was awakened in the middle of the night by his loud challenges in unknown languages and by bullets crashing into the darkness. Probably there was never anyone to challenge, but as I came to learn more of the Kurds and their ways I realized that an over-zealous sentry was better than a sleeping one—particularly on Spilik Pass.

There are in Kurdistan nomad tribes who migrate every autumn from the mountains to the plains as the winter snows drive them down, and who return again in the spring to the high hill-pastures on the frontier far beyond Rowanduz. Partly by right of ancient custom, but more by the force of their arms, these tribes move with their vast flocks of sheep and goats and herds of ponies through the settled foot-hills to the lowlands, fighting their way when the local inhabitants oppose them. When I saw the straggling flocks of the nomads, well guarded by their shepherds, taking heavy toll of the scant dry grass of the local landowners, I was reminded of these lines of a well-known Australian ballad writer:

Now this is the law of the Overland that all in the West obey,
A man must cover with travelling sheep a six mile stage a day;
But this is the law which the drovers make, right easily understood,

8. The New Road up Spilik Pass

9. Spilik Pass Policeman, Guerges and Hassan

10. Mule Caravan Transporting 'Juss' to Kani Rash

I Camp on Spilik

They travel their stage where the grass is bad, but camp where the grass
is good;
They camp, and they ravage the squatters' grass till never a blade
remains,
Then they drift away as the white clouds drift on the edge of the saltbush
plains,
From camp to camp and from run to run they battle it hand to hand,
For a blade of grass and the right to pass on the track of the Overland.

One day some time after the new road had been extended from
Shaqlawah to Spilik, I was returning from Arbil when I heard that
there had been a brush between the local Surchi tribes of Spilik and
the Hurke nomads, who nearly every year came into conflict with the
villagers of the foothills. Several women were engaged in this fight, for
they are just as warlike and as good shots as the men. I arrived in my
car at the camp to find my Assyrian road-foreman, Deriouish by
name, fully armed with rifle and bandolier. This was strictly against
orders, and I made him take them off at once.

'But, sir,' he said, 'there has been a fine fighting here between the
Surchi and the Hurke tribesmen. Khidher Agha with his Surchi was
shooting very nicely, sir, from these rocks, and the Hurke men and
women were shooting from down there. I am near the middle, sir,
with my road-gang, and I am bringing my rifle and shooting at both
sides to make them stop, please. But no, sir. Eleven men altogether are
getting killed, and four women. The mounted police coming from
Batas and stopping them a few hours ago. Khidher Agha, he is fighting very nicely, sir, shooting good, sir,' concluded the Assyrian
enthusiastically, for he had the hill-man's eye as to how such fights
should be run.

'Well, in future, Deriouish,' I said severely, 'you cut this shooting
business right out. These are private fights and you are not allowed to
join in. Let me hear no more of this sort of thing or you will be
sacked.'

He saluted and went away grinning happily at being let off so
lightly. He belonged to one of the famous fighting tribes of the
Assyrians, and he wanted me—and the Kurds—to know it. That was
the first time I heard of Khidher Agha, and it was not to be the last.

The thousands of migrating tribesmen, passing for days with their
endless herds of animals, were often a great hindrance to our work,
for they found our partially formed road the easiest path to travel
over and in wet weather they churned the earth of the unfinished road-
bed into hopeless mire. Moreover they liked the new track so well that
they camped beside and on it and were reluctant to move their flocks
to let a car pass.

These nomads had never seen a car before and were greatly amused

E
65

by mine, which I had sent for as soon as the progress we made with the road had warranted it. I sometimes gave them a lift. On one such occasion a picturesque Kurd, fully armed as always, had the back seat all to himself. I felt something uncomfortable poking into me between my shoulders and looking round found it was the barrel of my passenger's rifle. He was sitting back smoking quite unconcernedly with the butt of the weapon between his feet and the muzzle in the middle of my back, but was quite agreeable when I took his rifle and told him in unmistakable language he might point it somewhere else (for it was almost certain to be loaded). At the end of the journey he felt something was due to me in apology for his carelessness, so presented me with two pomegranates. It was all he possessed other than his long thin pipe, his patent lighter that all Kurdish men cherish, and his rifle and dagger.

Another evening I came back to my tent on Spilik to find a gruesome gift awaiting me. A human skull rested on my tea-table! Benyamin Yonin, the overseer, presented himself with a beaming smile.

'We found him under a rock, sir, and thought you would like him as a souvenir of Spilik Pass. He has been dead only a few years, sir,' he added hopefully, when he saw my enthusiasm for skulls was lukewarm. Now all the religious sects of the East are equally rigorous about collecting and burying their dead. Bodies must be recovered at whatever risk and properly interred. So what waif was this who had met a lonely death on Spilik, unknown to his friends? I ordered the skeleton to be properly buried, skull and all.

After this it became the custom for my men to bring dead bodies to my tent. In a land where rumour and fact get so mixed up they doubtless felt that the actual corpse prevented any possible doubt on my part as to the victim's being really dead. If, as was usually the case, the man had been murdered, the chief culprits were often the most active in this 'habeas corpus' business, apparently in the hope that they would thus prove their innocence. But their ready accusations and stories usually made me place them under arrest along with any others I might suspect, until such matters could be referred to the nearest district police post which was at Rowanduz.

CHAPTER VI

The Brigand, Hamada Chin

The village of Kala Chin lay above the Spilik caravan road over the Pass where the track wound along by the deserted fort of Kani Uthman. The men of Kala Chin had a reputation for pride and bravery as befitted their lawless profession. For centuries they had been robbers and brigands, levying toll on the travellers and caravans that passed over Spilik on the long journey from Arabia to North Persia. The brigand chiefs called their trade a kindness to humanity, for, said they, the rich and heavily laden are assisted on their way relieved of all encumbering baggage! Moreover, might not a merchant's wealth, his cloak, nay, even his boots, be considered only fair payment for the privilege of traversing the famous Spilik alive?

As the pass overlooked the old road for many miles, caravans could be seen while they were still far off, and the brigands could wait behind their natural ramparts of rock till they were certain of the business of those who approached. Should they prove to be merchants they might be merely robbed and let go, provided they submitted without fuss; but should they be armed forces or interfering officials they could be shot even before they knew that enemies surrounded them, for there was no better ambush in Kurdistan than the rocks of Spilik.

The chief of the village was Hamada Agha, once a ruthless swashbuckler, now an old man less active than in the wild Turkish days, but said to be as cunning as ever. He was believed to be the instigator of the many schemes that were carried out by his son and lieutenant, Khidher Agha, whose shooting abilities had been so much admired by my Assyrian road foreman on the occasion of the fight between the Surchi and the Hurke tribes.

When I first came to Kurdistan I had little time to think about the chance remarks I had heard concerning the evil reputation of Spilik Pass and I had unwittingly pitched my tent almost within a stone's throw of the most notorious village in the land. But I was soon warned of the possibility of danger by one whose opinion I could not lightly disregard.

I had asked my friend, Squadron-Leader Bryson of the Air Force, to spend a few days with me in Kurdistan. It was perhaps one of the ironies of warfare that Bryson who had two and a half rows of decorations on his tunic, had fractured his pelvis in an ordinary accident with his car far out on the flat desert. I hoped he might come to the hills to enjoy a better climate for convalescence than the intense heat of Baghdad, but he replied that he was fit again and on duty. He could not join me, therefore, but he gave me a useful hint. He had at one time been Special Service Officer for this district, which meant that he had thoroughly investigated the behaviour and intrigues of the people and knew the character of every tribal chief.

'Beware', he wrote, 'of that ——, Hamada Agha, and his offspring of the village of Kala Chin!'

A warning from Bryson would not be given without reason, for on his reports air-squadrons and infantry battalions might be moved about like chessmen. My work, however, kept me fully occupied, and I confess I paid but little attention to his letter. Nevertheless, I made some inquiries concerning Hamada Agha and the recent history of the Surchi tribe from my overseers and servants, who proved to be only too willing to tell me of their exploits, for the Oriental loves to relate (and exaggerate) deeds of violence.

It was thus that I learnt much of the history of Spilik that I have recorded in the last chapter; and also heard details of the implacable attitude of this robber clan towards that Englishman who had the misfortune to be the first British administrator to come amongst them.

The story has some dramatic incidents. When Mosul was captured by the Mesopotamian Expeditionary Force in 1918, the Rowanduz district passed nominally into British hands, and a certain Political Officer, Captain W. R. Hay, was given the difficult commission of keeping it in order. Perhaps his most troublesome task was that of controlling the brigands of Spilik.

He once succeeded in capturing Hamada Chin after a stabbing affair, and imprisoned him. In revenge, on the day of his father's release, Khidher attempted to murder Hay by shooting at him through the window of his house at Arbil, and only the prompt action of Captain Lymington, who happened to be in the house at the time, saved his life. For although unarmed, Lymington attacked the would-be murderers the instant the first shot was fired. When they recognized their assailant they fled, for no man in Kurdistan was more feared by evil-doers than this officer. So on this occasion the vengeance of Hamada Chin was thwarted.

The British Political Officers in Iraq knew the importance of personal contact with the tribesmen and their chiefs, and, regardless of the risks they ran, spent much time journeying through the country, usually with only small guards of native recruits, trusting to their own acumen and knowledge of the people and to sheer daring (which the

The Brigand, Hamada Chin

Kurds greatly admired), to see them through in safety. Many courageous men died bravely in the course of their administrative work in those early days, but by the manner of their life and death they won for their nation a name for fearlessness and fair dealing and, for those who followed them, a greater safety.

Captain Hay on several occasions journeyed beyond Spilik to visit Rowanduz, always one of the most troublesome spots under his control. From his own written accounts he seems to have regarded this turbulent area with the special affection of a parent for the most wayward child, even though he risked his life whenever he went there. When he was returning from Rowanduz in August of 1920, an adventure more alarming than usual befell him. He was passing through the Rowanduz Gorge—accompanied by a bare dozen horsemen separated into twos and threes along the ten-mile track in the narrow defile— quite unaware that a band of assassins lay in ambush behind a great rock where the path twists along by the side of a stream. Three of Hay's men who formed the vanguard well ahead of the rest of the party rode unwittingly into the trap. They were ordered to surrender and pass on in order that the Englishman might follow, unsuspecting of the ambush. But the three retainers proved 'loyal to their bread', as the Kurdish saying goes, and the man who rode first shouted defiance and opened fire upon the assailants. He was at once shot dead and the other two were seized, stripped and beaten.

The shots that were fired caused Captain Hay and his companion to halt and, after reconnaissance, to send back to Rowanduz for a detachment of the Levies who were at that time under the command of Lymington. When, pistol in hand, he arrived with his little force on the scene of the brutal deed the assassins had disappeared, and the journey through the gorge was completed in safety.

It speaks well for Captain Hay's popularity that this villainous attempt on his life and the killing of a loyal henchman were strongly denounced by all the Kurdish tribes. The men of Kala Chin were of course loud in their protestations of ignorance of the whole affair. But it is difficult to keep secrets in Kurdistan, where every man knows every other, and at last it was whispered that the leader of this mysterious band of miscreants, who had vanished as if into the rock of the mighty gorge itself, had again been none other than Khidher, son of the brigand chief, with the intriguer Nuri Bawil (who had his own reasons for greatly resenting the presence of the British in Kurdistan). Once more had Hay narrowly escaped death at the hand of the implacable Hamada Chin, and once more had Lymington defeated the brigand's plot.

When the rebellion, of which these attempts on the life of one of Britain's Political Officers had been but a minor event, was finally suppressed, all the rebel leaders were pardoned, Hamada Chin among

The Brigand, Hamada Chin

them; for Hamada had been no worse than many others during that period.

But because he was pardoned the old brigand saw no reason why he should reform his lawless ways. One day he was in the Arbil office of the Administrative Inspector, Captain Clarke—'Chakbo', as he was called by the tribesmen—who was endeavouring to settle a dispute which had arisen between him and one of his neighbours. His past had been quite forgiven and he was being shown every consideration in the case when, suddenly, incensed by some remark of his opponent, the aged Kurd drew his dagger like a flash and would have plunged it into the body of his enemy, had not Clarke—knowing the Kurd and his ways—foreseen the attempt and caught his wrist. The drawing of a dagger during arbitration is an unpardonable offence in Kurdistan, and means a feud until death with the other litigant. Moreover, the British Administration could not but regard such conduct as crime, so the decision was given against Hamada Chin. That chieftain then departed, infuriated with Clarke and with the British in general; and a proud, scowling—yet picturesque—old brigand he looked as he rode off to his mountain home. He and his ancestors had defied Turkish governments, and he would continue to defy this British administration.

Englishmen secretly admire such men whatever their duty and the law may say about a matter of this kind. Accordingly Clarke sought no further punishment for the impetuous chieftain, and with great courage he not infrequently visited Kala Chin as the guest of the brigands. Such was their increasing respect for this officer that the general conduct of the chief and his followers began at last to show marked improvement.

When the Rowanduz road first began to penetrate the mountains, the question which exercised the minds of such men as Clarke was how would the lawless tribesmen behave towards the road-engineer and his unarmed working parties. Doubtless they knew that the building of the road meant the end of their ancient independence. It may be remarked here that the road-line was admittedly not the best one from a purely engineering point of view, but wound hither and thither through the territory so as to pass near or through the villages of the most dangerous men, in the hope that contact with civilization might persuade them to become more peaceful. I was, however, warned by Clarke of the possibility of opposition to my work on the part of any or all of these 'specially honoured' tribesmen.

One day I had been busy checking levels with my Indian surveyor far beyond Spilik Pass. Usually when I required a horse on odd occasions such as this, I hired the first that offered, and I could not expect uniformity of performance. I had found that the horses of the plains could not be made to stop galloping; on the other hand, the ponies of the mountains were often never allowed to gallop at all and were as docile as donkeys. Perhaps just as well, you would say, if you could see some of the dizzy tracks round the precipices in the gorges.

This morning there was no horse available and I walked up from the camp alone, leaving instructions that a horse was to be found and sent after me. I was detained on the work till dusk, and as there was no sign of the horse I had ordered, I borrowed a pony from the surveyor and rode back up Spilik towards my camp. It was a lonely, eerie path over which no caravan passed after sundown. This evening all was silent except for the drone of night-beetles. The gnarled and stunted oaks and the wild mountain-pear trees, hollow and shattered by parching droughts and winter snows, raised their crooked branches like the spectres of dead victims of that track, and in the dim light of the stars they seemed to wave me back as from some impending danger. I rode idly along, rapping the ribs of my pony with a stick and thinking of the many deeds of violence that had happened hereabouts. The path wound past a huge rock on which passers-by had piled pebbles (some said as incantations against the evil spirits of Spilik), and as I rounded the rock, there in the middle of the track stood a lantern, and behind it a crouching figure with a rifle. I rarely carried firearms except on the fortnightly pay-days when I brought money up from Arbil. It seemed a pretty hopeless show, but I felt that if I must be killed, I had best put a bold face on it; so I rode steadily towards the light and said loudly in Kurdish: 'Who is that?'

'It's me, sahib,' answered a familiar voice. 'There was no horse, so I came to meet you. This track is dangerous for a man alone.'

The sinister crouching figure whom I had thought to be an assassin was none other than the worthy Guerges who had come with rifle and lantern many miles over the lonely pass to escort me home!

Even the anxiety shown by my servants, and their belief in the perils that encompassed us, failed to forewarn me of the totally unexpected way in which real danger from the village of Kala Chin was to present itself; and this was how I first came in contact with Hamada Chin.

My bearer, Hassan, had hired for me an old grey horse. When I attempted to put the animal to a canter, his foreleg struck a rock and, as he collapsed, I was catapulted over his head on to the stony ground. I thought he was killed, but fortunately neither of us was the worse, and, in a bad temper, I remounted and rode on. I found that the staying power of that horse on a long journey was marvellous, especially considering his age. On one occasion I was pressed for time with a fifty-mile ride before me, yet after nine continuous hours he was still untired. In his youth he had probably been a very fine performer, but those days were past, and I took another mount for the remaining seven hours of that hot midsummer's day.

The Brigand, Hamada Chin

The hire of a horse in Kurdistan varies according to the kind, condition and age of the animal, and also whether fodder and a man to tend the beast are supplied by the owner. This horse had a gaudy Kurdish saddle, but little else besides his endurance to recommend him. A rupee and a half a day was, therefore, fair payment to offer; but when the owner himself, whom I had not seen before, came to collect the money and found that I offered only twenty-one rupees for fourteen days' hire, he gave me a terrible look, his hand went to his 'khunjar', or dagger, and for a full second he seemed to have a mind to kill me. Then he spat upon the floor, a most deliberate insult, turned on his heel and strode away.

'Hassan,' I said to my bearer, 'tell that unpleasant old man that I have twenty-one rupees to give him before evening. If he doesn't like that he can go to the devil and take his horse with him, for he won't get one anna more. I don't want to see him if he comes tomorrow, and I don't like his manners. Tell him so.'

In the evening the old man returned and told my servant that if I had little better to offer for the hire of his horse than the wage I paid my coolies there was going to be trouble.

'Good,' I said. 'Bring him here. Now ask him just what trouble he intends to make.'

Again those baleful eyes were fixed on me, and I returned his stare with equal fury. The man looked so wrathful that I began to think that there was perhaps something behind it all that I did not understand. He still fingered his dagger handle as if ready to spring, but he held himself in check. His red-dyed beard sank suddenly on his breast, and he muttered something unintelligible.

'What does he say?' I asked Hassan. 'Is he cursing me?'

'No, he just says he will take whatever you offer him.'

'Good,' I said, handing him twenty-one rupees. 'Let me get his receipt for the money. His name?'

'Hamada Agha of Kala Chin,' said my servant.

'What,' I exclaimed, in amazement, 'this cannot be the famous brigand of Kala Chin!'

'He is surely Hamada Agha, sir. We have not seen him before as he is getting old and sick and goes out little. He says that had he wished he could have shown you long since who was the chief of Kala Chin and of the Spilik Pass. He has done you no injury because "Chakbo" of the British is his friend, and asked him to help in the road-work; so he lent his horse. He says it is a great insult to him and his village to offer a coolie's rate for the horse of the chief of Kala Chin. It is now perhaps old like its master, but it was once the finest and fastest in Kurdistan, as many of his enemies could testify.'

So here was the notorious Hamada Chin! He had lent his horse, his own horse, as a chieftain to his guest (for I was his acknowledged

The Brigand, Hamada Chin

guest as my tent was on his ground). This was not the hired mule of a caravanchi.

'Had you visited him when you entered his estates, as was due to his position,' Hassan continued to interpret, 'he would have feasted you with honey and the fattest goat of his flock, but again you insulted him and his people by ignoring him. Nevertheless, at his orders his tribesmen have left you unmolested. Today, had he been a younger man he might have killed you in his anger—but he says it has now abated!'

There was every reason to believe these words, for the Kurds are very impulsive and care little for the results of their actions.

'Tell Hamada Agha', I replied, 'that I did not know who he was or I should have shown him the respect due to a chief. As for the payment, I shall raise it to what is befitting the hire of a chief's horse. The animal may be old, but like his master is still valiant as when young. I have indeed done Hamada Chin an injustice and offered insult through ignorance, but, insha Allah, God willing, perhaps he will forgive me. "Chakbo", and indeed I myself have good reason to look upon him as a friend.

'If he will pardon me and still hold open his invitation, I shall visit him and accept his hospitality. I trust that long after he and I are dead, his prospering tribes will speak always of Hamada Chin, terrible in war on his swift grey horse, yet greater still in peace, for he has made friends with the British and the Government of Iraq and helped in their works; and his tribes and flocks have increased and multiplied as never before.'

For years I passed and repassed over Spilik in the course of my work; often I was forced to halt overnight there with large sums of money I was taking to the road-head for payment of labour; yet neither I nor my men were ever robbed, and my relations were always of the friendliest with Hamada and Khidher and the men of Kala Chin—such is the remarkable and, in my experience, friendly character of the Kurd.

CHAPTER VII

Gali Ali Beg

I had set out the new road-line over Spilik Pass, and the work of moving the great boulders into long walls which would enable an evenly graded road to be built on the sloping mountain-side was proceeding satisfactorily when orders came from headquarters for me to join Captain Franklin, the Inspecting Officer of Police, in an extensive tour he was about to make through the Rowanduz district to select sites for police posts in the mountains towards the Turkish and Persian frontiers.

I was glad of these orders. If an engineer is to be sure that a road is located on the best possible route he must have a good knowledge of the whole of the surrounding country. Moreover, as Rowanduz was to be my station for some years to come, part of my job would be to carry out other works of the Department in the district. I wished, too, to seize every chance of getting to know the tribes-people better; for, apart from the interest I was beginning to take in the Kurds and their ways, I needed to find out what were the prospects of securing labour for the road-sections that lay ahead, and whether any of the tribes were likely to be hostile, as this would mean I must ask for armed protection for the work.

It was suggested that on the tour I should visit the Kurdish governor of the Rowanduz district, the famous Sheikh Sayed Taha, and try if possible to win his active assistance. I knew that nominally he was pledged to support the road because it was an official project, and his was an officially recognized position; but what his real feelings towards it might be I had as yet no means of knowing. Sayed Taha was in very truth the ruler of this province, and up till now little restraint from Baghdad had been imposed upon him, though the proposed police posts and above all the road I was engaged upon were calculated to break the mountain stronghold of this clever and imperious man—one of the last of the great barons of Kurdistan.

He was a man with a great reputation. For a Kurd he had been well educated, and he knew more than a little of the art of government. He was of high Kurdish descent, and in addition was a 'Sheikh', a title which has quite a different meaning to the ordinary Arab word, for in

74

Gali Ali Beg

Kurdistan it denotes a man with special religious power. Though the designation 'Sayed' means that he was a descendant of the Prophet this is a much more widely shared distinction. The Kurdish people believed Sheikh Taha could work miracles, and they came many miles in order that his hands might be laid upon them to heal their sicknesses. To Englishmen he usually denied that he possessed any such powers.

Far from being a religious 'faqir', however, he was, in every sense of the word, a man. He stood over six feet in height, was of powerful physique and loved to display his great powers of endurance by long journeys on horseback and by difficult feats of mountain climbing. He rode magnificently, was no mean performer at polo, and was the best rifle shot in the country—having something of the reputation of William Tell for marksmanship. It was said that he could stand ten cigarettes on end and at thirty paces, using an English service rifle, which he always preferred to the Turkish or Russian weapons, could hit each cigarette in turn without a single miss. I never saw him do this remarkable feat, and doubt it; but, as a hunter of bear, leopard or ibex, he was far famed. Every autumn he spent several weeks in the mountains, and sometimes invited one or two of the Levy officers to join him. They always came back full of admiration for his endurance and skill.

I knew that the success of my work as a road-maker, and even my safety, depended largely on the attitude of this man towards me. If he chose, he was powerful enough to ask for my removal from the district on one pretext or another. Or if he thought the new road would be dangerous to his power, he might easily arrange for my disappearance in some less official way. He was responsible for the conduct of the tribesmen, and any weakness in his administration might encourage lawlessness and interference with my work; altogether he was a man to be reckoned with.

So I welcomed the prospect of a tour through the domains that he kept at peace by the force of his strong personality, and thought that if I had the opportunity of talking with him in the midst of his own people, I should be able to convince him of the unquestionable value of the road to his country, however much he might distrust present politics and resent the sapping of his power.

Before the date of the proposed tour I met Sheikh Sayed Taha quite unexpectedly on Spilik Pass. A long line of armed and mounted men were filing up the old caravan path amidst my workmen, who were busy on the new roadway. They paused from their labour to salute the celebrated chieftain as he passed, and the name 'Sheikh Sayed Taha!' was murmured up the hillside, leaving me in no doubt as to who the traveller might be.

He was accompanied by a large retinue of servants, clerks and interpreters and a train of mules laden with bulky purchases. The party was returning from Baghdad where the Sheikh had gone to talk with King Faisal and the High Commissioner. It was seldom that he deigned to visit the deserts and cities of the South.

Mounted on a great black stallion which picked its way carefully among the jagged limestone rocks, Sayed Taha looked indeed a true chieftain prince of the wilds, yet when he reached me he dismounted and greeted me in very good English. I am taller than most people, and had already found that in Iraq it pays to look as imposing as possible when dealing with local rulers, but I felt almost insignificant before this big, smiling diplomat who asked polite questions while he eyed me keenly.

'How is the road progressing? When will it reach Rowanduz? What can I do to assist in expediting the work?'

Whether or not Sayed Taha really wanted to see the gates of his ancestral stronghold shattered was a matter which puzzled me. Quite possibly he believed as I did that it would eventually benefit his country, though he himself might fall by it. He was evidently either a great bluffer or a game loser, probably both.

A potential king of Kurdistan, feared if not loved by his subjects, fate had forced him to submit to the government which British influence upheld. After all, he had something to thank us for. If the Turks could have captured him he would have been executed, for as a leader of rebellious tribes, he had been a thorn in their flesh for years. He would also have been arrested by the Persian Government if they could have laid hands on him. Again, the Arab ministers in Baghdad would have been delighted to crush him if the High Commissioner had allowed them to do so. High though he stood among the Kurdish chiefs, his was a lonely grandeur, for he was surrounded on all sides by possible enemies. The British were his only protectors—and he knew it.

Nevertheless, his position was a difficult one for us to uphold. The Sheikh had his own police force, called 'Shabanas', who were armed and paid with government money, yet there was little or no check on the collection of revenue from his district. These 'Shabanas' helped to guard my work and stores and did it well, giving me no cause for complaint, but it was said elsewhere that their actions were often highhanded. It is a custom among both Arabs and Kurds that any man, whatever his character, may throw himself on the mercy of a tribal chief, who is then bound to adopt him into the tribe, treat him according to his rank, and protect him from his enemies with armed force if need be. I was told that among Sayed Taha's men were many malefactors from the surrounding districts who had fled to him for sanctuary. Certain it is that there were some strange characters in the Sheikh's following, though for that matter my own labour gangs contained men who were probably little better. When men came asking for employment I made no inquiries about their antecedents; I knew that many of them were ex-criminals; but, as long as they wanted to work and would work well, I was only too anxious to take them. My policy emulated in a humble way that of Henry Ford, who writes: 'Our employment office does not bar a man for anything he has previously done—he is equally acceptable whether he has been in Sing Sing or at Harvard, and we do not even inquire from which place he has graduated.' I had to make one or two exceptions to my rule, but of that you will hear later.

Sheikh Sayed Taha, having paid his diplomatic compliments and taken stock of the engineer, remounted his stallion and passed on over Spilik, leaving me still uncertain of his real thoughts concerning the road which was pushing forward into his domains. Later on, however, I got to know him much better, and his good will towards me proved invaluable. He understood right well how to manage his own people, ruthless though he was; but, like others of these hillmen, his proud and independent spirit finally brought misfortune and downfall upon him.

Captain Franklin with his force of twelve mounted police duly arrived *en route* for the tour of the frontier with the Kurdish Commandant of Police from Arbil, and we proved to be a most friendly party during the days of journeying we spent together. Nearly all of us were mounted on mules, my own a sturdy animal, small and tough, while Franklin's was a huge female brute, as big as a hunter, with a habit of wailing at frequent intervals like a lost soul in torment.

To me it was a memorable journey. First came the Rowanduz Gorge. I had heard many accounts of its grandeur, not only from the enthusiastic Hassan, but from all who had ever seen it. Nevertheless, I thought that when I should come to study it with the impassive eye of a maker of roads I should find it commonplace enough—but it was not so.

Kurdistan is a country of high mountain ranges lying parallel to each other, approximately north-west to south-east. Beginning with the foothills near the Tigris, each range rises higher than the last till finally the elevated Persian plateau is reached with its fringe of towering peaks.

Between the ranges lie long valleys, down which run rivers and streams. But the really unique feature of these ranges is the number of mighty gorges that the rivers cut in their endeavours to escape from this mountain system to join the Tigris. Often enough these ravines are not straight clefts; they wind in the most curious fashion and have endless ramifications. The Rowanduz is the best known and perhaps the grandest of them all. It has no less than five branches through which tributary streams flow to join the Rowanduz River, and each of these is itself an imposing canyon.

Gali Ali Beg

Look again at the map and you will see that the Rowanduz River enters the first arm of the gorge on the north-east side of the Kurrek Range at Rowanduz town and flows mainly westward, but twisting repeatedly at sharp angles and enclosed for many miles between almost perpendicular walls of rock. Farther on, as it passes beneath the Baradost Range, some few miles to the east of the brigand village of Kala Chin, the gorge opens out into a valley that is wider from side to side but even more completely inaccessible. In this valley the Rowanduz meets the Greater Zab flowing from Barzan and the remote highlands of the Hakkiari province in Turkey where the Assyrians once had their home. Every Assyrian speaks with pride of the beauties of this land and the legends of these Nestorian Christians claim the upper Zab as the true site of the Garden of Eden.

When the Rowanduz and the Greater Zab flowing from opposite ends of the same valley meet, head on, the confluent waters turn at right angles into the solid rock, and bursting through the mighty Bekhme Gorge emerge on to the lowlands of the Harir plain. The river pours through the chasm over jagged reefs in boiling cataracts and whirlpools, between rock walls which in places almost close overhead. In flood seasons it may carry more than half the waters of the Tigris. At Bekhme, where it escapes to the plains, I judged that a dam for hydro-electrical and irrigation purposes could be built under almost ideal conditions, and near by on the Harir plain thousands of homeless Assyrians might then have been settled and have established industries, if we had thought fit to continue to control Iraq. Such visions of a peaceful security for these people have, however, never materialized.

In this fifty-mile maze of gorges and canyons an explorer may follow one of the grandest formations of nature to be found in the world. The Bekhme Gorge itself is impassable for animals, and only a man with the agility of a cat dare undertake the dangerous passage, scrambling over the huge boulders and round the ledges on the precipices where they overhang the torrent. This journey has been undertaken more than once, but no man has yet followed the Rowanduz River through all its winding defiles, and of course it has never been properly surveyed. There are but few Kurdish villages along its rocky yet often beautifully wooded sides, and the villagers who live there are wild, primitive creatures even as Kurds go. Many are cave-dwellers, still living under rocky vaults with their sheep and goats, just as they have done since the birth of the human race.

Only from a few points on the tops of the precipices in this deeply cleft belt of highlands can one see down into the depths where river meets river and from which comes the ceaseless roar of surging waters. I am possessed of a curiosity that drives me to see all that there is to be seen; yet, though I lived for two years in the Rowanduz Gorge, it

Gali Ali Beg

was months before I was able to find ways down even into that section through which the road was to be made; and never was I able to scramble along all those vast ramifications of 'galis', such arduous climbing, almost perpendicularly up and down, did it entail. My investigations in the depth of the ravine enabled me to map out the shortest possible route through the labyrinth and obtain fairly easy gradients for the road. From an engineering point of view this is as it should be, but I knew that those who might eventually travel through the gorge by car would see relatively little of the grandeur that lay around and above them, just as passengers through the Simplon catch but glimpses of the beauties of Switzerland.

But this detailed knowledge of the gorge I obtained later on. Now as I sat on my sure-footed mule and jogged along by Franklin's side I realized only its immensity.

From Spilik we followed the old caravan track, which was then the only path that would take us through to Rowanduz, and descended into the valley of the Alana Su down the steep shale slopes beyond the old fort of Kani Uthman. Ahead of us rose the towering range of the Kurrek Dagh, its leaning walls of limestone appearing to block the end of the valley down which we rode; but, as we approached, we saw a V-shaped cleft in the face of the rock into which ran the stream we were following. Passing through this hidden entrance to the gorge, we found ourselves in an impressive ravine where fine trees grew on the steep slopes on either side. A hundred yards or so from the rocky doorway we turned to the right and crossed a bridge, narrow and without parapets, that shook beneath the tread of our mules. The animals, however, seemed quite unconcerned, and later on I found in Kurdistan many bridges that were far more hair-raising than this one.

The track, which here had been partially formed into a roadway by the work of the Indian Sappers and Miners was overshadowed by a beautiful canopy of foliage. It wound through the bottom of the canyon, twisting with the stream. The huge rock behind which the brigands had waited for Captain Hay was pointed out to me. It was big as a two-storied house and had been christened George by the Sappers. Later on, the motor-road was blasted through the very middle of it, and it was found to be prolific in fossil ammonites, as large as footballs.

Now we came to the only bit of flat land in the whole gorge, a few acres of level ground at the foot of a precipice, and at that time the camping place of the Sapper Company to which I have referred. I was to live for two years in this spot, officially labelled 'Mile 65', but better known as the Camp of Gali Ali Beg, the Kurdish name of the great gorge itself.

The track led up out of the bed of the Alana Su by a steep and rocky path, and here the work of the Indians was left behind us. We climbed some six hundred feet or more and, as we rose higher on the south wall, I began to get some notion of the extent and complexity of the mighty rifts and their branches, and to realize how narrow they were in comparison to their depth. I felt I could almost reach out and touch a towering pyramid of rock that rose opposite where we stood and must have been some thousand feet in height. On the peak of this pyramid was a little look-out post built of boulders where I have since often waited at dawn for ibex. It looked quite close, but to reach it would mean a long and difficult climb, for the main gorge lay between.

Higher and yet higher mounted the caravan track. A side trail branched off leading on over the summit of the Kurrek Dagh, but the main road to Rowanduz which we followed turned to the left, and rising more gently now, wound round steep and sharp re-entrants overlooking a river which could be seen as a silver strip almost vertically below. I pointed out to Franklin that this river could not be the Alana Su we had left, for it was flowing in the opposite direction and I was told that this was my first sight of the Rowanduz Chai, the real river of the gorge.

As we descended beyond the highest point of the track, Franklin checked his mule and pointed across the gorge to a strange and unexpected sight. Through a narrow slit in the opposite wall the Balkan River delivered its waters. Framed between towering cliffs we saw in the distance green plains and a ruined bridge of many arches, beyond which rose a conical mound that was once perhaps a fort of Darius or of Alexander. The smooth plain, bathed in sunshine with no living thing visible upon it, seemed a land of peace and promise compared to the grim precipices that hemmed us in. It was almost as if we were looking through a window into another world. As we moved on the cliffs closed together again and the scene vanished as suddenly as it had appeared.

It was about here that a Kurd of the party who knew the place turned toward the cliffs and shouted, and the echo of his voice came back to us in ghostly fashion as if some traveller who had died upon the track were imprisoned for a thousand years within those rocky walls and cried to be released. A few yards farther and we looked out over a maze of yawning chasms, their depths shadowy even with the sun at its zenith.

'What do you think of this place, Franklin?' I said. 'It looks pretty hopeless to try to make a road through it. Can you suggest anything else we could usefully do with it?'

He stood and regarded the weird scene in silence for a time and craned his neck to try and see down into the depths of the canyon, then answered dryly: 'Well, I've only one suggestion that might help you; it'd make a most sporting golf-course, though I shouldn't care to have to hunt for my ball off the fairway!'

11. The Alana Su joins the Rowanduz River

12. The Caravan Track in the Rowanduz Gorge

Gali Ali Beg

We sat farther back in our saddles as we dropped rapidly into the gorge again, riding gingerly round the great bluffs that overhung the river beneath. Once I dismounted and kicked a stone from the track and slowly counted seven before we saw it strike the water far below! Just so long would it take for a man to fall if his mule slipped on the smooth rock of the narrow path. But mules are cautious creatures, and our beasts hugged the mountain-side with the utmost care. Only camels and horses from the plains earn the just reward of carelessness on this dangerous bluff. Bones lie in heaps on the sharp rocks below.

After this the track descended steadily, and I thought we should soon be riding alongside the swirling torrent of the Rowanduz Chai. Instead, we turned suddenly southward up a cleft where we were almost deafened by the roar of water which poured down the steep ravine to the Rowanduz Chai below. The track crossed and recrossed this torrent, in one place by a natural bridge of rock beneath which the water had tunnelled its way. As we climbed the thunder of water became ever louder, and then we saw that the mountain-side on our right was a mass of foam. A veritable river was pouring from the solid rock overhead. This was the famous spring that Hassan had once tried to describe to me in Diwaniyah and which was spoken of from end to end of Kurdistan. It is called Kani Bekhair, meaning 'the useless spring', because it cannot be made use of for irrigation as there is no arable land near it. The ruins of a building close by showed, however, that once it had been used to turn a Kurdish flour mill. These water engines are strange contraptions, though similar in principle to the Pelton wheels commonly used in most up-to-date hydro-electric installations. The Kurds have even invented an automatic arrangement for feeding the grain to the millstones, each revolution of the stone allowing a small quantity to pour into the central hole. One comes upon many of these mills still grinding wheat and barley flour in Kurdistan, but the mill of Kani Bekhair has long been out of use. There was no house or village to be seen, and the spring wasted itself over solid rock.

Only a 'chaikhanah' stood on an island amidst the running water, and here we rested gratefully and sat and drank tea in the shade of its thatched roof. We were told that in the burning heat of summer nowhere in all Iraq could there be found a more refreshing spot to sleep, for the air was cool from rushing torrents of ice-cold water all round.

'Does anyone know where this Kani Bekhair comes from?' I asked.

But no one did. The source of this river that springs from a mountain-side is quite unknown. That it must be fed by surface water is proved by the fact that it becomes discoloured in the wet weather, but no river of anything like its size is known to disappear into the earth in the mountains near by. The spring is perpetual; it waxes and wanes

F

according to the seasons, but it never dries up and its temperature is remarkably constant.

We climbed into our saddles again and filed off up the steep path that led out of the valley. After climbing some hundreds of feet up a shale track we reached a ridge and saw once more the plains near Diana, which we had already glimpsed that day through the 'window' of the Balkian Gorge. In the nine miles we had travelled from the entrance of the gorge of the Alana Su the track had risen and fallen like the temperature chart of a malaria patient, and I could see that the route we had followed was quite unsuitable for widening into a motor road, however well it might serve as a footway for animals.[1]

What a land was this in which to attempt to build roads! We paused on the crest of the ridge to rest our beasts after the long zigzag ascent from the spring, for the track had climbed at an almost impossible gradient and had passed up through a narrow cleft that the baggage mules could barely negotiate, and where they slipped frequently on the smooth rock.

Franklin mopped his brow, for we had been walking to rest our mules—a procedure that the police escort regarded as some form of English madness till they were curtly ordered to do the same themselves.

'You will need escalators on this section of your road,' he said, 'for I refuse to drive my car up that place. As for the rest of the track we have come over today, I wouldn't tackle those curves on the edge of the precipice even if you provided me with a parachute, and if it comes to the local taxi-drivers with their steering axles tied up with fencing wire, you know what would happen if you drove with one of them.

'If the Americans had this place anywhere near Coney Island they would build a switch-back railway on it that would be the world's thriller, and they would have a modern Blondin doing a tight-rope turn across the gorge with a wheelbarrow.

'Seriously, the moving picture people could stage magnificent scenarios and hair-raising dramas with Sheikhs and Primitive Passions, and all that sort of "movie" stuff. But, speaking as a layman, I should say that a road-engineer is surely rather up against it. What do you propose to do?'

'Well,' I said, 'the track we came by certainly seems to have disadvantages as a natural speedway. A road *could* be made, but I must reserve judgement till I have been through the bottom of that canyon, if it's possible ever to find a way into it; perhaps we can make a road to Rowanduz elsewhere.' I was thinking of the glimpse I had had of the Diana plain in the far distance through the wall of the gorge. There

[1] Later on this track was widened and greatly improved especially to allow of the easy migration of the Hurke flocks, for the Hurke had fewer enemies on this than on the other routes that they sometimes used.

was surely a possible route if one could once probe the bowels of this extraordinary valley.

We rode on past the remains of Turkish barracks built from the friable rock of the hillside, till a few houses appeared on a rocky face that sloped away below us for a thousand feet to a river in the distance. Before us was a great panorama and I could see that, of all places in the world I had ever visited, Rowanduz was about the most difficult to reach with a motor road.

CHAPTER VIII

Forts on the Frontier

Rowanduz is a strangely situated town, dominating the eastern approach to the gorge just as effectively as Spilik Pass, fifteen miles away, dominates the western entrance; for there is no track passable for caravans other than the one paved with slippery boulders that leads through the old bazaar beside the water-channel at a breakneck angle of descent that caused even our mules to stumble.

In this land of mountains, rivers, gorges and natural ramparts, the town could have been built in no more commanding position. It lies between two mighty chasms on a narrow tongue of rock that slopes down from the high range of the Kurrek Dagh. This tongue as it descends becomes a strip scarcely one hundred yards in width, which falls steeply until it reaches a flat platform of rock by the confined banks of the Rowanduz River, which here turns sharply into the canyon that bounds the promontory on the west. The stream runs between sheer walls five hundred feet in height with scant foothold, even at the bottom by the water's edge, for any animal larger or less nimble than the mountain sheep and goats which the nomad tribes sometimes drive this way. This was the beginning of the Rowanduz Gorge out of which we had climbed some three miles lower down at the Kani Bekhair spring. The second canyon on the eastern side of Rowanduz is that of the Handrin Chai, just as deep and awe-inspiring as its neighbour.

High on the steep and narrow slope and perched thus between two great precipices is the town of Upper Rowanduz. At the foot where the canyons almost meet are the ruins of the nearly deserted Lower Rowanduz. Between the upper and lower towns winds the ancient track which all caravans from Turkey and Persia had to climb. These caravans, as they passed through the town, paid dues to the local officials, and the great flocks of the nomads were tallied for taxation before they entered the gorge. Rowanduz thus collected a steady revenue—occasionally for the Government, when there was one, more often for the local administration or ruling chieftain.

From Lower Rowanduz two tracks diverged. One crossed the Rowanduz River by a narrow bridge without any parapet, above a sheer ravine some eighty feet in depth. Over this bridge came travellers from distant Turkey, and from Diana and the Kurdish villages of the north. The second track led up the valley to a spring called Kani Jindian, and thence over the pass of Zin-i-Sheikh to Persia, now only some forty miles away.

Rowanduz looks out on mountains on all sides—jagged and irregular peaks, nearly all of them over eight thousand feet in height, snow-capped for six months of the year; though even in summer, when their summits are bare, they are no less magnificent. Across the river which winds snake-like below the town, rises a high ridge of shale on which stands a massive fort, built, it is said, by Kor Pasha, the blind ruler not only of this district, but of the greater part of Kurdistan a century ago. Like most prominent Kurds he was eventually killed, in this case by the Turks, who finally overthrew him. Beneath the fort is a large storage tank for water, which was full even that midsummer when I visited the place, but the building itself was tottering, for it was said to have been badly shelled by the Russian mountain batteries in 1915.

The Russians, with some Armenians and Assyrians who had joined them—my servant Guerges was one of these—destroyed most of Rowanduz, and the lower town by the river still lies mainly in ruins, for only when the new road restored its importance did the towns-people begin to rebuild the place. I heard often from Guerges about the sacking of Rowanduz.

'I have twice burned Rowanduz,' he would say with the air of Julius Caesar. Modesty was never one of his virtues. I warned him that the less said about such exploits the better, for I wanted to be friendly with the Kurdish people; it would not help matters to have them taking revenge upon my servant.

However, the burning of Rowanduz had not been anything like the Fire of London. The houses have stone or mud-brick walls and the only inflammable part is the roof, which consists of beams and thatching, covered with mud and stones well rolled in to give a waterproof surface. Yet the destruction of the roofs at the onset of winter when they cannot be repaired, and the robbing of the season's grain, means dire distress to the people of a Kurdish town.

Rowanduz does not possess any noteworthy architecture as does the citadel of Amadia, the other ancient Kurdish stronghold in the mountains north of Mosul. Its buildings are crude and simple as the mountain itself. To withstand sieges such places must always have their own water-supply—though this may be anything but sanitary and is the common cause of widespread typhoid and dysentery. In Rowanduz the little stream which our party followed down through the narrow bazaar was far from clean by the time it had run a few hundred yards between the houses, even though it began as a crystal brook on the Kurrek mountain-side. My interest in the necessity for purer water was soon to be stimulated when I myself contracted a sickness that must have been due to drinking from some such infected source, and a year later I found great pleasure in laying pipes to supply clean water to Rowanduz.

The town is romantic in its history and in its very atmosphere, for it has always been a place of grim deeds and bloody retribution. Its greater and its lesser rulers alike have nearly all met with violent deaths and even today this reputation is being well earned.

It is not a big town—there is no room for a big town—but it is an important place, as it is the seat of administration in this district, and in it lived several notable people. The leading townsman at that period was Ismail Beg. Though not yet thirty he was a man far-sighted and ahead of his time. Nine years before when quite a youth he had been appointed by Captain Hay as local administrator, but now, for reasons as yet unknown to me, he did not hold any position of official responsibility in the district. He was, however, a Deputy in the newly established Iraq Parliament in addition to being the most powerful tribal chieftain of Rowanduz.

There lived in Rowanduz also Sayed Heusni Effendi, the editor of the local Kurdish newspaper—written, illustrated, printed and bound with his own hand, and the only one of its kind in the world. He wished to accompany our party on the tour we were making, for like journalists the world over he did not want to miss any good copy that was going, and rode along with us armed with a formidable-looking notebook in which he drew sketches with considerable talent.

The 'Rais-el-Beladiyah' or Mayor of the town was Mohammed Ali Agha, a veritable Vicar of Bray in the way he managed to prosper serenely, be there Turk, Russian, Briton or Arab in power in Rowanduz. Later on it so happened that one of my road camps was established near his home and this portly old man often used to call in to see me, usually to ask for some favour or article that I could not grant him. Yet we rubbed along fairly well for I made a point of doing for the people of Rowanduz whatever service I could. I used to arrange with him about trips for the schoolboys to come and visit the work and have an outing (not forgetting a good feed for them afterwards).

I found that all the townsmen became increasingly friendly as time went on, but on this first visit they seemed to me a 'dour' lot of people, so like are they in their reserve and taciturnity to the hillmen of Scotland. They have not the graceful manners of the Arabs, nor the same flattering eloquence to an unknown guest: yet I was to find that they had many more solid qualities. They were described to me as more miserly than the Arabs and less willing to be generous hosts, but I discovered that there was little truth in this, even though there was no doubt that the average Kurd has to live very simply and sparingly. His country is rocky and unproductive and there is little flat land fit for cultivation. They are a poor yet proud people.

Forts on the Frontier

We smoked and drank tea and coffee with the notables, answering their few gruff but quite friendly questions till Sheikh Sayed Taha joined our party. He had come to escort us to his famous summer resort, the Spring of Jindian, where a great feast had been prepared. It was dusk when we left the town, riding in single file behind the tall horsemen who led the way up the bank of the river. What a relief it was after being among oppressive cliffs all day to ride once more through a wide and open valley! The darkness deepened. Galloping tribesmen appeared, reined up suddenly with horse-shoes striking fire on the rocks, spoke to their chief and disappeared into the darkness again. I wondered with some misgiving what all this portended and where we were being taken. In reality it was just the normal fuss of making hospitable arrangements for our entertainment, and I cannot speak too highly of the kindness with which the Sheikh invariably received his guests.

We were ushered into his banquet hall—the cave in which rose the magic spring called Kani Jindian. The name means literally the 'spring of the genii'. This weird spring disobeys the laws of all rational springs, and Kurdish tradition says it has done so since time began. It flows and ceases half a dozen times a day—quite the most temperamental spring I have ever heard of. It comes from a deep recess in the solid rock of the Handrin mountain which is 8,600 feet in height. It starts and stops as it pleases, sometimes sucking back down the funnel at the rear of the cave, sometimes welling forth in a great torrent that overflows its channel and submerges the floor of the cavern. There is no regular interval in its fluctuations. The only explanation I can think of is that the water may come from some subterranean lake having a connection through the mountain with the air, so that winds or the barometric pressure may be responsible for the variation of its flow. Some of the springs of Kurdistan are sulphurous and some are thermal, but there seems no evidence of any geyser action here for this water is pure and ice-cold. It is used for irrigation and for driving the flour-mill that stands where its waters leap into the Rowanduz River.

After the feast, which was concluded with luscious grapes drawn up in great baskets from the icy depths of the spring, we slept outside the cave beside the fickle stream where it entered the gardens below, and at dawn we took leave of our host who sent with us two of his men to act as guides and to be security for his own good faith towards us.

The day's march found us far to the north towards Turkey, outside the village of Shaitaneh (meaning, I suppose, 'the Devil's village', for 'Shaitan' is the same word as Satan). Here the first of the police forts was to be erected. The headman seemed not overpleased when he heard what was to be done, so when I got back to Spilik I sent my tactful overseer, Ramze Effendi, to Shaitaneh to take charge, and with a small detachment of his late enemies, the Assyrian Levies, he kept peace there, for Ramze had a friendly, unobtrusive personality and a high sense of integrity which influenced the hostile and suspicious tribesmen more than blustering force could do.

We were now upon the fringe of what was said to be a dangerous locality, for we were within the sphere of influence of Sheikh Ahmad of Barzan, a somewhat fanatical chieftain who, though not openly hostile to the British, had not been particularly friendly in the past. In addition to the building of the police posts a road would sooner or later be made into his country to connect the isolated posts together. Then, perhaps, this redoubtable Sheikh might be induced to leave his highland fastnesses and discover the world that lay beyond his own hilltops. In the meantime his decisions and subsequent actions were of great importance to our projects.

I was beginning to have faith in the saying that no man is entirely bad; and I had been impressed by the fact that though my Department had already begun the building of a large block-house at Bleh, to the west of the district we were now entering, the work had not so far been opposed by Sheikh Ahmad. The commencement of this work had been the subject of much military consideration and two columns of Assyrian troops were mobilized at different points and ordered to advance, one from the east and one from the south, to capture the proposed site. My immediate senior, Major Perry, was notified that he must be prepared to co-operate and be ready to start building operations when the troops had taken possession. But the most carefully prepared military plan may go awry. Owing to changes in the time-table of operations the engineer reached Bleh before and not after the military conquest. When the troops arrived, one column from the east, the other from the south, scouts sent out ahead and flank guards advancing warily, prepared for some deadly ambush, they found the engineer had already pitched his camp on the site and was calmly going ahead with his building surveys!

In truth it has often been proved in Kurdistan that a small party, especially such harmless folk as an engineer and his workmen, can move about without interference where armies may be violently resisted. This was well illustrated when the Iraq army was eventually sent to patrol this territory, and at once came into conflict with Sheikh Ahmad. The Arab army would certainly have been defeated and perhaps wiped out, but for the timely intervention of the R.A.F. which saved it.

From Shaitaneh it is a long day's trek to Kani Rash—some twenty miles by the route we had to follow, over many steep passes and deep ravines. To give ourselves ample time to examine the country for sites for the police posts we left before dawn.

It is strange to set off on mule-back along a mountain path in the darkness, following close behind the dim figure of the rider in front, through stunted oak trees, over valley and spur, feeling the ground sinking or rising as the grade changes, but seeing almost nothing. Horses and mules can see fairly well in the dark, so there is no need to worry much except to look out for overhanging branches. One glances back along the caravan line, lit with the glow of a cigarette here and there, hears the tinkle of a mule-bell in the transport behind, and then dawn slowly breaks. Soft shafts of light gleam over the mountain-tops from the east, the long straggling train of animals becomes every moment more distinct, the rim of the sun at last appears and the golden ball leaps clear above the hills and mounts higher and higher into the sky as we jog on and on into the blazing heat of midday.

I was used to long rides by this time, but Franklin, though a hardened veteran of the Kut-el-Amarah siege of 1915, and a man of tall powerful physique with a reputation for endurance amongst the Arabs and the Kurds, was just fresh from his office and cursed heartily all the way. I admit that on the last stage of the day's journey my own temper was strained as much as his. While we carried on our investigations we had allowed the baggage caravan with the tents, food and servants to go ahead with orders to wait for us at the Biraz Gird River some few miles from Kani Rash. When we eventually reached the river after nightfall, tired and hungry, we discovered that our orders had been misunderstood and they had gone on. We had been without lunch except for a water-melon given us by a kindly Assyrian peasant. To add to our discomfort the mosquitoes were ferocious and we were not cheered by being told it was a particularly bad district for malaria. Franklin, being a police officer, was very exacting in his orders, and rather than overlook the matter he recalled the caravan already camped far ahead, even though we probably suffered more from this injunction than the offenders, who were already rested and fed. It was midnight before we eventually had our evening meal and could turn into our camp-beds.

The Biraz Gird is unfordable in flood seasons and near our camp was the site of an old bridge. A few of the piers still stood, for they had been built of good masonry, squared rock cemented with lime mortar. We were told an interesting tradition of this bridge, which was said to have been built by Harun al Raschid. The great Caliph was renowned as a builder throughout his wide dominions; and (possibly by the magic help of the genii), he is said to have constructed a bridge or a mosque in every place he visited. In Kani Rash near by is a mosque excellently built in the same squared masonry and lime mortar as the bridge, quite unlike the rough houses of the village where mud is used as cement. The name Kani Rash, they said, was derived from Raschid, and along the river is another village called Hauruna, obviously, we were told, another part of the Caliph's name. These facts were told us as proof that the story is correct and that this bridge was really the work of the central personage of the *Arabian Nights'* tales. As likely as not the structure was built in a night as was Aladdin's palace, but the ravages of time have undone the work of the ancient wizard. In its day it must have been a very useful bridge, and I suggested we should recommend the erection of another one in the same place even if we had to use slower and more orthodox means.

Indeed, the construction of the block-house for the police at Kani Rash was no simple matter. Here also, as at Shaitaneh, a small body of Levy soldiers was stationed, and, though they would have been quite unable to resist a determined attack in force by the Barzan tribes, their presence gave the workmen confidence, for the Levies belonged to Britain, which meant much in Kurdistan. In addition they held a strong position once the walls of the building were up, and they were good soldiers. As I have remarked, it is difficult to catch an Assyrian sentry sleeping.

The little force was in helio communication with the post at Shaitaneh, and Shaitaneh in turn with the main Levy Camp at Diana, so news of an impending attack could be flashed to headquarters in time for assistance to be sent. Fortunately, as it turned out, there was neither attack nor demonstration against the post throughout the course of the work.

Apart from the question of defence the transport difficulties were considerable. A kind of cement called 'juss' was required, made by roasting the alabaster (calcium sulphate) rock which is found in these mountains till it becomes a kind of plaster of Paris. This material had to be carried from Shaitaneh on mule-back and nearly a hundred mules were continuously employed on this job. Mules are sufficiently valuable animals to tempt any Kurd to turn bandit and drive them off. Other requirements, such as doors, windows, roofing and fittings had to be brought from far-off Baghdad and money had to be taken up for the payment of wages. I had learnt the lesson taught us by Faisal Ad-Dawish at the Basaiyah massacre in the south, so it behoved me to take every precaution. I myself visited the place more than once during the period of construction and took pains to ascertain whether there was any ill feeling in the district towards the Levy soldiers, or our workmen and their overseer, and if so, why; for troubles so often had small beginnings. All rumours or bad reports of the men's conduct were looked into, and changes made so that the right men were obtained for the work. Anyway, the redoubtable tribesmen of Barzan left us alone and even lent their own animals to help us.

Two days after leaving Kani Rash we came at sunset to the Battalion Headquarters of the Assyrian Levy Troops. I had begun to look upon these Assyrians with much respect and I had already met some of their British officers. The camp had a wireless station and was built alongside the natural aeroplane landing-ground. It was well fortified, sur-

Forts on the Frontier

rounded by pickets and a good deal of barbed wire and was neat and ship-shape in every respect. The businesslike challenge of the sentry as we entered, the guard on duty under the Union Jack, which was slowly lowered to the bugle-call as the sun set behind the mountains while all in that little community stood stiffly to attention, made an impressive spectacle in this most remote of all British outposts. As the last echoes died away we went forward to the Mess along an avenue where willow trees grew at intervals beside the irrigation channels on either side, and long rows of tall sunflowers stood in bloom.

After the weeks of solitude I had spent on Spilik Pass, followed by our arduous trek through wild and scantily populated country, it was strange to be pitchforked into a civilized environment again.

We were met by a big, smartly uniformed officer with cane and the red plumed hat of the battalion, who was afterwards to become a familiar friend in this strange land. A real Londoner, he greeted us in the serio-comic manner that I later knew so well, and partly in expression and partly because of his witty buffoonery, he was, to me, always distinctly reminiscent of George Robey.

'Hello chaps! You're Franklin and the engineer bloke, I suppose? Well, I'm Alf York. You sent a helio message from Shaitaneh, didn't you? Surprisingly it got here before you did, in spite of our signallers having handled it, so we wirelessed Mosul for extra beer. It hasn't arrived yet, but come and try a pint of yesterday's! Glad to get it used up; we find it doesn't keep well this hot weather. Seems to evaporate, specially if taken off ice and put in a mug alongside one's elbow.'

Captain York was accompanied by a couple of small fox-terriers who sniffed suspiciously at our legs as we dismounted, but forgot us entirely and gave way to a noisy chorus when three pet bears suddenly galloped up. They were young ones that had been captured in the mountains and they bounded up to us in the hope of getting the usual lump of sugar, but York warned us to beware of their playful embraces if we didn't want our clothes ripped to pieces.

Most of the officers at Diana seemed to be Scotsmen from well-known regiments, and I was delighted to find McTavish, whom I had met at Hillah, amongst them. Several had seen almost as long service in Iraq as Franklin himself. The Levies had been a considerably larger force and were at the time being gradually disbanded. There was only one other battalion left in the country—at Sulaimaniyah, farther south. A section of the force were now acting as guards to the Residency in Baghdad and to the extensive R.A.F. Headquarters at Hinaidi.

Owing to the disbanding, many of the officers were leaving to rejoin their regiments in other parts of the world. With their tin boxes strapped on mules they rode off from this wild outpost, reluctantly leaving the men they had drilled and led for many a year. At Shaitaneh I had spoken with an Assyrian officer of the battalion about a certain captain of the Argyllshire and Sutherland Highlanders with whom I had recently conversed on Spilik when he was on his way home to Scotland. 'We liked him well, sir, and we wept when he left us,' was the touching comment of the Assyrian.

The force was fully equipped for instant warfare and the training of the troops was most rigorous. Under the British officers were Assyrian officers—mostly the hereditary leaders of their tribes, for the Assyrians are a tribal people, much like the Kurds in this respect. Captain York introduced me to Yacu Ismail, the senior Assyrian officer under his command, and many were the adventures that we three were to have together.

The Assyrians are a strange remnant of a race whose history is veiled in much mystery. Archaeologists say it is not certain whether they are, as they claim to be, descendants of the ancient race of Sargon and Sennacharib. Nevertheless it is well known that the peoples of these lands keep their names and their lineage pure for thousands of years, and it seems by no means impossible that they may be true sons of that great race of antiquity.

Today the Assyrian is a hardy son of the mountains, though tradition says that in past ages they were plainsmen. There is no doubt that they were the foremost scholars of early Mohammedan times and founded the very first universities long before any were known in Europe.

Long though they have been Christians, Mohammed himself, in recognition of their learning, granted them a 'Firman' which gave them religious freedom. They were at that time the greatest of all Christian nations. Their missionaries converted whole communities as far afield as China and the coasts of India, where there is still evidence of their labours; their emissaries discussed religious matters with the Pope. They may have good grounds for asserting that their Nestorian form of Christianity is the most simple and unchanged of all forms, having come down unaltered since the very days of Christ.

It is strange that they should have survived all the terrible waves of persecution of Christians, and yet today, while under British protection, seem in danger of extinction as a race. Neither Mohammed nor the Caliphs nor the all-conquering Mongols nor the Seljuk Turks did them much harm, and only in the last two centuries have they been driven for refuge into the inaccessible Hakkiari mountains, and it is only in the last twenty years, during and since the war, that they have been reduced from a nation of over sixty thousand to some twenty to thirty thousand survivors, and scattered without homes or leaders.

The Assyrians of today have been rendered almost desperate in consequence of their recent terrible losses and suffering, and it is little wonder that when properly armed, equipped and trained as British soldiers they have become a formidable fighting force; and they have done their utmost to win the esteem of the British nation they served.

The village of Diana adjoined the Levy camp and in it the greater number of the surviving Assyrians lived at that time, partly for protection, partly because the village had become the centre of their national activities and their few industries. Some, however, lived in the villages near Batas, and others were being established in the somewhat malarial district round Kani Rash, and in several other districts as well.

Diana had been Christian for many years, though the land belonged to Ismail Beg of Rowanduz. He was, of course, a Kurd and a Mohammedan, but was by no means oppressive as a landlord and was highly regarded by his tenants, who found that his protective influence secured their safety. Every year at the end of the Mohammedan fast of Ramazan they visited and paid court at the house of Ismail Beg.

The journey from Diana to the Persian frontier and thence back to Rowanduz was almost equal in length to that which we had already travelled, and led us through country where a couple of years later my chief work was to lie. The Berserini Gorge was then impassable even to mules, and we struggled up the long climb of two thousand feet to the Dergala Pass, descended into a side valley of the gorge, climbed up another great spur and finally jogged wearily up the long steady ascent to Rayat and the pass Zini-i-Sheikh on the Persian frontier, six thousand feet above sea-level.

Here lay the districts of still other important chieftains who played their part in the building of the Rowanduz Road in later years. I could see that a vast amount of work would be involved in cutting a road through such continuously precipitous country. I felt, however, that the organization and machinery that could conquer the Rowanduz could also make a way through these passes, though it must mean long and patient years of labour.

But I had now lost some of my interest in scenery and wild tribesmen, even in engineering problems, for I had contracted dysentery shortly after leaving Kani Rash. Instead of being able to avail myself fully of the splendid opportunities of the trip and the hospitality offered by the chiefs we visited, I lived mainly under the kind but strict ministrations of Franklin, who allowed me no solid food, but fed me on castor oil, brandy, and the sour 'liban' or 'mast' as it is called in Kurdistan, which has remarkable curative properties for many complaints. This treatment relieved me, though it could not cure me, and when at last we got back to Spilik I went on with Franklin to Kirkuk to secure the treatment I was by then badly in need of. It proved to be of the 'starvation' variety, and at length, when I appeared to be cured, I was not loath to press for permission to return to my work. This hastiness was foolish, for the trouble came back and I did not throw off the sickness completely for several months, though I managed somehow to carry on with the job.

CHAPTER IX

Men of the Middle East

The first stage in the building of the road over Spilik was now practically finished and it was rapidly lengthening to connect with the Sappers' work in the gorge, so I left Benyamin Yonin in charge there and started a new front of attack—the widening and surfacing of the narrow pioneer track from Arbil to Shaqlawah.

Thus the great project was at last in full swing. News of the work spread through the country like wildfire, and men came from near and far, hoping that they would be needed. I had six hundred to cope with at the Pirmum Dagh—the high ridge the road crosses beyond Banaman—and but one overseer there to help me. To handle these large gangs efficiently was not an easy task. We had no office and no surplus staff at Banaman; the work was our one objective. I was engineer, paymaster, doctor and lawgiver to the coolies and skilled labourers of my working gangs.

It was fortunate that my overseer, Sabri Effendi, who had been another of Sheikh Mahmud's rebel leaders, proved almost as good as Ramze. His influence did much to keep the men contented, but there were of course always a few who were troublesome to control and others who were dishonest if they thought they saw a chance. At first I could not know each man individually, and at times some fellow would give a false name in order to receive another's pay. This offence, if discovered, meant a thrashing—not a severe one, for I found it was usually enough to put the rascal to shame before his fellow-workers. Others among the coolies had to be fined for laziness when they failed to complete their daily task under the piece-work system we used, though unfortunately I could do nothing to reward those who worked especially well—as for the most part they did.

In spite of severity in matters of discipline they seemed contented enough, and we had neither strikes nor lock-outs. To my great joy when they saw the road gradually advance as the result of their efforts, they developed a real enthusiasm for their job, an enthusiasm that never deserted them till the road finally reached the pass on the Persian frontier four years later. I became increasingly impressed by the tenacity of purpose of these simple people and by their capacity for

learning specialized work, and I soon found that they were well worth
the trouble of their tuition.

Moreover they were an entertaining lot. They were of three main
nationalities—Kurds, Arabs and Persians. Let me try to describe each
in turn.

There were several gangs of Kurds from the neighbouring villages,
dressed in the greyish goat's hair cloth of the hill-man, wide pantaloons
and knotted waist-bands in which they kept their money and valuables
and the inevitable curved dagger or 'khunjar'. If the latter (a nasty-
looking weapon) is meant for show only, it is tucked slantwise well
down into the folds of the waist-band; but if it may be needed for
instant use it is placed higher up on the front of the breast, so that it
can be drawn with the lightning rapidity for which the Kurds are
famous. I was told that in Turkish days they were forbidden to wear
the khunjar and if a man refused to surrender it he might be shot, so
strict was the law. We did not worry about this matter, however, but
trusted to other methods to maintain peace. My coolies might wear
their khunjars on the road-work as they pleased, without question,
and in the early days of our work the Kurds would arrive with rifles
and bandoliers of bullets slung over their shoulders and the khunjar
prominently displayed in their waist-bands. Later, when they found
that there was really no use for them and that these ornaments merely
got in the way, they took to leaving them at home. In tribal warfare
protection against dagger or sword thrust depends on a curious
pleated waistcoat, which for its purpose is almost as good as a coat of
mail. It is made of felt, tough as hide and nearly an inch in thickness,
and, as it is warm my Kurds often wore it in the winter. Their peaked
leather shoes were of local make and the dark-grey fringed turban
wound round the small skull-cap, completed the costume.

These village Kurds were unaccustomed to hard toil for long hours,
but they soon got used to working away steadily. At first, of course,
they had to be given the simplest of jobs, such as bringing rocks for
the masons. Also in the case of nearly all new men their work was
seriously interfered with by their habit of stopping for frequent intervals of prayer. I ignored these breaks unless I considered the prayer
was being prolonged for deliberate slacking and very soon they followed the example of the other workmen, gave up these interruptions
and entered into the competitive spirit of the work.

They knew no language but their own particular dialect of Kurdish
which, quite apart from the added difficulty of the many dialects, is
not an easy language to learn. Kurdish is closely related to Persian and
is possibly the original of that language, but there are so many
dialects that quite often Kurds from different districts cannot understand each other. But on the road-work at least I did not require a
large vocabulary, all I needed to say was, 'Hurry up! Bring big stones,

13. The Old Berserini Bridge

14. Kurdish Villagers

15. Rowanduz from the Air

bring plenty and bring them often!' for the Kurds are a sensible people and set little store by oratory. In this they are quite unlike the Arabs, who expend half their energy in chattering and singing their shanties, and require perpetual verbal goading to keep them at a job. Of course, there can be good Arab workmen, and bad Kurdish workmen, but I am speaking in general.

There were quite a number of Arabs on the road-work. They came in the summer and left again in the autumn, for they did not care to face a Kurdish winter. They belonged for the most part to poor tribes from the plains round Mosul and either had no lands to cultivate or else, possessing land, were too lazy to work it and preferred to leave farming to the attentions of their women-folk. They were typical of the poorer agricultural class of Arabs to be found throughout Iraq, and to reach the road-head had travelled over one hundred miles from their homes, carrying their belongings tied up in a cloth and slung over their shoulders on a stick, much in the style of the English tramp. Their clothes were the very simplest of garments. A long white shirt, usually made of coarse cotton or goat's hair woven by the women on their primitive looms, hung loosely to the feet. Over this they wore the dark abba or cloak, which they could pull up to cover their heads when they walked or squatted in a cold wind. Their head-dress was the typical mottled red and white 'kefiyah' hanging over the shaven skull and held in place by two turns of black rope called the 'agal' which balances on the head. They nearly always went bare-foot. Their feet had hard horny soles that defied the camel-thorn of the desert, but being without boots their movements on the sharp rocks of the mountainous regions were considerably restricted.

They were genial chaps, these Arabs, more humorous and talkative than the Kurds, and more skilful at evading hard work. They usually brought with them their absurdly small-bladed agricultural shovels with little wooden cross-pieces for the foot to press on. Of course, these tools were quite useless in the rocky ground, but the Arab smiled cheerfully when he was given a pick or a crowbar to toy with and brought his ridiculous shovel along again next year just the same. I believe they liked carrying them about.

They received the same pay as the other workmen, but spent very little on good food and tried to save as much as possible to take home to keep them in idleness during the winter. As a result they were of poor physique—often almost starved. I did what I could to make them eat decent food, but beyond seeing that it was available at a reasonable price, and telling them they looked an underfed lot, I could do little. A general kitchen, or a compulsory rationing with a corresponding deduction from their pay, was out of the question where the gangs were so scattered and the foods of the different people so varied.

The Arabs disliked the mountains and said so. They were not much use at handling rock, and so were always put to dig earth when there was any to be dug, a monotonous business. Yet they came back year after year, toiling up the ever-lengthening road after the spring sun had melted the snows, till I got to know each one by name and would ask why such-a-one was not along this year.

'Oh, God bless your honour, he died last winter,' they would answer cheerfully, pleased that I took such interest.

Sometimes I would chaff them by saying, 'But I told you chaps not to come back again, because there would be only rock-work ahead. No more earth to dig. Besides, you said you were afraid of the Kurdish people, who might rob you and kill you!'

'True,' came the reply, 'but we've been working for you a long time now. You grumble at us, but you always give us work and look after us. And the fact is we find robbers never attack anyone on this road.'

So I would discover some section of the road where they would do useful work for yet another summer.

But the most important of all the workmen who mustered at roll-call were the Persian Kurds, the regular or professional labourers who stayed always on the road because they had no homes elsewhere. I gathered that many of them were bad characters who had been cast out of their native villages, and so had wandered into Iraq in search of employment. They could get through twice as much work as any other class of labourer and became very skilful in handling crowbars and picks and manipulating large rocks into position in the road-bed with only half the effort the other coolies put into it. They were nearly all bachelors, these fellows, with no wives or homes to worry about (so they said). They spent more of their pay on good food than did the Arabs—and contentedly gambled the rest away.

If the attire of the Kurds and the Arabs was picturesque, that of the Persians was even more curious. They were clad to some extent in Kurdish and Arab garments but in addition wore heavy European boots (often falling to pieces), and second-hand Western apparel of every description. Where they got their coats and trousers I never knew, so complex is the system of barter in old clothes in the Near East, and so many hands had they passed through.

I could easily imagine that the man who appeared always in a Brigadier's tunic had acquired it from British military sources in some way, honest or otherwise. But where the coolie who appeared in a morning coat with long tails of a cut popular about 1850 had secured it no imagination could discover. Nor where the dark coat, branded on the shoulders in large white letters 'L.N.E.R. Guard' had come from. Whenever I saw the owner of this garment coming up the road with his pick I felt I ought to begin a feverish hunt through my pockets for a lost ticket to Edinburgh—in case I should get put off the train. Another wore a lady's imitation sealskin coat that possibly once walked down Bond Street, but it had left much of its fur behind since then, and its owner sported bandsman's trousers adorned with faded red braid.

Nearly every one of these Persian Kurds had some weird garment of European origin. Such treasures were all greatly prized and kept in neat repair by their owners, who wore them day and night for the better part of a lifetime. Their underclothes were also much patched, but were washed often and kept clean in spite of the arduous work.

Many of these men had been previously employed on some kind of engineering labour either by our Department or by the Oil Companies or the Railway Department. In consequence they took a very intelligent interest in their work. Some could produce their discharge certificates showing what their capabilities and conduct had been. I always gave a man who asked for it a signed statement of his service under me, for it would be useful later on both to him and to any employer he might approach.

Touching this practice I was amused to hear from a new-comer in the R.A.F. how on one occasion he had motored with friends to a lonely part of the road and had halted for lunch near a Kurdish village. Suddenly he and his companions became aware of the presence of a number of armed tribesmen close beside them. Considerably startled and unable to speak any Kurdish they waited, loosening their pistols. The leader of the Kurds came up flourishing not a dagger or rifle, but a document which he thrust forward with great pride. It said Aziz Agha had worked for two years and given every satisfaction—and the signature was mine! The villagers only wanted to know whether the visitors would like some grapes, and the headman could not miss the opportunity of showing off his complimentary certificate.

It was mainly the Persian coolies who mastered the complicated technique of rock-blasting and bridge-building, though a few of the Arabs also became first class at these jobs.

An important skilled trade was that of the stone-masons, chiefly Assyrians, who took the rocks that were brought in by the coolies, trimmed them roughly to shape with hammers and built with them walls of uncemented masonry to the height of the final road-level. These walls were sometimes twenty feet or more in height where the road led round steep faces and they had to be firmly built to carry the weight of the steam-roller which afterwards rolled the final dressing of small stones and crushed rock into a smooth surface. On top of this (as we had the funds available) came the bitumen dressing.

We began at Banaman with the first units of 'plant and machinery' that in later years swelled into an up-to-date array of road-making appliances.

We were sent a steam-roller, a stone crusher and a tractor. This last hauled stones by day and drove the engine of the stone crusher by night. I took great pride in these three machines and loved to show how much they could do even with unskilled drivers. Of course, for a time they only added to our troubles. The men who were put to work them were frequently injured. The 'second' on the steam-roller did not know Stephen Leacock's first law of natural science, 'If you put your fingers between rotating cog-wheels they will go on and on till the machinery is arrested by your suspenders.' Fortunately in this instance the man only lost the best part of his right hand. Another put his arm too far between the jaws of a stone crusher. I began to feel thankful that we had no circular saws about, as I wanted to have a few whole workmen left.

When such accidents occurred I had to dress the wound as best I could with the help of the first-aid outfit and then take the casualty in my car to the Syrian doctor at Arbil, who repaired the damage as well as might be. In every case I attempted to obtain adequate sick-pay and compensation for the unfortunate workman, and in the course of a year or two this was sometimes granted by the Minister of Finance. It seemed almost as though a special Act of Parliament had to be passed to deal with each accident, it took so long. The sum involved was often as much as eight pounds!

A most spectacular show was staged one day when our steam-roller ran away. Some irrigation engineers were visiting the work and met me just beyond the section under construction.

'By Jove, you are making progress here,' said one. 'Your steam-roller performance on the other side of the hill was an eye-opener to us. That driver's a perfect marvel of a man. He took those downhill bends at thirty miles an hour with perfect ease; and he shaved past our car with only six inches to spare. Finally we saw him driving down even faster round a sharp corner right out of sight. Remarkable achievement. How did you manage to train a man to do stunts like that in so short a time?'

My hair stood on end. No steam-roller was allowed to be driven faster than five miles an hour (and my visitors knew it well enough), a higher speed was both useless and dangerous on such a road. Worse than this, I had only that morning put my best driver on the sick list and entrusted the roller to the partially-trained assistant, who had evidently got mixed as to which way the levers moved. I pictured a bent mass of wheels and boiler and spurting steam with a crushed man somewhere underneath. But I thought it as well to keep such visions to myself. Evidently the motorists had heard no explosion, and I thanked Heaven for the six inches that had saved their lives. I replied casually:

'Oh, yes, we manage to pick splendid drivers among these coolies. And we have to make the most of our one and only steam-roller on this long road. Can't let it dally about, you know. Too-ra-loo, you chaps, call in on your way back,' and waving the party frantically on I stepped out at a lively pace in the direction from which they had come, only to find that the damage incurred when the engine eventually did stop was no worse than a broken front fork which we were able to repair ourselves in our workshop lorry. This workshop lorry possessed a lathe and other tools and was a war-time heirloom that had come to us from Baghdad; and very useful it proved to be.

That steam-roller was luckier than a second one which left Kirkuk to come up to us, a brand-new machine straight from the makers in England. The man who had been deputed to drive it to Arbil had been the driver of another roller on the plains; he was warned that mountain roads were not the same thing, but the East (like the West) is full of hearty optimists. His gold teeth glittered as he laughed these warnings to scorn. Did he not know how to drive? Had he not been driving for years? Was there any English steam-roller that he could not learn to manage in five minutes? Of course not! Steam-rollers! He had been born in one!

There is something very impressive about the eloquence of the true optimist. Many gold bricks are sold in London every day of the week by just such self-assured and confident men. But they mostly have the prudence to be elsewhere when the trouble begins and not to be involved personally when their propositions finally topple over as did that steam-roller some six miles out of Kirkuk into the bed of a river! It turned completely upside-down. The wheels pointed heaven-wards, the bent funnel lay over sideways, and the driver crawled out of the mud a sadder and a wiser man. Even when hauled out and righted that roller never again looked the same debonair machine, and never could be persuaded to forget its indignity, but bore a grudge against our Department for years.

All serious injuries occurring on the work were seen to at once, but for minor injuries and ills I had to open a dispensary and treat the men every evening. My remedies came out of a portable box supplied by the Health Department and supplemented by my friend, the Syrian doctor at Arbil. From this box and its typed instructions it almost seemed I could treat any condition whatsoever, medical or surgical, short of a major operation. My patients almost invariably went away happy and restored to health. In the box were bottles of iodine, quinine, boracic acid, aspirin, Epsom salts, morphia (marked 'poison'), castor oil and potassium permanganate; there were scissors, bandages, catgut and splints; if I had all the rest of the pharmacopœia and the instruments of Guy's operating theatre I could have done no more than with my little box.

Here is a typical case. An Arab comes in groaning: 'Sahib ani khasta,'—I'm sick, sir.

Me: Whereabouts?

Arab: Wallah, batni—my belly (holding the offending portion of his anatomy).

Me: Very good (pouring out a liberal dose of castor oil from the two-gallon can and seeing that he swallows it). Now, how's that, feeling better?

Arab: 'Kullish Zen, Sahib.' (Lots better, God bless you, etc.)

He is almost certainly cured there and then. Such is the power of faith! Incidentally, the more unpleasant my ministrations the more faith my patients seemed to have in my treatment.

The fever patients were given quinine (they were mostly malarial), the injuries cleaned with hot water and iodine, the sore eyes washed with boracic (trachoma is a very common affliction).

Anyone who looked really sick was sent off to the Arbil hospital, but most of them were healthy enough and had only minor ailments.

As we moved farther from Arbil and medical aid, I established hospital tents where men who needed it might lie up and get good food and some kind of attention. Tribesmen sometimes came in from their battles far off in the hills to get their wounds dressed, and their faith in my primitive medical service was often most touching.

The checking up of 'muster rolls' and the working-out of pay sheets also took up a good deal of time in the evenings. I sat in my little tent (tents were scarce and my own was ragged and no better than those of the coolies), and computed the amounts due to each man according to his attendance and his rate of pay, while scorpions and large brown beetles clinging to the sides of the tent took stock of my columns of figures.

The actual payment of the men every fortnight was a long and troublesome business. The six hundred-odd coolies were divided into gangs of about twenty with one man in charge, called a 'tindal', who was responsible for the work of his men and for the tools which were issued. If tools were missing and no explanation forthcoming their value had to be deducted from the pay. And there were still other complications. Occasionally when there was a flour shortage we had to purchase it in Arbil and issue it to the gangs in part payment of their wages. Of course, each man knew just what his own wages should be and if by accident he was underpaid he said so at once, though if he was overpaid he took what the gods offered and said nothing.

Payment was not simplified by the fact that half the muster rolls as prepared by Sabri Effendi, were written in Arabic or Kurdish and I had to keep remembering that 0 may mean nought in English but in Arabic it stands for 5, and that 7 in Arabic means 6 in English; thus 70 meant 65, but 91 actually *is* 91, for these latter symbols agree with our own!

The condition in which the money was sent from the Treasury in Arbil was appalling. Iraq spent years considering the adoption of a new currency before it was finally brought out, and in the meantime we handled the foulest paper money I have ever seen or wish to see. Bundles of ragged and torn Indian notes; dozens of them in two or more pieces which had to be sorted out and stuck together with stamp paper or pinned so that the numbers on opposite corners tallied, though other parts might be missing. They were dirty beyond description, the legend upon them often all but obliterated by ink or stains or even blood. They went through many strange hands and saw many strange happenings in that land of violence.

I had to count these notes, a thousand or more each time, before accepting them from the treasury officer, who also handed over several thousand silver rupees and smaller coins. That pale Arbil teller, an emaciated victim of tuberculosis, never made a mistake in his count and we trusted each other absolutely. He always gave me the cleanest notes he had, such as they were. It would have been an easy matter for him to have foisted short count on a busy and impatient engineer, for once I accepted the bundles the responsibility was mine entirely.

Sometimes I had to take only silver when no notes were available and then I returned to the camp with sacks of coin that the car could scarcely carry. At other times there were only notes and no silver which meant paying the men in batches so arranged that their combined wages added up to an even sum of five or ten rupees. They shared the money out afterwards quite fairly and, strange to say, never fought over it.

Every man as he was paid had to give his thumb-print in triplicate so that records could be kept. Taking six hundred thumb-prints in triplicate is a long job that often took me far into the small hours of the morning to complete. By the light of a single hurricane lantern I would slog away at it, hundreds of dim figures standing patiently all around me in the darkness. As the season advanced, it often poured with rain and the muster sheets got smudged and filthy if I wasn't very careful.

One could try and hurry through the job but it hardly paid, for when they left my hands I had not done with these muster sheets and accounts matters. Questions would come from the Iraqi auditor:

Query: Kindly explain why Ahmad Murad of last muster is now written as Murad Ahmad.

Answer: Because they are, and always have been, two different men.

Query: Kindly explain why Kerim Khan has given a right-hand thumb-print instead of a left-hand thumb-print and is paid inclusive of Friday holiday.

Answer: Because he has no left hand and is employed as a store's watchman.

Two years later comes another checking of the same sheets:

Query: On sheet no.——dated——Abdul Kadir's days worked do

not total correctly; payment was eight annas in excess, kindly recover and credit imprest, and do not repeat such errors in future.

Answer: Abdul Kadir died eighteen months ago, error regretted, recovery impossible.

Query: Recover from relatives and credit imprest as instructed.

Answer: Abdul Kadir had no relatives in Iraq, came from Persia.

Query: Then kindly rectify error, and discharge all Persians.

Answer: Abdul Kadir had a naturalization certificate, so is an Iraqi subject. Eight annas duly credited *vide* my accounts. Nationality of labour under investigation, etc.

Query: Etc., etc. (*ad libitum*).

After every labourer had been paid there was always a squad of men to be dealt with who claimed some payment they had missed by previous absence. In most cases when all the facts were elucidated their claims were found to be justified, and I seldom discovered deliberate dishonesty once the men knew I was out to treat them fairly.

The time to look out for lies and exaggerations was not in such matters, but rather when private quarrels were brought for arbitration. Then a man's blood is up. I might make him swear an oath upon the Koran or upon his son's head or by the throwing of pebbles or any other holy thing, yet would he perjure himself at such a time. Generally, however, after the expenditure of much patience on my part they would come to some amicable agreement along the lines I suggested.

At last 'the day is done and the darkness falls from the wings of night', the surgery is closed, the wages paid, the wranglers pacified and dispersed, and my bed is taken out under the starry canopy of heaven. All around me on the stony ground lie my men, descendants of once-powerful civilizations—Arabs, Kurds, Persians, Assyrians, Armenians and Indians. They are huddled here and there in the warm moonlight, needing no covering or bedding. All sorts and kinds of humanity as we are, believers and infidels, we cast all our troubles into dreamland and lie there sleeping the sleep of utter exhaustion that follows on twelve long hours of work through the fierce heat of an Iraq summer's day. In the distance can be heard the steady rumble of the stone crusher on its midnight shift, but we sleep unmindful of it, and of the bites of mosquitoes and the cares of the morrow. We may differ in appearance and dress, in language and customs and religion; but in sleep as in death all men count alike in the major scheme of things.

CHAPTER X

The Depths of the Canyon

The Kurdish winter of 1928 found us established in the Rowanduz Gorge at the camp of Gali Ali Beg. There we were to remain for more than two years, so formidable a barrier did the cliffs and rivers of that gorge prove themselves to be.

Yet these were two intensely interesting years, and we knew that the success or failure of the whole road-project lay at Gali Ali Beg.

After some months of investigation a way was found through the very bottom of the gorge where it was at first thought that no road could hope to go. (The route originally proposed was that of the high caravan track.)

The work of exploration of the depths was not devoid of thrills. Below the camp the Alana Su stream falls in cataract and waterfall over rocks and through shady caverns richly hung with maidenhair fern, till it pours in a stepped and fan-shaped cascade into the Rowanduz River. This is a beautiful dell, heavily wooded, with crystal springs of trickling water, and near the lower end the stream is crossed by a natural bridge where a huge rock has fallen in some bygone age. The surveying of this side gorge had its difficulties, but I did not anticipate that the actual road-work would cause much anxiety except in a few places.

The main canyon was a different matter. To get into it at all seemed almost impossible. It could not be entered from the lower end of the Alana Su owing to a great rock bluff that fell sheer to the point where the waters of the two rivers joined and over which the Alana Su tumbled in that last glorious waterfall.

From the caravan road we could make out goat and ibex paths leading down the precipice faces and following along by the edge of the river. I studied these from several vantage points and decided that at one or two places it might be possible to climb down by following them, and once down, it looked as though the lower part of the gorge might perhaps give easier foothold; but the descent proved hair-raising and I shall never forget those first climbs down into the rift, nor the perilous ledge at the bottom.

The day on which we first reconnoitred the depths is to me indeed

The Depths of the Canyon

memorable. I had descended with a party of picked men from the caravan track, following goat tracks that had proved well-nigh impossible, and we congratulated ourselves when at last we stood where the ledge began at the bottom of the gorge; but any hopes we may have entertained of a pleasant stroll by the water's edge were soon dashed. The ledge narrowed and narrowed as we progressed along it, and we had to cling tightly to the occasional stunted fig trees that grew from the crevices where springs of water trickled out. These springs added to the danger by making the narrow path slime-covered and slippery. Finally the ledge became overhung by a projecting strata of rock, and we had to stoop for a dozen yards, then crawl forward first on hands and knees and in the end on our bellies, often with one foot hanging over the edge that fell sheer to the rocks and the foaming river below. At long last, after some two hundred yards, the ledge widened a little and we were able to stand upright again. Mountain leopards no doubt found that track easy, but I felt vastly relieved when all my little party were round in safety.

Beyond came a high climb over a jutting bluff where water showered down from a great spring above, the spray shimmering in rainbows among the long pendants of fern when shafts of sunlight penetrated the gorge at midday.

Still farther on we descended to river-level again and found our way almost completely blocked by an immense torrent that poured out of the precipitous mountain-side, just as did the spring of Kani Bekhair. After some reconnoitring we managed to cross it by leaping from rock to rock though one man was nearly swept into the river by its terrific force, and was grabbed by a comrade at the last moment.

This spring came as a complete surprise to us, for from the old track high above we had seen no sign of it the week before; and even more amazed were we a month later when it stopped as suddenly as it had started. I presume it ran only after a season of extra heavy rainfall, for it never again became anything more than a trickle. It was as though some wizard of the mountain had turned it on full blast to impede us, and finding that he had failed, had turned it off again.

In Kurdistan no spring seemed devoid of some unusual feature. There truly must have been spirits within those mountains!

We came now to a place where, to our astonishment, it seemed that a track had once been built by human hands. It must have been many centuries old, for even the local Kurds had no knowledge and no tradition of it. Yet here clearly enough were the remains of two bridges, the pier of one still standing. And there were sections of stone wall that had once been the built track. For the most part it had been completely swept away by rock slides from the precipices above. At these points the smooth limestone gave no foothold at all, but fortunately we had come provided with ropes and steel bars and we were able to improvise means to make progress.

Scrambling along we got to the jagged rocks directly beneath the old caravan track now several hundred feet overhead; and we came upon grim evidence of the toll of life demanded by the dangerous path above us. It was an eerie place. Great cliffs all round, the rushing river beside us and, at our feet, the broken bones of men and animals, and crumpled fragments of military equipment and of merchandise that had hurtled down from the track above. Standing there we thought of our adventures in getting to this dread spot by the route we had followed, and of the worse ordeal of getting out—if we ever could— from such a Valley of Death. We felt hemmed in, trapped for ever in this prison of nature.

As we looked anxiously around our minds were brought back to the business of the day, the finding of a way through the gorge; for there, across the river, was the opening in the rock through which poured the waters of the Balkian River. It was, in fact, the 'window' through which we had seen the green plains near Diana on my first journey along the upper track. And I knew that through this side gorge the road must go, whatever the difficulties of cutting a road along its precipitous walls.

The only way into the Balkian Gorge was from the Diana end, for the Rowanduz River in front of us was impassable until some kind of a bridge had been built, so we retraced our dangerous path down the main gorge, fortunately again without serious mishap.

The most disturbing of all my exploratory experiences was to occur during the investigation of the Balkian Gorge. As I have said it had to be approached from the far end which meant a long detour through Rowanduz to begin with. On this journey I set out one wet morning accompanied by Major Perry of our Department, who had just returned from leave. By the time we reached the entrance to the Balkian Gorge, the rain had turned every rivulet into a torrent.

Dismounting we left our one attendant outside the gorge with the horses, but had not gone far when the indistinct track we followed divided. In order to explore both branches in the shortest time we took one each, for they looked as though they should join again later on; but they didn't, and, narrow as the gorge was, we lost each other.

Sheets of rain obscured everything and the roar of the river, rising ever higher and higher in brown fury, drowned all shouts which might have brought us together. I hunted everywhere, high and low, and scrambled on till the side gorge met the main canyon of the Rowanduz River, but could still find no trace of my companion. It was anxious work, for he knew even less than I did about the complex system of canyons around us. Moreover, the tracks I had followed were often not a foot in width, and in that heavy rain extremely slippery. One careless step, one slip, and no man would come out alive from the boiling flooded river.

At one spot, under a rock which lay well above the river, a party of unfriendly looking Kurds, complete strangers to me, were sheltering. I noticed that they were all armed and for some reason were handling their long rifles, so I loosened my automatic which I invariably carried on such unusual expeditions as this, far from my base camp.

Again I went through that gorge hunting for any sign of my companion, for I realized that he might be lying injured, perhaps unconscious, and I searched up and down the track by which he had left me. Finally I began to think that the Kurds I had seen might have robbed him and thrown him into the river, but could see no way of finding out, for when I thought of questioning them and asking their assistance they had mysteriously disappeared.

I was worried beyond words; night was not far off and something had to be done before dark. If Perry were injured or lost he must be found, and if there had been foul play the culprits must be caught. So I went back to the coolie who was minding the horses at the entrance to the gorge and scribbled a message to Captain York of the Levies telling him what had happened, and saying that a search party was imperative before darkness.

The coolie quickly grasped the urgency of the matter and ran off on foot like a hare, for he could make better speed thus than on horseback, so slippery was the hillside.

The man had been gone only a short time when suddenly my companion appeared out of the dark opening of the ravine, soaked to the skin and weary as I was, but uninjured! He had thought that I was the one who was lost and had hunted miles along the main gorge in the belief that I must have gone there. Even so, how we had missed each other in the first place I don't know. His anxiety had been as great as mine, and though we grumbled that this was no place nor weather for hide-and-seek, our mutual relief can be imagined after such a day.

It was now almost dark as we mounted and rode for the Levy camp to cancel my message for help. It rained still, a torrential downpour that fairly leapt from the muddy ground.

We had gone some distance and in the dim light were approaching a small stream that we had crossed in the morning and which we knew would now be considerably swollen, if not impassable. Suddenly a sharp challenge rang out and we reined in to that most ominous of sounds—the clattering of breech-bolts in a dozen rifles. We were covered from all sides and Assyrian soldiers seemed to rise from every mound and bush around us, from out of the earth itself. Then we saw that the torrent in front of us was alive with khaki figures up to their waists, up to their armpits in the muddy water, but struggling through

The Depths of the Canyon

with the determination of men bent on grim business, careless of all things but their orders to take every man, dead or alive, who came from the Balkian Gorge.

It was not long since my message had been delivered yet here was a fully armed company (in the darkness it seemed like the whole battalion), already far from their camp and prepared for anything. I realized then, if I had not thought about it before, that the Assyrian Levies were a force to be reckoned with and I felt a little anxious as to our reception from their officers after bringing them out, after all unnecessarily, and in such weather.

'Damned glad to see you both,' said the deep voice of Captain York out of the darkness. He sounded serious for once.

'Signal-sergeant Yokhana, get a message through to the camp that both engineers are safe. You see,' he explained, 'B company are standing by awaiting instructions. I must send up a pistol flare also to recall the platoon who have gone to block the other approaches in case any suspects tried to get through and escape. Yes, the men would have enjoyed a scrap, but I'm jolly glad neither of you fellows are floating down the Zab to Baghdad on a night like this—too wet to drown pleasantly. Let's get home to the old log-fire and that beer I left behind me.'

Captain York relaxed into his old vein once more.

'Hardships? North Sea Patrol and all that? Give me Kurdistan for luxury and comfort! You can't beat the old soldier with long service in cramped stations for knowing how to look after himself. But as for you fellows, you look as happy as two hens in a duck-pond,' he laughed and made some more untimely jokes about our bedraggled appearance as we set off for Diana.

And we knew that in spite of all the bother that we had caused him, our friend was brimming over with his usual good humour—and we were deservedly fair game that day.

Others were not so fortunate as we had been in escaping the clutches of the Rowanduz Gorge.

A party of my men tried to climb along the lower slopes of the main gorge where I had first penetrated, but foolishly went without ropes or gear of any kind. One man fell into the river and was immediately swept away out of sight. The rest of the party managed to climb up to the caravan track again and were returning sadly along it when to their amazement they saw their companion far below sitting huddled on a large rock in midstream. With some difficulty he was rescued, but it was a lesson none of us forgot.

Still another of my men, when clearing rocks on the upper-track, slipped over the precipice at the deadly danger spot where I had seen the litter below. Scarcely a bone in his body was unbroken when his mates eventually recovered it for burial. Some said he had been shoved over. Perhaps he may have been for all I could ascertain about the matter.

In spite of these tragedies connected with the place, there was a thrill in the idea of conquering the gorge that spurred the men to greater efforts in their work. In fact the road-construction proper was forging ahead with scarcely a hitch.

The winter which was coming upon us would, I knew, be a time of fierce storms and bitter cold in Kurdistan and it was essential that the preliminary survey to the pass at the Persian frontier should be completed before the deep snows lay upon it, so I left Gali Ali Beg in charge of my trustworthy Indian Supervisor, Sujan Singh, and set out eastward.

As related, we had met with pretty bad going in surveying the Rowanduz Gorge, but, ten miles beyond Rowanduz, we were faced with the Berserini which was almost as bad. No caravans passed through it; instead they made a long detour with a two-thousand-foot climb. Such goat tracks as did exist in Berserini were difficult in the extreme. There were few sections where one could ride even on mule-back, and to take our pack animals into the place, as we had to do, meant endless loading and unloading and crossing and recrossing of the river, which fortunately was at its lowest at this season.

Such transport difficulties made our progress very slow. However, as the survey work took time and consideration, this delay did not matter much.

It was a most striking and stately ravine. The gorge was on the whole more open than the Rowanduz, though in many places great cliffs overhung the stream. It would take many tons of explosive to blast out our roadway, and to cross the river several long bridges would be needed just as for the Rowanduz. The river except for one or two short cataracts, was smooth and peaceful as an English stream, and willow or 'chinar' trees hung gracefully over the quietly-flowing waters. Fish jumped by the score—a veritable angler's paradise.

In both the gorges fish made a welcome addition to our very limited menu. They were troublesome to eat as they had dozens of curiously-forked bones, but one got used to this and they tasted delicious if freshly cooked. When I had time for fishing with a rod I found it excellent sport, but I hardly dare confess to the expeditious if unsporting methods we often adopted when we were really in need of food. You would have forgiven us had you been there; very little explosive sufficed and we had to swim for every fish as it floated, though they often recovered in time to escape us.

On either side of the gorge, intercepted by mighty steps of sheer precipice, rise wooded mountains reaching up to the barren summits where winter snows linger for months. Among those far-off crags the ibex holds undisputed sway, and beyond the farthest visible peak lie range upon range of mountains stretching to the high no-man's-land where meet the frontiers of Turkey, Persia and Iraq.

At this time somewhere in that unruled territory dwelt Simco Ismail, the most notorious of all Kurdish outlaws. For many years he was a king of this natural fastness, safe from punishment for his crimes. Then in 1930 the Persians laid a trap for him and he walked into it, tempted by the bait they offered.

It happened this way.[1] A letter had come to him from Tabriz professing to offer him full pardon and giving him the governorship of Ushnu province near the frontier. So, accompanied by the chiefs of the nomad tribes whose spring pastures were in his no-man's-land, he went to Ushnu. Here he was given command of the garrison and invested as Governor. A house was put at his disposal and special Persian clothes were issued to him and his followers.

For three days Simco ruled and received homage. Meanwhile the garrison was secretly increased and the Persians laid their plans. Some among his followers spoke to him of the danger of treachery, but he would not listen. Was he not surrounded by his own men and were not the Persians sending for the chiefs of all the Kurdish tribes in the district to come to Ushnu to acclaim him?

A message was brought that an important Persian personage was on his way to visit him. Preparations were made and Simco, accompanied by the nomad chiefs and all their followers went out to meet the official. They waited long at the appointed place and then a horseman came galloping to say that the visitor could not arrive that day. His car had broken down. Simco accordingly turned back to re-enter the town.

The Persian garrison armed with rifles and machine-guns had meanwhile been stationed on the roofs of all the buildings and lay in ambush. Some presentiment of danger came to the Chief as he walked back towards the town. He declared he would leave with his people for his mountain home as soon as dawn broke. But this wise decision came too late. As dusk fell and he approached his house at the head of his party, suddenly from all sides the Persians opened fire.

Thus died Simco Ismail with twelve Kurdish chiefs and many followers. Had it not been dusk few of all the Kurds who had been lured to Ushnu could have escaped.

The Kurdish people drew up a petition to Great Britain and Iraq which asked in English 'that a noble race like the Kurdish be saved from our oppressors. Which human conscience will accept such a treachery as this, that many great chiefs without fault be so murdered?'

By the time this massacre took place I had been in the district long enough to have become friendly with a few of the nomad chiefs who

[1] This is from a translation of a Kurdish account of the matter.

came down every autumn from the mountains and returned in the spring driving their flocks along the new road; there was one, Khorshid Agha, with whom I often talked and he was amongst those killed. Though no one held any brief for Simco, who had, some years earlier, treacherously murdered the Assyrian Patriarch, the Mar Shimun, yet I regretted the death of the unoffending peaceful chiefs who unfortunately were with him and who had already shown friendship towards me. It seemed to me a poor way of administering justice, a way that could only breed hatred.

Beyond the Berserini Gorge we rejoined the caravan road. Here it was apparent that the work of constructing a roadway would be less difficult and bridges of any size would not be needed. Yet the obstacles were considerable. Sharp ridges of rock from which the Turks had bitterly resisted the Russian advance on Rowanduz, barred the track and still other gorges stood in the way, shorter and much less imposing than the Rowanduz or the Berserini, but diabolical from an engineer's point of view. The last was closed at one end by a great wall of rock, which, to our surprise, we found to be pink and white marble.

Then at last we came out on high country where glaciers of a past age had left huge boulders. At the head of a wide valley, not many miles away, rose the king of the mountains of Kurdistan, the Algurd, 12,249 feet in height, already deep in its winter mantle of snow.

It was snowing hard by the time we reached Rayat, the frontier town and customs post that nestles on a promontory of land between two rivers. I had sent a man ahead to warn Ali Agha, the headman, of our coming, for a Kurdish host always likes to know when he should expect guests, that he may have food ready, and offer the best that he can provide.

Ali Agha came walking through the snow to meet us, an old man possessed of much dignity. I had with me Younis Effendi, a well-known Kurd, who (like Ramze and Sabri) had been a rebel leader under Sheikh Mahmud, and was now a capable and trustworthy overseer. I knew I could depend upon this man to help me in dealing with the chiefs I met on such a survey as we were making. Younis introduced Ali Agha and we exchanged greetings. There was a beauty and simplicity about the language of the Kurdish chief that seemed in keeping with majestic surroundings.

'Salaam alekum, 'bkher-hati—peace be with you and welcome,' he said as he bowed his head and placed his hand upon his breast. 'Let your honour of the Government enter into the house of your servant. Food, cigarettes, tea and all I have are waiting for you. You have come far, you are cold and in need of rest. Enter my humble doorway, sit with me by my fire and go no farther tonight.'

I answered in the best Kurdish I could muster and asked after his health.

16. Berserini Gorge

17. Shaikh Ahmad of Barzan with his Chieftans

18. Assyrian Children

'Na wallah chaw bash nia—my eyes are troubling me,' he replied sadly. Trachoma is prevalent even in the most remote villages of Kurdistan.

He led me into his richly carpeted 'diwankhanah' or guest-room, warm and dry, where a large samovar of tea steamed cheerfully. As I entered I slipped off my heavy wet boots in the doorway, for it is a rule that one must not dirty one's host's carpets, and as I walked to the seat of honour at the head of the room the other guests who had been seated on cushions rose. With crossed legs I sat down beside Ali Agha, and we once again exchanged greetings, our hands laid upon our hearts. Only now did the other guests re-seat themselves.

There were several, for word of the approach of the engineer had spread through the village. I was introduced to the mudir of customs, the schoolmaster and the neighbouring chieftain, Sheikh Allahadin. The local 'bash chaush', or police-sergeant, had hastily donned his full uniform. Any who knew Arabic or Turkish greeted me in those languages to show off their superior education. Someone even knew a few words of English. But for the most part we spoke Kurdish, a working knowledge of which I was by then acquiring.

We sat thus in the warm room and were handed tea in little glasses heaped with sugar cut from a conical loaf with a small bejewelled axe. A large cylindrical stove roared in the middle of the floor and was fed continually with sticks of mountain-oak that burned like tinder. Food was brought in and when at last the meal was ended we smoked together until the guests departed.

Ali Agha and I sat on and discussed his private affairs. He asked advice about this and that, simple matters such as his health and the education of his son. Finally he bade me a dignified good night and left me alone with my Kurdish overseer, Younis Effendi. I was soon in my camp-bed and fell asleep before the hushed voice of my companion had finished his nightly prayers to Allah.

On looking back it is strange that I felt in no danger sleeping thus alone and unguarded. Both Ali Agha and Younis might well feel justified in taking vengeance upon me as a representative of the Government. Younis had been in Sulaimaniyah when our aeroplanes had bombed that city and he had told me many grim details of the bombardment that seemed to call aloud for revenge.

Ali Agha's small village had also been bombed; why, I could not find out, for he was never a rebel as far as I knew and perhaps his village was mistaken for another. The story is told that one bomb fell near his house on the open hillside and made a large hole in the ground from which welled up a spring, evidently from some hidden stream under the barren surface. When good relations were restored (they had never been really broken in this district), a touring officer paid Ali Agha a visit. It happened to be a dry autumn, and the officer was taken to see the spot where the bomb dropped. It still ran water, but was now only a trickle.

'This hole, so near my house, was made by one of your British bombs,' said Ali Agha, and paused significantly, his retainers grouped on all sides fully armed. The officer, rather taken aback, wondered what was going to happen next.

'I wanted to ask you,' said Ali Agha, 'is that bombing business all over now?'

'Yes, of course,' was the anxious reply, 'there will be no more bombing of your village.'

'A pity,' said Ali Agha sadly. 'I was just thinking that if you could drop a few more bombs like that one we might get some more springs of water in this dry weather!'

Beyond Rayat is a hill upon which were once the extensive barracks of the Russian Army and the graves of many soldiers who died during the retreat from Rowanduz. The actual pass and the Persian-Iraq frontier lies farther off at the saddle of the dividing range.

This frontier tract was bleak and dreary as I saw it, snow-covered that late November with blizzards sweeping down upon us from the heights of Algurd as we struggled on with the survey work. Fortunately we completed it on the very day that heavy snow began to fall—snow that would remain there till the following spring.

We took leave of Ali Agha and came rapidly down from those frontier highlands pursued by rain and sleet till the cold ate into our bones as we sat astride our mules. I decided at last that it was more comfortable to walk, and strode ahead with such vigour, in order to keep warm, that the caravan complained they could not keep up with me. All through that rainy day we kept going steadily, making our bolt for home. Late at night, soaked to the skin, chilled and weary, we reached a village. No man had gone ahead to tell of our coming, and I could not consider it courteous to call so late on such a night without having sent word. Accordingly, I suggested we should attempt to camp outside round a fire. But Younis, whom I knew I could trust in such matters, said that hospitality to all travellers was a sacred obligation in Kurdistan; so we entered the village, the dogs making a great uproar.

The people who were all asleep woke at the sound and seized their arms, but Younis rode forward and asked for the chief. He was not there, they answered, but away visiting some tenants and only a minor relation was in charge of the village. This man took us to his guest-room, which was cold and cheerless, and said we might stay there if we wished. He seemed, quite justifiably I thought, to resent being disturbed at such an hour.

Then suddenly the anger of Younis Effendi burst forth.

'What would your chief say to such conduct towards visitors?'

cried the furious overseer. 'Is this not Kurdistan? What sort of hospitality do you call this? Bring a fire, bring food, bring rugs and bedding. Be quick or we shall refuse to stay and shall tell the world of your meanness and your mannerlessness!'

This was brusque language to use in a strange village but Younis was a Kurd and he knew the unwritten laws of his people. The man went away humiliated, mumbling apologies, and soon returned to make us comfortable with all we could desire.

Such is the strange and generous code that every tribesman lives up to. When I returned to Gali Ali Beg, I gave orders that if he had need of it, any Kurd who passed my camp should be given shelter and food and the same treatment that I had met with on my journey in this country where such bad and yet such good traditions can go hand in hand.

CHAPTER XI

All in the Day's Work

The work at Gali Ali Beg went on unceasing, day and night. There were about a thousand men employed on the road during the late autumn, though in the winter their number was considerably reduced.

Little by little they were becoming familiar with the blasting work and acquiring the skill necessary to drill deep holes into the hard limestone, using no other instrument than a long, tempered steel bar. When, during the following summer, proper rock-drilling machinery and steel bridge parts arrived from England the work forged ahead more rapidly, for only then was it possible to cut a roadway round the vertical precipices and to cross the rushing rivers. Nevertheless, even before we had any machinery we were able to make considerable progress with the primitive appliances that were available.

Drilling holes is the all-important part of rock excavation—the explosive does the rest. At first it took two men nearly a full day to drill three feet into the rock with the steel bar. The hole was charged with native gunpowder as that was all that we could get, and a strip of rag soaked in nitre had to serve for a fuse. By the time gelignite and a supply of safety-fuse and detonators arrived we had learnt that if he were properly trained one man alone could drill a ten-foot hole in a day, provided his bar was correctly gauged and tempered by a really good blacksmith.

Such a blacksmith was Ahad Rahim, the Turk. He must have been a descendant of the smiths who forged the Damascus blades, so highly prized by the Crusaders, for he was a past master of his art. His steels were as finely forged and tempered as those from the manufacturer's workshop. I have always admired and encouraged a clever craftsman, and so I spent many an hour with Ahad Rahim at his forge, testing out every device that we hoped might improve our rock-drilling methods, primitive as they then were.

Each bar had chisel-shaped ends. Drilling was accomplished by lifting and throwing the bar into the hole where it pulverized the rock and then bounced up—giving rise to its name, the 'jumping-bar'. As the hole deepened the powdered rock had to be removed by pouring water in and sucking out the white slurry that formed.

116

All in the Day's Work

For this job we had to invent a special pumping device (consisting of a short length of pipe with a foot-valve on the end of a long iron rod), and make them in considerable numbers. The men brought their own little tea kettles to pour in the water. It was all rather comic, for they were bespattered with white mud from head to foot. They were paid according to the depth of hole they drilled and cared little for appearances. As they worked away in a compact group on some high rock the ringing sound of the steels in the resonant holes of varying depths made a quaint pipe-organ music that echoed in the gorge, and was especially melodious to the ear of the engineer-in-charge.

Hundreds of holes were often drilled in a day, and by four o'clock in the afternoon were ready for loading. Gunpowder is easy to use, but the handling of gelignite in quantities gives one the worst kind of headache and sickness I have ever experienced. For hours I have lain too ill to move after some special blasting effort for which I had to prepare the charges myself. Fortunately for some reason the men seemed less troubled by this nitro-glycerine sickness than I was. They became more accustomed to it, I suppose.

The process of firing the hundreds of charges was always exciting and had to be conducted with great care so that no one was hit by flying fragments of rock. The workmen were sent well outside the danger zone; police whistles were blown loudly as a warning; the section where the charges were laid was barricaded off at either end by watchmen with the orthodox red flags. The tribal Kurds and the caravans who wished to pass through may not have understood the meaning of red flags, but they certainly understood the word 'bomber', which locally meant anything that exploded, be it shrapnel shell, aeroplane bomb or blasting charge; and they didn't dispute the warning of that significant word.

When all was clear, some half-dozen of the most agile men each seized a glowing stick from the fire and began touching off the fuses, running madly between the holes. The lighting of a fuse took a second or two, especially if in some awkward place, on a high ledge for example as many of them were, for the line of the road was anything but smooth and level before blasting commenced. The 'blasters' as they were called were specially selected and trained, and they got extra pay for their dangerous job. They had to run like greased lightning rapping out sharp warnings to each other if a fuse missed and the work was delayed! The first charges exploded long before the last were lit. Detonations with flying rock came on behind them, following like some pursuing demon within the mountain.

In haste for life and limb they cry in Kurdish, 'Wallah! Wallah! Zu! Zu!' (for God's sake, hurry, hurry). 'Bilagel! Bilagel!' shouts back an Arab blaster in his own language.

How they rush on and how they enjoy it! Every man must be at least two hundred yards from the first charge before it explodes, and the fuses burn quickly. The explosions ring out with a deafening reverberation in the narrow canyon. The age-old rocks are torn to fragments. The very earth itself is shaken as charge after charge takes up the thunderous chorus. Great blocks of rock lurch from their ancient settings and crash into the river below. Debris flies skyward and rains round the sheltering places where the coolies lie under cover. He is a foolhardy man who pokes his head outside his cave while the barrage is at its height!

There is nothing to be seen of the party of blasters with their torches now. They are far away and have probably completed the lighting of the fuses up to the end of the section, and have sprinted for cover like the ibex that tears across the mountain-tops above in wild alarm at this strange noise, dreadful as the winter avalanche that so often engulfs him. The whole gorge is invisible in a fine dust that rises like the steam of some volcanic eruption, and the air is full of the acrid nitrous fumes of the explosives.

When, as was sometimes necessary, several hundred holes were charged and lit in one day, it was like some great battle of heavy artillery. The gorge roared and shook, explosion following explosion in an endless syncopated sequence, now a single small one, now a cluster, now a veritable earthquake. No wonder the Kurdish tribesmen thought the engineer something of a magician, if explosions count for anything!

As suddenly as it began, the din ceases. The last rock hurtles to its resting place and all is silence. Slowly the dust drifts away and men come forth and gaze on the results of their day's labour, the line of the road torn and rent with upheaved masses of rock lying at all angles.

The scene may not be approached at once. An interval must be allowed in case there is some charge still to explode. First of all come the blasters, carefully examining every fuse to be sure it has burnt. One with a long bar probes each shattered and unstable rock mass to ensure that it cannot slip and fall suddenly on the workmen when they return.

When the blasters are satisfied with the inspection, their whistles blow loudly once again and the men come back to clear a path for the waiting tribesmen and caravans, who pass on in wonderment, amazed that the ancient barriers which have hindered men and animals since time began have melted away before their eyes.

One blasting, of course, was never sufficient to clear a roadway; the process had to be repeated time and time again, sometimes it took many weeks to shift the high rock buttresses that blocked our way. The men would begin far up, perched like flies or held securely by ropes, drilling out a ledge for foothold on the face of the great cliff. Then we improvised derricks which drilled on the principle of the oil rigs, and made holes thirty or forty feet in depth. In such places we always worked night as well as day shifts so that the progress of the whole work might not be held up longer than need be.

I made myself a stone and mud house at Gali Ali Beg to shelter me from the winter snows and to safeguard the office records and the cash chest, which for safety I kept buried under my bed chained to a rock anchorage in the ground. I built my two rooms in the usual Kurdish manner, thatched them with sticks and leaves plastered with wet mud into which we rolled pebbles to prevent cracking when the mud dried. It looked perfect, as such roofs go, but I had failed to realize that in Kurdistan it could rain almost without a break for weeks on end, and I had not then learnt that a roof to be water-tight must have a certain amount of clay in the mud with which it is plastered. I had used the soil that was handiest which lacked the all-important clay. It withstood the first storm or two gallantly, but when the rains really set in, my roof leaked everywhere and I could find no dry spot in either of my two rooms, all my possessions being soaked. I was for the time completely cut off from the outside world, for the road with its earth surface was quite impassable for a car; it was hopeless to think of getting corrugated-iron roofing sheets from Baghdad.

I hoped that when the snow came matters might improve but the heat of my stove thawed the snow on the roof and the drips fell just the same. Eventually as I could not sleep with large drops of water falling into my ear at irregular intervals, I rigged up a tent over my bed and slept undisturbed, though there was still grave danger that the whole house might collapse once the walls became thoroughly soaked.

A short distance from my house we had erected a similar building to serve as an explosive store and here we kept two tons of gelignite. Beyond that again was the police-room, where lived the guard supplied by Sheikh Sayed Taha, and the gaol in which I had often to hold one or two of the coolies while the crimes of which they were accused were being investigated, or until they could be sent on to Rowanduz. Farther off were the quarters of the overseers and, in a separate camp, the tents of the coolies.

It would have been wiser to have stored the explosives well away from the camp, using caves, as we afterwards did, for this purpose. Gelignite, especially in winter when it is frozen, is extremely sensitive to shock of any kind and we ran the constant risk of being blown up. A single bullet from the rifle of some hostile tribesman or a dissatisfied coolie might detonate it, or the collapse of the roof might have the same effect, and then there would be little left of our camp beyond a very large hole in the ground. But that first winter I preferred to keep things as compact as possible for defence purposes. I was not then fully assured of the goodwill of the local chiefs as I was later on when the tribesmen themselves guarded all my explosives and stores.

All in the Day's Work

It was a strange and lonely place, this camp at Gali Ali Beg, when the winter storms swirled through the gorge and I sat alone, under the tent in my leaking house planning and estimating for the big push that would come in the spring. There were bound to be difficulties. To try to foresee how to overcome these was part of my routine job. So I spent long hours checking over excavation quantities and planning each step in the making of the road, while my tin stove glowed red and raised clouds of steam as drops from the roof fell on it until the whole house became like a Turkish bath.

Coiled up by the stove lay my woolly Kurdish dog, Ghunnie, a beast with something about him of an Esquimaux huskie and something of an Alsatian; perhaps not very far removed from a wolf, but a good companion and a splendid watch-dog at night.

In a corner, his feathers ruffled snugly up, sat a pretty blue pigeon. I had been given three in the autumn, but one day as they flew about outside a great eagle swooped down from the rocks overhead and seized one in mid-air. Despite my counter-attack with the service rifle I always kept within easy reach he came again and killed another, so that now only one of my pets was left.

I shot that eagle later on, as he sat on a rock across the stream. I had 'sighted in' the rifle with some practice rounds as I needed to become accurate with it for the ibex season; so, even though it was a long shot, I got him and rejoiced when I saw the giant bird flap heavily and crash to earth. He fell like some disabled aeroplane, his great wings being wider from tip to tip than my arms could stretch.

A policeman of the camp guard who had been watching shouted his admiration.

'A wonderful shot across the river,' he cried.

'Why so specially wonderful across the river?' I asked.

'Because the water draws the bullet down. Always it does that, and one has to make allowance, didn't you know it?' he asked, for this was a common belief in Kurdistan.

This shot gave me a reputation for marksmanship, which I was happily able to maintain even when it came to the use of a shot-gun on the chikaw or mountain partridges. The Kurds themselves never even try to shoot moving game. They wait for sitters. These birds are quite hard to hit, both because of their colouring and of their habit of hurtling through the air downhill at such an incredible speed that even when killed stone dead in their flight, their bodies will travel on right to the bottom of the gorge. As a table delicacy they proved as plump and tender as chicken and an excellent addition to our rather monotonous fare, which was usually goat's meat.

Sometimes as I sat alone at night, working out my figures, I heard the roar of a snow-leopard high up among the crags. These beasts never came into the camp as far as I knew and, unless wounded, will not usually attack a man; though when they do they are said by the Kurds to be the swiftest and deadliest of the feline kind.

Occasionally in the evening Sujan Singh, the Indian supervisor, who had been with me since we started the attack on Gali Ali Beg, came to report some matter of discipline. If anything he was overstrict in labour matters, but he himself was a man of surprising energy and he expected it in others. His knowledge of the workmen was almost uncanny. He knew every one of the thousand-odd coolies by name and could tell me something pretty much to the point about the character and history of each. To Sujan Singh the rapid progress of the work was in great part due, for he took on his shoulders much of the training of the locally recruited staff. 'Ser-i-spi' (whitehead) the coolies called him, because of his white Sikh turban; and they 'got busy' when they saw it coming.

It was unfortunate that changes in the Iraqi Government in Baghdad frequently entailed changes in my road personnel. Often no sooner was a new man trained than he was transferred or discharged. Worse still, the few skilled Indians I had at the beginning were repatriated to India; and of five ex-rebel Kurdish leaders who joined the road-work only Ramze Effendi was left with me throughout the whole undertaking. The Assyrian overseers and clerks were also regarded with disfavour by the nationalistic government and were eventually discharged, though luckily not till the greater part of the road had been completed.

Apart from the unquestionable loyalty of the Assyrians they were very capable at their work. I found that for some unexplained reason Mohammedan coolies would often work better for the Christian overseers than for one of their own religion. The opposite relationship also frequently held when Christians seemed to prefer to work under a Mohammedan overseer. There was one young Assyrian called Leon Mar Shimun who belonged to the famous family from which the head of the Assyrian people was always chosen. He had been educated in France and was a youth of exceptional trustworthiness whose one concern seemed to be the welfare of his men. The Arab coolies wished never to work for anyone but this young man and complained if transferred to the charge of other overseers. Indeed, on the road-work, I observed nothing of the racial animosity between Arabs and Assyrians that existed in the towns. For one thing all were too busily occupied.

That first winter, when we became practically isolated from the outside world owing to the mud, I was impressed with the absolute necessity for building a road with a very solid foundation of boulders. Every kind of earth road was useless by the time two months' rain had fallen on it. One drove a car only at the risk of leaving it bogged for the rest of the winter—even if it could be persuaded to move a few miles along the roadway. At first most of my winter visits to Arbil to fetch the mail and the money for the wages had to be made on mule-back—usually a three-days' journey, and sometimes much longer when the streams proved unfordable and I had to wait for them to subside. Almost all of these rides were made in drenching rain, and the mountains, though now glorious in snow-bound grandeur, rarely showed through the clouds. There were no travellers, no Kurdish cultivators, no shepherds, hardly anyone at all out and about in such weather, as I rode in solitary state over the sodden plains and snowy passes, with only a servant and a policeman as escort.

At night I stopped wherever I could get shelter, preferably at a halting-place I had built at Shaqlawah, but the swollen rivers often prevented my reaching it. At such times I was forced to go to the nearest 'chaikhanah' by the roadside and share the single room that sheltered man and beast alike, for the animals could not remain out-doors in such weather. I would have my camp-bed arranged in a remote corner beside the animals, the inevitable cash-box beneath it. Though I had shelter I could never expect a night of tranquil slumber. The smoke of the fire built in the middle of the floor beneath a hole in the roof that served for chimney was always thick and blinding, in-sects of many descriptions were numerous and active throughout the night, and I lay with my pistol under the bedclothes by my hand, fully loaded and the safety-catch set for instant use. One can see a lot through half-closed eyes, and it is easy to shoot through bedclothes without perceptibly stirring a single muscle of the body to take aim. To keep one's pistol under the pillow is quite useless for such occa-sions when an assailant's khunjar is much quicker than the sleeper's gropings for a weapon kept under his head. All this I had learnt from Bentley at Diwaniyah, and well did I always follow his advice.

The more surprised the company were at my unexpected descent into their midst, the safer I felt. My servant and the policeman took it in turns to stay awake by the fire keeping a careful watch on our fellow-lodgers to see that they hatched no plots. When I could feel satisfied that all was well—one develops an instinct in such matters—I would snatch a few hours' sleep till wakened by a snorting in my ear or a flapping in my face as my animal protectors, horse or hen, moved their position. I was awake on the instant to discover what had dis-turbed them. As a matter of fact I was never interfered with. The people had, I think, come to regard me as a kind of 'dervish', a man who leads a humble and austere life for preference. They could see no other reason why an officer of the Government should make long journeys through mud and rain and flooded rivers seemingly for the mere fun of it.

Once I was forced to take refuge in a village which had been severely punished by the Levy troops for the treacherous part the headman had played during the rebellion. Lymington had narrowly escaped death there, and with his own hand had seen to it that the people should remember. It was dark and snowing heavily when I arrived. My defenceless condition was obvious enough. Yet these Kurds, fierce and unforgiving as they are reputed to be, invited me to share their evening meal, and I was given the key of the guest-room when I retired to bed that I might lock myself in if I wished.

I felt often enough that I was luckier than I deserved to be. From the very nature of the job I often had to take risks, put up a bold front and just hope for the best. Even in my own camp I was surrounded by men of the most doubtful character. I could not even know that the camp sentries were to be relied on. There were always some thousands of rupees in the cash-box on the return journey from Arbil, and the Persian and Turkish frontiers were near at hand, offering a sure asylum.

They were all tough customers, these men who worked for me, men with nothing to lose and everything to gain by the robbery and violence they were reputed to practise. They could, moreover, get about the country in a speedy, secret way that no troops could emulate. Take, for example, this feat of Rustam Khan, who helped Guerges in the kitchen at the subtle art of living with the greatest comfort and the least effort.

The rivers rose higher and higher as the days and weeks went by, till one day the official postman of the camp who made a weekly trip to Arbil with relays of good horses, returned a few hours after he had set out, saying the journey was now out of the question. It was most important to get my mail and accounts through, so I called for a volunteer who would attempt the task the postman had abandoned. To my great surprise Rustam Khan was the first to volunteer. Like Guerges he was a man with an active if shady past, and apparently he wanted to show his mettle; for he took the mail and walked the whole way to Arbil and back, fording the rivers I know not how. In record time he was back in camp again with letters from the outer world. It was a fine performance.

Again, there was Gurgor, the grizzled uncouth old 'shibana' or policeman of Sheikh Sayed Taha, looking villain enough to please any movie-play director. He never wore more than half his police uniform, if so much—Kurdish clothes were good enough for him; and his reputation for dark deeds over half a century kept all men at a respectful distance when he patrolled the camp. 'Shoot first and challenge afterwards,' was Gurgor's motto as a sentry, and the vast clan of the Hurke nomads filing day and night through my camp went quickly on when they recognized the ominous figure squatting on the ground with rifle over knees, eyeing them hawk-like.

He was an inscrutable fellow, this Gurgor, and I could never tell just what were his feelings towards me or feel perfectly safe alone in his company. One day I was about to set off up the steep side of the gorge. There were said to be chikaw easier to shoot near the snow-line, and I wanted to investigate a track that led, I was told, right up out of the gorge on to the Kurrek mountain above.

'I am coming with you,' announced Gurgor and, without even waiting for my permission, he came.

It was a long stiff climb up that track, but I was very fit and hardly noticed that my pace was too severe for the old Kurd who plodded along behind. At length we reached a winding ledge round one of the inevitable precipices. Below us was a sheer drop, and far down, so many little white points, was the camp we had left. The rocky ledge was worn smooth through centuries of use by man and beast. It was clearly, therefore, an important route, probably a secret way of escape in time of trouble when the main exits of the gorge were held by an enemy.

'Let us sit down,' commanded Gurgor. 'You walk too fast for me,' and he squatted by the brink.

Now I love mountains, but not precipices, and was most anxious to get on. Yet intensely as I disliked it, I could do little else but settle down beside the old man to let him rest, though I confess I would have preferred any other companion.

Sitting there like a shrivelled vulture and pointing out places with the barrel of his rifle, Gurgor began a long account in an almost incomprehensible Kurdish dialect of the wicked history of the great gorge beneath us.

I grasped little of the tale, but that worried him not at all. He would turn suddenly with flashing eyes, his hand would grip his khunjar to dramatize his narrative, and he would look eagerly to me, as old men do, to applaud or dispute his conclusions. He told me of the chieftain, Ali Beg, who had been a great governor and had made the caravan-track through the gorge, thereby giving it his name, Gali Ali Beg. For the most part, however, the tales were monotonous accounts of violence and bloodshed in the valley beneath us. Finally came the story of Hassan Beg.

Who Hassan Beg was or where he lived I never discovered, but this Kurdish worthy had, it seems, plotted to hurl a stranger to death from the track we were on, apparently because the unfortunate victim had discovered the secret way.

'That was the very place,' said Gurgor, and pointed at the spot where I was sitting. 'Hassan Beg stabbed his enemy from behind, just as I might shoot you now.' Here Gurgor swung his rifle to cover me and he went on with his story. 'He fell, apparently a dead man, and his blood trickled to the edge. Hassan Beg went back to kick the corpse over. Suddenly as he dropped into space the dying man gripped his murderer by the leg and down they both went together.'

Gurgor leant eagerly forward to point to the spot where they had first struck the rocks beneath.

'Yes, yes,' I said, 'very interesting, but if you are rested let's get along. Do you think you could shoot the chikaw nestling on that rock away to your right?'

I felt I had heard enough of Kurdish murder stories for one day, and had sat perched in this awful spot quite long enough.

'Never,' answered Gurgoe; 'no man could shoot one at such a distance.'

'Well, you watch,' I said. I was out to try anything that would break the evil spell the old man's tales were casting over me, making me wish to fling myself into the chasm.

Just as with the eagle, I chanced to make a wonderful fluke shot that sent the bird cart-wheeling down from its rock. They are small creatures to hit at a hundred yards' range, and the Kurd gaped with surprise.

'Off you go and get it,' I said, trying to pass the shot off as a commonplace affair with me.

With eyes aglow he ran along the wicked ledge we were following, and at length climbed down to the dead bird which he brought back in triumph.

They were perhaps rogues who dwelt at Gali Ali Beg, but I often felt that I actually lived more safely because of their presence. Through the long winter nights it was at least stimulating to the imagination to be in such a place among people to whom violence was commonplace. My greatest recreation during those evenings I found in reading. A friend had sent me one book peculiarly fitting to my environment— Dorothy Sayers's famous collection of *Great Short Stories of Detection, Mystery and Horror*. I read it from cover to cover.

Yet even murder, as practised in the East, can have its lighter side; and the funnier aspects of my extraordinarily varied camp duties kept me from ever getting 'nerves' at Gali Ali Beg.

I always wanted visitors from the outer world to carry away the impression that, whatever Kurdish character might once have been, under my beneficent influence *my* camp was as peaceful as a Sunday School. The annoying thing was that the impression I was trying to convey was often shattered under my very nose so to speak. There might be no such happenings before or afterwards for weeks, but it would almost seem that murders and fights were staged especially for these visitors. Perhaps midway through a dinner given in honour of a touring Advisor or Director (both most exalted officials) a sinister prostrate form would be brought to my doorway by a crowd of shouting coolies, and I would have to leave my guests to make a few investigations and arrests. Take the murder of Ali Baba, for example.

One evening an Irish Medical Officer from the Levies called at my camp, and as we sat smoking and chatting outside my tent thoroughly enjoying a quiet evening, I became aware of the ominous approach of the police-sergeant, Abdullah Chouish, who was in command of my very meagre police force, of which Gurgor was a typical member.

'Well?' I said, as he saluted with a heavy clicking of heels.

His important manner warned me that there was at least murder afoot and I was not mistaken. Behind him carried on poles by four coolies was a long dark object wrapped in sacking.

'This is the man, Ali Baba, who was missing, sir,' he said in a loud confidential whisper, glancing sideways at Murphy to see the effect. 'We found him in the river where he's evidently been some days. Only just floated now though. I've found some marks on his head,' he announced with professional pride. 'What are your orders, sir?'

Murphy had scarcely been expecting entertainment of this sort, but Iraq is proverbially a place of unexpected happenings, so he knocked out his pipe and came with me to make the necessary examination.

Ali Baba, a Persian coolie said to possess money, had been missing for some days. There were good reasons to believe he had been murdered, but his tent-mates declared he had gone back to his own country. This seemed hardly likely since he had not collected the pay that was due to him. Moreover, shreds of the missing man's clothing and stains of blood had been discovered on the rocks beside the river, close to the water's edge. There was no trace of the body, and I hardly expected it would turn up. On the clothes of Ali Baba's tent-mates were found bloodstains which they declared were from a goat they had killed for meat. No one among the coolies could confirm this story and the camp butcher asserted that he had supplied these men with meat quite sufficient for their needs. I had had the gang, who were all noted gamblers, arrested on suspicion.

And now here was the body which we thought had been swept away by the river. It had been discovered gyrating slowly in a sluggish whirlpool behind a great rock. It was an unpleasant sight, but was without doubt the missing Ali Baba.

Murphy and I examined the gruesome object together. It was a job commonplace enough to him; a medical officer in Iraq gets plenty of such tasks. We agreed there were definite signs of injury inflicted before death and bruises that suggested a struggle.

'Abdullah Chouish,' I said to the sergeant, 'do the arrested men still plead innocence?'

'Yes, sir.'

'Then you must go down amongst the coolies in the morning and try to get more evidence. They must be talking among themselves, and there must be someone who knows something.'

'I will find out all about it, sir. I will go among them disguised,' he answered, drawing me mysteriously aside so that none might overhear.

All in the Day's Work

'Can you really manage to disguise yourself so that even the coolies won't guess?' I asked, for Abdullah Chouish was a well-known figure.

'Can I?' he replied scornfully. 'Am I not a detective as well as a policeman? Leave it to me!'

Next day I was engaged upon my rounds and had for the moment forgotten the case. At midday I was passing the camp chaikhanah where a few of the coolies were congregated and noticed a curious figure sitting in their midst drinking tea. It was a large man with a Kurdish turban on his head and over his shoulders a long Arab gown drawn in at the waist by a leather belt from which hung the regulation ·45 calibre police revolver. From below the gown projected legs arrayed in khaki breeches and puttees, and on the feet were large hobnailed police boots!

'Well, I should never have known you if you hadn't saluted, Abdullah Chouish,' I said. 'Got any clues?'

So I know now what a great Kurdish detective looks like when hot on the scent!

Like most cases of the kind in Iraq, this murder was referred from court to court, but apart from the blood on the clothes of the accused, which was shown to be human, it was held there was no conclusive proof, and the men were liberated.

I had done my best, however, to get them hanged. Imagine my surprise, therefore, when they came cheerfully back to the camp calmly expecting me to re-engage them on the work! For once I refused men employment. They seemed aggrieved at my decision and stayed about the camp for weeks hoping I would change my mind. But discipline had to be preserved somehow if only as a warning to their companions; and I liked to feel that even if I couldn't hang a murderer I could at least give him the sack!

CHAPTER XII

A Christmas Eve in Kurdistan

There was so much to be done along the great length of the road now under construction from Banaman to Gali Ali Beg and beyond, that I had fallen into the habit of forgetting that there were certain holidays to which we were entitled; but I had definite orders to come down from the mountains to Kirkuk for Christmas, and one may not overlook the wishes of a considerate superior. As a week's dry weather had made the road almost passable again, I set about making arrangements for my brief absence.

I had failed to take advantage of all the holidays allowed, partly because we were much too busy and partly because the official notification of any date usually failed to reach our remote outpost till some time after the day itself was gone.

It must have been a hard job for those in charge at Baghdad to have to arrange holidays to suit every religion in Iraq. There were holidays in plenty for the Mohammedans, especially about the time of the fast of Ramadhan, in most of which the Jews and Christians participated. Also there seemed always some sect fasting or feasting, praying or making pilgrimages to one or other of the countless shrines that were scattered from end to end of the land. Mohammedans are supposed, at least once in their lifetime, to make the pilgrimage to Mecca. This is the big affair and gives a man the title of Hajji, but there are also many local pilgrimages. The Shiahs of Persia used to make the long journey to their most holy city of Najaf taking with them their dead for burial. When I was in the south I used often to see their caravans winding across the desert laden with coffins. These were usually carried by camels, but latterly drivers of motor lorries took up the business too. The Shah has now put an end to the custom, as it took much money out of Persia owing to the high payment for burial sites at the important mosques in Iraq. The Shiah Mohammedans practise the fanatical Hassan-Hussein rites, and those among my coolies who were Shiahs (mainly the Persians) made quaint banners and had days and nights when they beat themselves with sticks and swords; they then indulged in a great feast for which they collected donations from any who were willing to give. Even the most intelligent

19. Shaikh Mahmud

20. Half Tunnelled Roadway in the Rowanduz Gorge

of these workmen professed unshakable faith in present-day miracles which, they assured me, were commonplace in specially holy places, such as Najaf and Kerbala.

'Have we not seen with our own eyes men taken up from the earth by the hand of the Prophet himself?' they would say.

The Sunni Mohammedans, among whom are the Kurds, are less credulous. They worry themselves little about pilgrimages (I do not recollect ever having met a Kurdish Hajji), and are content to bury their dead in their local graveyards on the hillsides, each grave marked only by a long upright slab of undressed stone without even an inscription upon it. The headmen and the townspeople usually observe the fasts; the poorer folk don't seem to bother much about them, and I believe working men are given a special dispensation in the matter.

Even after the authorities had appointed holidays to satisfy all Mohammedans they had still to allot certain days 'for Jews only', others 'for Christians only', and doubtless some for Yezidis (the Devil-worshippers) and for all the various other religions, had I but the full roster.

The Jews were the most exacting of all in their observances. No Jew may work on a Saturday, and perhaps that is why so few ever came to my camp as workmen. There were quite a number living in the villages near the road under the protection of the Kurdish chiefs who seemed to treat them well.

Among the many Christians who came to work for me, I found that there was an even greater variety of sects. The Armenians, who were quite the best motor-car and tractor drivers available, belong, I believe, to the Greek Church; there were also the Chaldeans, a sprinkling of Roman Catholics and Nonconformists, and, more numerous, the Nestorian Assyrians. These different kinds of Christians held their festivals at different times. There was no one holiday that could be said to be general—not even Christmas. Ever since the missionary efforts of Dr. Wigram, the Assyrians have official connection with the Church of England; nevertheless, they have a Christmas and a period of fasting that is all their own.

I cannot think there was any religion of which we could not produce some representative on the Rowanduz road. Even among the few Indians no two were of the same sect. The supervisor was a Sikh, the surveyor a Hindu, the steam-roller driver a Mohammedan 'mullah', and so on.

My servant, Guerges, held a flexible faith and a most convenient one. He said he had been born a Christian, but he had found it disadvantageous not to be able to participate in the times of worship and rejoicing of other men. So at the Christian festivals Guerges was Guerges, at the Mohammedan he was Abdullah Ismail, and at the Jewish he became Shaul Elishu!

A Christmas Eve in Kurdistan

In quite a different class was the devout Mohammedan P.W.D. storekeeper at Arbil, Abdullah Effendi, who was really a Scotsman from Glasgow. This man had developed a deep belief in the traditions and principles of the Islamic faith and had become a most respected Moslem. By his conversion he sought neither betterment of position nor any worldly object, but only humility and a deep satisfaction in his own conscience. He often expressed to me his regret that so few Mohammedans live up to the high principles of their faith. In spite of his religious beliefs Abdullah Effendi insisted upon remaining a British subject and a loyal Scotsman, even though he knew this meant he must lose his employment in the Department and leave the country. He is now, I believe, in India.

As to the question of whose Christmas it really was that 25th of December 1928 I concluded it would take too long to find out. Instead I thought of the subtle scheme of asking my staff and all others on the road whether they would like a holiday. Men on a daily rate get no pay when there is no work done, and it was not within my power to pay them for any holiday, though I knew how hard they had been slogging away, week in and week out, without a break. Even so, their vote on the Christmas holiday question was never in doubt, the countless different religions came forward with one reply:

'Your Christmas is good enough for us,' they said.

Starting at road-head as dawn broke on the morning of the 24th I paid them off and gave leave to the staff. The Roman Catholic Assyrian, Leon Mar Shimun, went off for Mass to Diana, though he feared that as they were all Nestorian there, they might be unable to give it him till the Nestorian Christmas a fortnight later. He could but go and see what might be done about it. The Armenians and Chaldeans likewise set off for Diana to see what religious benefits were available for them. The other workmen merely sat about, mended their clothes, collected winter firewood or went shopping to Rowanduz: some fished in the river, and all seemed contented one way or the other.

At last all at Gali Ali Beg were paid and disposed of. With the car packed high with the assortment of bedding, cash-box, policeman, spare tyres, typewriter and office files, with which I had always to travel, we set off to splash our way through the mud of the long roadway—the winding sixty-five-mile trail to Arbil. With all the joy of escape from the perpetual daily round of camp worries and with that eager anticipation of Christmas that takes one back to childhood's earliest memories, I thrust behind me any doubts I might feel about our chances of getting any farther than the bottom of the first long pull up Spilik Pass, and started in the true holiday spirit of nothing venture, nothing win.

Gingerly we crossed the narrow caravan bridge at the gorge en-

A Christmas Eve in Kurdistan

trance. It still did duty, even for motors, until such time as the new steel span should arrive. The total width of that bridge was some four inches greater than the distance between the wheels of the car and there was nothing whatever to prevent one's running over the edge on either side. The stream looked icy cold and was quite far enough below to give the car every chance of landing upside-down, with the driver inside, if she did go over. It was always a ticklish business getting across and I sent Guerges and Hassan ahead to watch the front wheels. They waved me left or right or put up a hand to stop me if I swerved the slightest fraction from the straight. To check matters up I often climbed along the mudguard to have a look myself at the position of the wheels relative to the edge. Somehow or other I always got over that bridge in safety, though I never failed to notice how anxious the servants were to climb out and leave me in sole possession of the car.

Then came the five miles of mud leading to the top of Spilik Pass, uphill all the way, the little Chevrolet ploughing away in first gear, boiling and frothing from the radiator like a thing possessed.

What a ride! Soon the car is smothered in slush, windscreen and all. At times she stops completely as she sinks axle-deep in mud. This deters us not at all. Out jump policeman and servants, I reverse along our tracks to get as good a run as possible and, in first gear, again charge the deeper mire in front. There is already one car (belonging to the Rowanduz Police Commandant) abandoned on this slope with a broken axle-shaft, but this is Christmas Eve and we must take a chance if we are to reach Arbil tonight! So I jerk the car through by dint of using the clutch with the engine racing, terrible treatment it is true but often surprisingly effective. We get through and away, the party leaping in from the sides, where they have been pushing desperately and yelling 'Y'Allah' as they heaved at the mudguards. They clamber in as best they can for I dare not stop. Farther on another halt and a tribesman wandering with his flock, and travellers from a passing caravan, are all forced by my indefatigable bodyguard to lend a helping hand. They push manfully and we are gone, leaving them staring after us splashed with mud and wondering at the devilish contraption which they call in Kurdish a 'trombil' (corruption of the word 'automobile').

Then we hit a sharp stone beneath the surface; a loud explosion follows. I have feared this and been expecting it. Many of the stones are razor-like on Spilik: that is why the side-lamps are festooned with spare tubes. Now to jack up a car in deep mud on a hill is a job that never improves one's language. The jack is never long enough and sinks almost out of sight, or slips and topples over as soon as the car is raised an inch or two. To achieve even this much one has to lie in the mud and pray hard. But we get through the job somehow, though

131

the tyres are already more or less in ribbons and patched and re-patched from previous journeys.

At last we reach the top of Spilik. Down the zigzag on the drier side we dash, and across the Batas plains, the skid-chains clattering madly in the mudguards. Here we make up some of the lost time, slowing only at Harir where the children crowd the roadway and never fail to shriek with delight when they see a car passing through.

We fairly race up the Mirowa Pass, the surface firmer than I had hoped after the rains, down the other side, taking the Mirowa River at twenty miles an hour before the splash has time to fall, over and on to Shaqlawah the half-way halting house.

Emmanuel Pawrus, the most cantankerous of my overseers, was there awaiting me. I had told him he could have no Christmas holiday on account of the trouble he always was to me; but now, on Christmas Eve, I relented.

'Pawrus,' said I, 'you are a troublesome malcontent and seem to be always quarrelling with the other overseers and with your men. Try what a Christmas holiday at home will do and see if it improves your mind!'

So I paid Pawrus and his men and went on to the village of Kora, where a metalling party under one Jacques Searty, an Armenian formerly of the Canadian Pacific Railroad, were forming and rolling the final surface of the macadam roadway that was forging slowly ahead from Arbil. Here at last we were to drive on a solid road!

The work of paying these large gangs took some time and there were the usual 'cases' to attend to, men injured, men unpaid and such-like. In due course it was all done and I took Searty along with me in my car. He was off to see his wife in Mosul and had in his lap a large and tranquil turkey quite unmindful of its Christmas death sentence.

As night closed in we speeded along the newly completed road with its hard rolled surface, up the dangerous hairpin zigzags of the one-thousand-feet Pirmum Dagh, down through the Bastura Chai running two feet deep after the autumn rains, pushing on through a driving storm of sleet and snow, the outside of the car and my belongings strapped between the mudguard and the bonnet caked with frozen mud. I steered for the last ten miles by poking my head out round the windscreen, it being impossible to see through the thick layer of ice and mud that covered it. The skid chains still clanked but the patched tyres held out somehow and, with the headlights beaming mistily, we came at last to Arbil, and the bare room above the P.W.D. Store.

The day's journey was accomplished and my Christmas mail awaited me. I read on and on till I had opened every letter and every parcel from my home at the ends of the earth. Cakes that *were* cakes, shortbread that *was* shortbread, even a plum pudding! All had made

A Christmas Eve in Kurdistan

the eight-thousand-mile journey from New Zealand in grand style, packed as they were in soldered tins.

With the roads in their present state there was no hope of reaching Kirkuk that night. It looked as though I must spend a lonely Christmas Eve. Then I recollected that I had an invitation from Captain Clarke to look him up if ever we chanced to be in Arbil at the same time. I made a quick change from muddy garments begrimed by changing tyres innumerable, to a lounge suit in which I at least looked more presentable and climbed again into my disreputable car.

It was a dark night, with scudding clouds chasing across the sky where the stars gleamed fitfully. I reached the house at the fashionable hour of eight-fifteen and was through the gate in the high mud wall before I saw that there were many lights in the windows and a clustering of servants round the cookhouse, which anywhere in the East from Malay to Cairo, means that a 'spread' is being prepared. I had the awful feeling that I had intruded upon company and was turning the muddy car about to scuttle off to my lonely room again, when Clarke's servant spotted me.

'Coming to dinner, sir?' he said.

'No, no,' I replied hastily. 'I didn't know the officer had visitors.'

'Haven't got visitors, but plenty dinner, sir,' the man assured me in that careless, generous way an Eastern servant has with his master's food.

I noticed then that there were no other cars. The matter was settled for me by the appearance of Clarke himself on the well-lit veranda, in immaculate evening dress.

What a strange setting! A wild winter's night in Kurdistan, a solitary Englishman celebrating Christmas alone in a large typically Eastern house built out on the flat grain-fields of Arbil, that oldest of all cities, whose high ramparts loomed up against the dark sky beyond the lighted house.

'Why, this is luck,' he said. 'I wondered whose car came in. I thought I was going to spend Christmas Eve all alone, and now you've turned up and I'm going to hear all the latest news of my wild tribesmen in Rowanduz. They say you get on so well together that I haven't even needed to pay you a visit yet. How's Hamada Chin?'

'Thanks to your influence up there we get along splendidly,' I assured him. 'But as for staying the evening, I fear I'm rather a gate-crasher.'

He led me into the house saying, 'I've this very moment rung for the soup. You're just in the nick of time. You must have had a long day of it, as I suppose you've come from Gali Ali Beg? I can see that your road is going to rob Kurdistan of all its old romantic isolation; it used to be a dangerous three days' mule-ride,' he laughed, as he mixed me a cocktail.

133

A Christmas Eve in Kurdistan

'I wish I could have offered you champagne,' he continued. 'I ordered some, but the rains prevented transport getting through, still this bottle has something of a Western flavour, don't you think? Here's to your health and to a pleasant Christmas Eve.'

In a corner of the room a gramophone was playing a soft *aria* of Beethoven, and the mantelpiece above the blazing fire was bedecked with Christmas cards, many Arabic and Kurdish ones amongst them, for even the Mohammedans joined in the spirit if not in the belief of Christmas. Some of the cards were the characteristic work of my friend, Sayed Heusni Effendi of Rowanduz, whose picturesque handicraft I always admired, especially when I thought of the primitive tools with which these delicate wood-cuts had been etched.

I was amazed at the care with which my host had planned his Christmas Eve in this isolated station. There were no guests he could have invited and he certainly expected none. Yet the room was decorated as any English home would be at Christmas time. One kept expecting a multitude of visitors to arrive and bands of waits to begin singing 'Good King Wenceslas' outside the window.

When Clarke took his place at the head of the table I was somehow reminded of the inimitable O. Henry's touching story of the New Orleans French aristocrat who sat alone in state in the banquet-hall of his ancestors in the same glory as of better years long past—and none came to his forgotten festival but a solitary passing tramp. I felt very like that tramp!

That evening of comfort and good food was in sharp contrast to my day of hard travel—and to Clarke's own ever-roving life. He told me that on the morrow he would be far out on the wet plains with his shot-gun. His greatest sport was duck-shooting and this was the season when the whole of Iraq teems with water birds that come from Siberia, it is said.

After dinner as we sat with liqueurs and coffee by the fire, I knew that I might hope for some sort of a story from this modest man who was widely known as one of the leading authorities on the language, customs and character of the Kurdish people. I already knew that he was spoken of from end to end of Kurdistan both for his judicial fairness and his daring. Many were the tales I had heard told. How he had been swept away in a flooded river and saved as by a miracle. How he had broken his thigh when climbing among the icefalls of the highest mountains where no others have ever ventured, and had for many days' march been carried by faithful tribesmen through the gorges and over the passes, strapped tightly to a ladder that the broken limb might not pain him, till finally he was delivered into the hands of a British doctor a hundred miles away on the plains and the tribesmen went back to their solitudes refusing reward.

By what miracle he had not met his death in the days of Sheikh

134

A Christmas Eve in Kurdistan

Mahmud's rebellion when for months he was alone with the rebels in Sulaimaniyah, none knew. He remained there as the embodiment of British power that stood between the Sheikh and his ambition for Kurdish sovereignty, and bullets sometimes spattered round him as he walked through the narrow streets of the hostile town.

The full story of Sheikh Mahmud and his long struggles which he believed to be in the interest of his people has not to my knowledge yet been written, though it is a most dramatic tale. That Christmas Eve I heard something of the story from the man who was for a time one of the chief actors in that mountainous amphitheatre of Sulaimaniyah (which lies one hundred miles to the south of Rowanduz). Some of it I had heard already from my overseers, Ramze, Sabri and Younis, who had served with the Sheikh.

Sheikh Mahmud had shown friendship towards the British when the army entered Kurdistan in 1918, but a year later his activities necessitated his capture and expulsion after a short campaign under Major-General Fraser. When it came to the question of appointing local rulers, however, there seemed no one better fitted to be put in charge of this district than its hereditary chief, so he was liberated and reinstated. This was by no means bad policy, for the man was truly a power among his people.

He was a religious leader of considerable sanctity, had the reputation of being a fearless warrior, and had survived so many fights that he was regarded with an almost religious awe. In fact, it was said that bullets could not harm him, as I had often heard from my overseers who had fought beside the famous chieftain.

'Before God,' said one, 'I have seen bullets pass right through his body and kill the man behind him, yet the Sheikh remained unharmed. He cannot be killed in war.'

He was also a man of his word, and when put on parole after his captivity, he would probably not have broken it and rebelled against any purely British administration. But when it was proposed to transfer him from British to Arab control he objected most strongly, for the Kurd and the Arab are ancient rivals.

For this reason trouble inevitably arose, and in 1924 Clarke, being a fluent Kurdish linguist, was sent to Sulaimaniyah as Mandatory Political Officer to attempt to keep the Sheikh under the jurisdiction of Iraq. This was indeed a difficult job because of the uncertainty of our own policy in the country, and even a man with the diplomatic skill of Clarke could not possibly avert trouble.

The Sheikh's followers, with infallible Eastern instinct, knew that our policy was a wavering one.

'The British are undecided,' they said, 'soon they will go and then we shall have no need to fear the Arabs!'

During Sheikh Mahmud's enforced absence, Sulaimaniyah had been

135

ruled with ability and forcefulness by Major E. B. Soane, a man who had great personal interest in and affection for the Kurds. He began to build the tribes into a progressive and industrious Kurdish state in a way that inspired the Sulaimanians to try to emulate our Western system of government and general advancement. But the great Soane was an arbitrary ruler, quite out of time and out of place in post-war administration. Receiving but little encouragement in his policy of creating a Kurdish nation, he retired from his official post to lead the quiet life of a student and a writer once again. He died soon afterwards.

It is certain that when Sheikh Mahmud was again given control of the district he was anxious to follow Soane's plan and reorganize and develop his country. We were then, however, beginning to give our support entirely to the Arab interests in the Iraq Government, and the Sheikh's followers had good reason for believing that our statesmen could not make up their minds what to do with the Kurdish districts. There seemed to be no assurance whatever that Britain, as Mandatory Power, wished to retain her influence in Kurdistan. Twenty-five years had been mentioned by the League of Nations as the desirable period of mandatory administration of Iraq, and on this the Kurds had requested to be placed under Britain rather than under Turkey: but they sought eventual independence and had not bargained on being left under Arab rule.

Sheikh Mahmud felt when this happened that his plans would be unduly restricted and his labours fruitless. He said that he and his people could not hope for prosperity under a Baghdad Administration, and he resented the Arab officials.

Towards Captain Clarke and other British officers he remained friendly and seemed anxious for them to stay on at Sulaimaniyah. It was decided, however, to transfer the British officers of the local Kurdish Levy troops out of Kurdistan and to disarm the men. The story goes that when the officers left, the disarming merely consisted in throwing the breech-bolts of the rifles down a well—from which they were readily recovered later by the troops themselves. Thus there remained in Sulaimaniyah a well-armed and disciplined force ready for the Sheikh to lead.

Though Clarke was ordered to stay on as Political Officer and Adviser to the Sheikh, the local notables now had the latter's ear and persuaded him to set up an independent government. The Turks were also believed to have promised to assist by sending arms. The Sheikh actually formed a Kurdish Government and even printed his own postage stamps—great rarities as only a few were ever issued. Some of my overseers were among his cabinet ministers and held various portfolios, such as Minister of Education, Minister of Customs and Excise, etc. This was about three years before they came to work for me.

A Christmas Eve in Kurdistan

These were perplexing times for Clarke. Friendly though the Sheikh was to him, it was obvious that he had no intention of being persuaded to accept the administrative instructions of an Arab Government.

The Sheikh was warned, however, that he must remain under the Government—be it Arab or not—and give up his plans for Kurdish self-determination. He was politeness itself in his replies and protested that he was a loyal servant of Britain. At the same time he was obviously scorning the instructions of the Baghdad ministers and not heeding the Political Officer's advice. Clarke therefore intimated that he was about to leave Sulaimaniyah, and he warned the Sheikh that this would mean that he would be regarded as a rebel from then on.

The Sheikh remonstrated:

'You must not leave me,' he said. 'You are my sincerest friend and my honoured guest.'

'Does that mean you regard your Adviser as a hostage?' exclaimed Clarke. 'If you think the Air Force won't bomb Sulaimaniyah just because you hold me here a prisoner you will soon find out your mistake!'

'So long as I had the Sheikh to myself,' Clarke explained to me that Christmas Eve, 'I could make him admit that he was courting disaster by his actions, but his own chiefs were usually able to talk him round to his old views again. He wobbled to this side and to that and tried to oblige everybody. It would have been amusing had it not been so serious. Of course I could not give him the assurance he asked for, that the British were going to remain in Kurdistan, for I knew it was most unlikely. You may take my word for it we won't be here much longer. I saw the old Sheikh's point of view and was only sorry I could not offer him a better deal. After all, one can't *make* the Kurds love the Arabs if the latter as rulers cannot inspire their proposed subjects with confidence.

'All the same, I warned the Sheikh in plain enough language that his orders were to remain under the Iraq Government, that he must sack his "cabinet" and cease his present administration—if not he would be treated as an open rebel.

'For a time he held me virtually a prisoner and would never let me ride far from the town. There was a man always with me, supposed to be a servant but in reality my guardian and warder in one. I got rather sick of his eternal company, and one day to test whether I was really captive or not I set off at a gallop as though trying to escape. After a desperate chase I let the fellow overhaul me.

' "I am going to Kirkuk," I said casually, "are you coming with me?"

'White and shaking he implored me to return, as his life would be forfeit if I made my escape.

'So I rode back to Sulaimaniyah and had it out with the Sheikh. I told him I was leaving—that he had made his bed and now must lie on it. With a good deal of obvious regret he finally agreed to my going. I believe he liked me personally. He asked me when I should return and I told him it would probably be in a few months' time with the Levies and the Iraq army behind me.

' "Well," he said, "either then, or when you come as an ambassador after I am King of Kurdistan, you will be equally welcome to my humble hospitality. In the meantime your house and your belongings shall be protected. Lock your door, bring me the key. When you come again I promise you that all shall be as you have left it. Though you march at the head of the force that comes to attack me yet will my men lower their rifles and spare the life of my honoured friend."

'I returned to Baghdad unharmed and put in my report. The upshot of it all was that when the Sheikh refused to surrender himself, the R.A.F. were ordered to bomb Sulaimaniyah, and they did it with severity.'

My overseers had told me something of the scenes in the town as bombs rained down upon the populace. The gruesome details they described, of the panic and the injuries to young and old under that deadly storm, were not pleasant to dwell upon.

Clarke continued his story.

'The Iraq Army was ordered to occupy the district, but at once these Arab plainsmen were outmanœuvred by the mobile hillmen. The Assyrian Levies, who are as much at home in mountain warfare as the Kurds themselves, were called into action and with the R.A.F. to help, the upshot of the rebellion could not be in doubt.

'There were many curious incidents connected with that campaign. Take this one for example. A plane had been brought down near Sulaimaniyah, due to engine failure or rifle-fire, and in order to rescue the gunner and pilot, a senior R.A.F. officer performed the daring feat of landing in enemy territory in the heat of an action. He picked the two men up and took off again successfully, while the rebels were trying to make up their minds what to do about this unexpected descent in their midst.

'It was a remarkable thing that, though he resisted desperately, the Sheikh continued to behave well towards us—in spite of the bombing of Sulaimaniyah. As an instance of this two British officers who had been captured were ill. The Sheikh who had housed them as well as he could, sent over a message asking that a doctor might be despatched to examine and attend them, adding that if they were found to be very ill they might be taken back to Baghdad. The doctor who made the journey within the enemy lines was received by the Sheikh with his usual words of courtesy and conducted to the captives. He made his medical examination and found that they had suffered little harm from their imprisonment. He felt he could not honestly ask for their

A Christmas Eve in Kurdistan

liberation on the grounds of their state of health, and said so. Nevertheless, they were eventually allowed by the Sheikh to go free.

'On another occasion a British officer of the Assyrian Levies was killed during an engagement with the hillmen. A letter of apology was sent to their O.C., Colonel MacDonald, saying that the death of the officer was greatly regretted, but that in the fight in question it had been impossible to distinguish who was who!'

Clarke laughed.

'Strange sort of warfare!' he said.

I remembered that at Diana I had once asked Colonel MacDonald about this campaign in which he had led the Assyrians to a complete and yet almost bloodless victory over the Kurds. The old Highland soldier, who had seen active service since Omdurman, tried to belittle his achievement in these words:

'My campaign against Sheikh Mahmud was a most gentlemanly affair. We stopped our battles at meal-times and there were always mutual expressions of regret if anyone got hit by a bullet. We had grand weather for it too, and those manœuvres were enjoyed by one and all. The leaders of the other side sometimes called in for a chat with us. Give me Kurds rather than charging Dervishes to fight against every time!'

It might have been otherwise had the Levies been less skilfully led. The Kurds can be fierce and stubborn fighters and their hill tactics would probably have carried the day against any troops who were not hillmen like themselves.

'You will note', said Clarke, 'that it was always Sheikh Mahmud's policy to emphasize that he was not antagonistic to Britain or, as he averred, to our continuing the Mandate. What he disliked, he said, was the idea of Arab rule and he considered that his own was as good as any other Eastern administration. Upon that subject it is not my business to comment. By the way, he kept his word about the safeguarding of my belongings.

'I had to take over the district when he finally capitulated. Sulaimaniyah was a horrid sight and you can imagine my surprise when I found that my house, which by a miracle had escaped the aerial bombardment, had not been looted by the tribesmen. Sheikh Mahmud when he gave me back the key said;

' "I trust that you will find that nothing has been touched, that nothing is missing," and after those months of warfare everything was exactly as I had left it. Such a manner of man was Sheikh Mahmud!'

'Well,' I said, 'he is at last vanquished. His district is well patrolled by the police force and studded with block-houses. He can do little harm where he now lives up near the Persian frontier.'

'Don't you believe that the influence of Sheikh Mahmud is destroyed,' was the reply. 'It is not. He can leap to life again just as he did before. And he will go down in history as the hero of the Kurdish people.'

I was to remember these words two years later, when grave charges were made by the Kurds that the parliamentary elections of 1930 had been falsified so as to deny them representation. The flame of rebellion blazed again and Sheikh Mahmud strode forth once more to battle. For the third time he was conquered, again after a struggle of two years, and as before not by the troops of the Southern Government he resented but by British air power.

This time he was handed over to the Arab Administration he had so steadfastly resisted, and Eastern governments do not release their captives as do the British. Like many another Kurd whose dreams for his country's independence have been shattered, he remains to this day an ageing prisoner in the hands of his enemies.

CHAPTER XIII

The Snows Melt

When spring comes to Gali Ali Beg, the barren country of Kurdistan, with its rugged mountains and grey rocks, bursts suddenly into extraordinary beauty.

Towards the end of March, almost in a night as it seems, the ground snows melt and the warmth of spring is in the air. The mists lift, and it is as though a veil that for months past had hung over the eyes of the beholder were suddenly withdrawn. In the clear air the mountains seem to stand nearer than ever before. Above the dark walls of the gorge the high snow-fields, like the white wings of some giant bird that has preened itself, stretch smoothly up into the brilliant cloudless sky; while the valley in all but the rockiest places becomes dense with green grass.

Those hill partridges, the chickaw, now awake and disport themselves in hundreds, intoxicated with the pleasure of spring and the food that the vanishing snows yield from the earth once more. There are water-fowl too, wild duck and teal, upon the streams of the plains (though never, strangely enough, in the gorge itself), and graceful herons wade in the swamps. Kurdish trappers come by with the skins of stone-martens and foxes, for these animals, and in fact all others are reckless and devoid of cunning in the spring—and their fur is in its most perfect condition. Even the stupid donkeys seem sillier than usual when liberated after their winter indoors. They prance and bellow tirelessly as they munch greedily at the fresh green grass.

The sheep and goats come forth from the shelter of the caves where the shepherds have kept them herded all these dreary months. They leap up the rocks and graze on every ledge with quickening movements as their bellies fill. The fat tails of the sheep swell again to store up food for the next hungry winter. At some sign of danger—perhaps because he has seen a wolf or a leopard among the rocks—the shepherd gives a curious whistle which calls his flock together. The animals run to him with instant obedience and group themselves round him, snuffing at his hands and clothes just as a dog might do. In this country the shepherd leads and never drives his sheep. He has sheep-dogs too, large and woolly-haired beasts like my Ghunnie; their

141

business is solely to protect the flock and well do they do their work if wolves come near.

Flowers of every colour burst forth amid the grass. Each day some new hue is predominant. An inaccessible ledge high up on the side of the gorge becomes brilliant with scarlet tulips, the roadside blue with irises. There are great lilies to be found in the darker crannies, and small orchids and beds of violets. On the hillside near Kani Uthman are acres of narcissi that show pure white in the distance like unmelted snow. On the Dasht-i-Harir beside the River Zab are huge red poppies and tall white daisies, for on the plains the flowers are quite different from those in the gorges. Except in the cultivated areas where the larger blooms appear, one walks on a carpet of myriads of small flowers. As the weeks go by the low rolling hills are lit with every hue, changing tint like giant chameleons as one variety of plant gives place to another, till at last all the land becomes brown under the summer sun once more, leaving only a short crisp hay for the autumn grazing.

I think the most beautiful sight of all is this Dasht-i-Harir. At its most verdant period it is cultivated wherever possible, and to clear the ground for ploughing each field has been bounded with wide belts of carefully collected boulders, sometimes piled into high pyramids. This stony land produces cereals amazingly. The crops of barley, wheat and rye rise as thick and high as any I have seen anywhere in the world; not in every field it is true, for many lie fallow in a riot of wild flowers. Seen from the high slopes of the Harir Dagh, the miles of fields with their irregular lines of boulders make the Harir Plain look as though a great patchwork quilt had been laid by giant hands over the grey dreariness of its winter surface. One realizes then why men have fought and slain each other during so many centuries for possession of these apparently useless lands.

None rejoice more in the flowers and the verdant spring than the Kurds themselves. Wherever I went I was presented with bunches of wild flowers and of still other varieties from their gardens. Strange as it may seem these tribal people love to grow flowers of every kind they can lay their hands on, and on no topic will they converse with more pleasure or interest. When I discovered this I arranged to obtain some small eucalyptus trees from a friend in the experimental farm at Baghdad, and 'swopped' them (and some English garden seeds that are common enough at home but unknown in Kurdistan) for any native flowers and shrubs that were brought me. I did so well by this barter that I made Kurdish gardens of my own at all my camps. The eucalyptus trees we planted grew readily, and I hope they still survive the Kurdish winters.

As I journeyed along the road I often stopped my car where the spring blooms were finest, and servants and policemen would jump out and come with me knee-deep among the flowers to pluck great bunches to decorate the car and to take home to my dingy mud hut in the gorge.

The stunted trees of the hillside are not to be outdone by the flowers in the unfolding of their spring beauty. Those clinging to the sides of the gorge, seemingly bare and dead for months, now give the dark rocks a less forbidding aspect, for they grow in every crevice. Then again there are fruit trees, and the first of these to start business is the wild mulberry. Its fruit is beginning to form while the pear, apple, peach, apricot and walnut trees will scarcely admit that spring has begun, but these in turn soon take up the chase in earnest. There can be no more enchanting sight than the extensive orchards of Shaqlawah in springtime. Here the tall 'ispandar', or poplar trees, punctuate a sea of blossom where bees are busily at work collecting and storing their honey in the hollow stumps—each horde carefully marked down by the villagers. The memory of the fruits of those gardens, sacks of walnuts, goat-skins of wild honey, donkey-loads of luscious grapes that one could buy for a rupee or so, remain with me today as among the material joys and compensations of my lonely life in Kurdistan.

In this country it will be seen that there are extremes of plenty and scarcity. Spring is prolific of the fruits of the earth as autumn and winter are destitute of them. Fortunately, the Kurds are by no means an improvident people. They put by enough for the winter and something to spare if possible, for there may be wars and troubles to provide against—indeed, there are almost certain to be in Kurdistan.

War and aerial bombing may mean the destruction of the whole village and the conflagration of the crops and grain stores leaving the people homeless and without food. Yet even more dreaded than wars are the locusts. They come like an invading army and are more difficult to battle against than either soldiers or aeroplanes. In whatever stage of their life-cycle they appear, as crawling, fresh-hatched creatures, as 'hoppers' that jump but cannot fly, or as the full-grown insect that may have flown hundreds of miles, their capacity for destruction is literally appalling. They move with slow advance over a frontage of many miles and everything in their path is consumed. Not a stalk appears above the earth, not a leaf on a tree is left; I have heard it said that disabled animals, and even small babies left unattended, have been devoured. Water channels and even rivers are no bar to their progress. Millions are drowned, but their floating bodies form a bridge for their comrades. The solid skin of the earth appears to be moving slowly about, and it is composed of locusts.

There is, of course, constant war upon them. In the hopping stage they can be killed by laying arsenical bran in their path; they eat it and die. More locusts come and eat these dead bodies and in their turn die. It takes vast quantities of the prepared poison and rapid, organized transport to catch the swarms before they fly. Many may be thus killed and great piles of husks of locust bodies are formed—and then, often enough, the invading army just passes over them on its way. They may also be burnt with petroleum or trapped in trenches lined with smooth metal sheeting—even the glossy pages of hundreds of the illustrated London weekly papers were used for this purpose by the resourceful English locust officer in Iraq. He organized a campaign that might well have led to the extermination of the pest had the Iraq Government fully appreciated the originality and value of his work.

If they reach maturity the hoppers fly and form a cloud that darkens the sun. They fly blindly against the windscreen of a car till it is thickly besmeared with their bodies, or they rest comfortably for a while on the mudguards gazing solemnly at the world about them. They show no fear of human beings. 'Kill us if you like,' they seem to say; 'there are a million others behind us.' It is said that some of the tribal Arabs dry and eat them, but I have never seen them used as food.

The building of the road not only assisted the mobility of the locust-fighting lorries with their poisons and petroleum fire-sprays, but also enabled grain to be readily transported from other districts to the starving people. A famine can be a terrible thing in the East, especially when serious epidemics accompany it, and a celebrated medical authority once said, 'To me, as a physician, Iraq is the most interesting country in the world, for it is a very paradise of disease.'

In the springtime, too, snakes and reptiles appear. There are large black ones and smaller mottled ones. Some few are deadly, but the majority, fortunately, are not. The river snakes, for instance, are practically harmless though they can be alarming enough to the swimmer who meets them. The Kurds avoid every kind and shoot them on sight. I was amazed at the rapidity with which a Kurdish Police Commandant once seized a constable's rifle and shot a snake into two pieces as it wriggled rapidly across the road in front of us.

Guerges had warned me that if I killed a snake, its mate would follow me and find me out, no matter how far away I might hide. That very day I had killed a large mottled one, and I laughed the warning to scorn. The place was miles away.

'Beware,' Guerges persisted, 'she will come. A snake is a magic creature and can perform the impossible. Else why is the medicine made from cast-off snake skins so potent that it cures all sicknesses?'

The Kurds and Assyrians both have implicit faith in this strange remedy.

That night as I lay dozing in my bed with the lantern still burning, I slowly became aware that there was another sound beside the incessant crackling made by the large beetles in the roof. It was a kind of gliding rustle among the dried leaves of the thatching. Faint as it was, I glanced up. Directly above my head there hung a long mottled snake, its flat head waving slowly from side to side as it looked about the room! I had heard that snakes came to thatched roofs to hunt for mice, but as it fixed its stare upon me I had a paralysing sensation of horror that this one had surely come for me. With an effort I broke the spell of those beady eyes, I rose stealthily, seized a walking-stick, and with a furious blow brought the creature wriggling in death to the ground.

'Did I not tell you that the mate would come and find you out?' cried Guerges triumphantly in the morning, as he gazed at the dead body of the snake.

At that time I was collecting snakes at the special request of an enthusiastic young doctor in the Medical Service in Baghdad. He is today an acknowledged authority on the subject. He wanted as many specimens as he could get, and had sent me a patent device for catching them and a bottle of formalin with which to preserve them, the latter totally insufficient for the size of the snakes I had caught. I did my best with spirits and kerosene to make up the deficiency and had a good-sized tinful collected.

The Director of Medical Services was one of my first visitors after the road was again passable for cars, and he asked me as he was leaving if there was anything I should like taken to Baghdad.

'Well, yes, if it isn't too much trouble,' I said. 'Dr. Corkill of your Department wanted some specimens of snakes, and I've got some for him here in this tin. I'd be much obliged if you'd take them down with you. The lid is quite secure.'

'Oh, snakes,' he said without enthusiasm, 'let's see them.'

I prised open the lid. The snakes *looked* all right, but I admit that the tin *smelt* very odd. I tried to explain that the snakes really *were* all right and always smelt that way in Kurdistan, but my arguments must have carried little conviction. Whether he had something against snakes as such, or just against that particular tinful, he did not say, but he flatly refused to assist his junior in the cause of science by taking my collection to Baghdad!

On my return journey from Arbil at Christmas-time I had been forced to abandon my car near the village of Kala Chin on Spilik. It looked a sad object, marooned there, each time I rode that way on mule-back. I was glad when the spring sunshine dried up the muddy surface of the road and I was able to drive it home. For two months and more it had been left there unattended, almost on the doorstep, as it were, of Hamada Chin and his notorious followers, yet, when I came to take it away not so much as a spanner was missing; such was the curious code of honour of these remarkable people.

It would have been quite otherwise had the road been in use by Armenian taxi-drivers during that period. Little by little my Chevrolet would have disappeared; first a few tools, then a wheel, then the engine, and finally the whole chassis. Like the locusts, bit by bit they consume every unattended car, or portion thereof, that lies in their way.

I know nothing quite so cool as the Armenian driver's way of appropriating other people's tools and motor parts. Supposing, for instance, I should happen to leave my car by the roadside near Arbil for ten minutes with a perfectly good set of tyre levers and a brand-new pump under the seat, I should come back to find that they had suddenly aged into old and bent and broken things. Some taxi-man has had a 'puncher' near by (translated from modern Arabic 'puncher' may mean anything from a puncture to a national calamity). I can see the marks of his flat tyre in the mud. With the freemasonry of the road he has helped himself to my jacks and levers and what not. When I overtake him and ask for my tools it seems he has merely made a slight mistake by putting back the wrong ones!

My own tractor- and car-drivers, most of whom were Armenians (who seem to have an inborn aptitude for mechanical work), were the worst offenders of all. They not only purloined the tools when it suited them but gave or loaned them to any driver friend who passed by. Doubtless a few annas could always be obtained for them in any bazaar. On my periodical inspection of tools I found that spanners and pliers and so on were always missing. It was a waste of time asking what had become of them—it invariably produced the usual Iraqi answer, 'Wallah m'aruf!' which means, 'How should *I* know?' so I merely commanded that they should be brought back from whatever bazaar they had been taken to, or there would be trouble.

To their credit, let it be said that these Armenian drivers were a daring lot of men who cared little for the risks they ran in driving their ramshackle cars in hilly Kurdistan. They had not even the most rudimentary training in motor engineering, yet they kept their cars going in truly remarkable fashion. All the troubles a car is heir to were tabulated according to an original vocabulary of their own. There was no word in any of the eight languages in common use in the district that would translate 'gudgeon pin' or 'universal joint'. So they classified a few of the causes of breakdowns and stuck to those. Suppose the engine stopped, the cause was always 'plugs' to begin with. They meant 'sparking plugs' of course and used up these inoffensive articles by the gross, breaking most of them by screwing them in and out with badly-fitting spanners. If the car still refused to move, though at least one cylinder of the engine was running, the next trouble to be looked to in the old model T Ford (which was the most usual type of car) was 'banz'. The 'bands' of the Ford epicyclic gear wore out in no time with the terrific loads they were forced to deal with on the hills. If a titivating of the 'banz' proved unavailing, the only remaining explanation was 'Wallah maksur!' This meant, 'The damned thing is *broken* somewhere!'

Usually strange grinding noises from the mainshaft, differential or rear axles might have already suggested this diagnosis. They would settle down there and then to the major operation of lifting the rear of the car, extracting the whole of the transmission and strewing the road with bolts and pinions. The offending part is at last discovered and held joyfully aloft streaming with oil.

'Dichlee (wheel)!' exclaims the Armenian proudly exhibiting a bevel wheel from which every tooth is missing.

It is at this point that the earlier mentioned acquisitive instincts of the driver show their value. Probably he has an old spare bevel wheel that he has purloined from some derelict chassis by the roadside. If not, it is practically certain that the very first driver who passes can produce one and is perfectly prepared to hand it over. How this masonic craft of taxi-drivers balanced out their individual working profits I cannot say; they would freely exchange anything by the roadside from a radiator to a complete engine!

At last a bevel wheel with approximately the right number of sound teeth to mesh with its neighbour is got from somewhere and the car is reassembled. The fact that ball-bearings are worn and loose and on the point of breaking gives not the least concern; even the broken teeth that still lie in the oil sump are of no moment, nor are the nuts and bolts that are lost and missing. They say, 'Why, there are always too many nuts and bolts in a motor-car anyway.'

So with hopeful joy everyone climbs into the car again—the passengers have all this while been sitting by the roadside admiring the magician at work—'plugs' and 'banz' are given a last scrutiny, the engine picks up rather hesitatingly on one, two or three cylinders and away our taxi goes again!

The mud had soon taken toll of these adventurous drivers who followed the road-engineer in a blind faith that all would be well on the newly-made track that disappeared into the mountains. That winter half a dozen cars besides my own were trapped somewhere along the route. I had not left the road in such a muddy mess on purpose, but the construction parties had gone ahead much too fast for the metalling party and the only steam-roller we had on the work. All we had aimed at and achieved in the first year was a connected track fit for dry weather.

With the spring, and as the road dried, traffic increased once more. Visitors and travellers became more frequent, caravans of merchandise passed through on the way to Persia, long lines of mules and donkeys brought supplies to the road-camp.

In the spring, too, the nomad Hurke tribesmen returned with their flocks and herds to the frontier mountains. They looked a formidable body of men when the leaders and their large armed escorts filed past on their hill ponies—picturesque in their Kurdish clothes and gaudy saddles, and fierce in martial splendour and bearing. I longed for a cinematograph camera to film them as they rode so proudly by. The Hurke are such a wealthy tribe, owning immense herds of sheep and goats, that they are really not so warlike as they try to appear—not nearly so aggressive for instance as the settled Surchi people and Hamada Chin. The Hurke stand to lose some of their flocks if they fight unnecessarily—though a year seldom passes that they are not engaged in a battle of some kind or other, usually forced upon them by less wealthy rivals.

As I have said, they did not interfere with my work and were very friendly towards me. Sometimes minor troubles arose between us, and then if I could not refer the matter to their chieftains, I just had to take what action I thought fit. Here is a case in point. A small party of tribesmen were shooting uncomfortably near my camp. What they were shooting at I do not know, possibly some wild animal. I had given orders that shooting was forbidden within a certain area round the camp and I sent a coolie up the hillside to ask them to stop. They replied that this had always been their hunting ground and always would be. So I despatched my small Assyrian sentry who was the only man available at the time to discover who they were and the name of their immediate chieftain. He did this and more, for he brought back with him their leader, disarmed and with his hands tied to his waistband behind, a sign of captivity. The Assyrian, like many of his nation, was a fierce little man and had suddenly arrested the nomad tribesman by sheer bluff, saying these were my orders. Though he was one against a dozen, yet to my surprise he had not been opposed. The tribesmen probably knew that their own chiefs would not approve of any resistance to my orders. The captive's dagger and rifle were returned to him as soon as he promised to take his party elsewhere.

Often enough, as I knew, the nomads had good cause to be hostile. I wonder that they were not more so. With our blasting we sometimes completely obliterated the old tracks for the time being, and the hill ponies with women and children on their backs occasionally stumbled and fell among the upheaved masses of rock. Also at the unaccustomed sight of a car they sometimes took fright and might bolt and throw their riders. It was my rule that cars and machines must always take the outside of the road so that the animals would not bound over the precipice; and the engines had to be stopped to lessen the risks. The tribesmen thus knew we were doing our best to avoid accidents.

They were less well-assured of our good conduct in other matters. My coolies invariably stole their sheep or goats when they got the chance. I would find goats caught up in thick bushes and under road-machines in the most mysterious fashion. Of course, no coolie could

148

ever explain how they got there. The beasts were so stupid, they said, they did such things by themselves! Occasionally the animals were actually seized from the tribesmen in my name and I discovered that my own servants were not guiltless of such practices.

I imagine that what happened was something like this.

'Oh, the engineer would like a sheep,' Guerges would say to some tribal chief, and in deference to me a sheep would be handed over.

Guerges and his pal, Rustam Khan, were known to do a lot of private trading with the coolies as a sideline to their official occupation in my kitchen. So after the sheep had been killed the two would sit and consider their ill-gotten gains and converse somewhat as follows:

Guerges: 'Well, Rustam Khan, it's a lot more than the officer can eat and more than you and I need.'

Rustam Khan: 'Still, remember the officer must get some of it. You've got to buy meat for him anyway you know. But it would surely be a pity to let the rest go bad. He wouldn't mind the coolies getting a small share of it, I'm sure.'

Guerges: 'True, Rustam Khan, you were always a good business man. Let us cut off the officer's portion and then see how much is left for the coolies. Here are the scales. He never objects when I enter in his "dufta" (personal account book) as much as a "hooka"[1] of meat a day. I charge him only a rupee for it and the coolies would hardly expect to have the officer's meat at a lower price than he, would they?'

Rustam Khan: 'That piece you've got on the scale is a bit light. You must be honest with your master, you know. Try this larger piece. Yes, it is practically a hooka. And we are selling the officer nice fresh meat specially selected by a Kurdish chieftain!'

When I found evidence of this sort of thing I was not pleased, and said so, and kept much stricter watch on camp and servants. Perhaps for this reason after some months Guerges decided he had saved enough money to return to Persia and he left me. He said that ours was a precarious life in that gorge (he never approved of the way I used to drive my car round the edges of the precipices) and he had to remember that he had a wife and child somewhere in Iran. So we parted with mutual expressions of goodwill. He wasn't a bad bearer, by any means; and his invariable optimism and assured knowledge of every subject under the sun never failed to amuse me.

In his place came the most trustworthy of all my servants, a Kurdish lad by the name of Hamid. Hard and wiry, he thought nothing of the longest and most dangerous of mountain-climbs or other expeditions. He was a Rowanduz boy and one of quite good family; his knowledge of local tribes was profound and his advice on Kurdish customs invaluable; moreover, he would have answered for my safety at any time with his own life.

---

[1] A measure of weight.

CHAPTER XIV

The Cave of Kospyspee

Though I had made a preliminary survey of the Berserini Gorge in the late autumn of 1928, in the following year I still had to spend much time examining the river valley up which the line of our road was to pass; this meant living for weeks at a time in moving camps far beyond the main headquarters of the road work. When out on such surveying expeditions we usually camped near Kurdish villages so that we could get food and find men to act as guides who not only knew all the tracks and passes but could tell me who owned the water channels and fields which a wide road would have to disturb. Needless to say, we planned the road to interfere as little as possible with existing cultivation, and the Kurds always appreciated this consideration of their ancient rights, for arable land is scarce in rocky Kurdistan.

In the evenings I would often gossip with the headman of the village near which my camp happened to be. Thus, one evening, I came to be sitting with my friend Aziz Agha, chief of the village of Berserini, and we drank tea and smoked cigarettes of peace and contentment in the fading twilight. From my camp we could still just see his village across the river. Berserini has an Italian sound about it, and the low thatched houses amidst the gardens on the rocky bank over the bridge looked picturesque enough for the shores of the Mediterranean instead of this deep, rugged valley hemmed in with towering mountains where winter storms strike so fiercely. The bridge of sagging tree-trunks on high piers might, by the grace of Allah, carry one man—or even one donkey—at a time! Later on, when I found that the position of this bridge made it useful to give access to the road from neighbouring districts I fixed it up properly, for the masonry piers, built probably hundreds of years ago, were still fairly sound, and the bridge needed only a few steel joists and new decking to make it serviceable for the mule caravans.

Part of the village had been destroyed by the Russians during the war and was not yet rebuilt. Aziz Agha boasted that he was a rich man before the Russians came but said he was now poor. There were certainly signs of his present poverty, for in the whole valley there were only two fields of corn being cultivated by his people. Aziz Agha had a leisurely way of being industrious. He hoped some day to rebuild all

150

the fallen houses—all six of them—or perhaps his son or his grandson might, who knows? Nevertheless he afterwards came with his villagers and took a very active part in the road-work. I always found that the Kurds could work well if they chose.

Aziz Agha said he was grateful to me for the road-work I was doing in his country and even went so far as to say that the Kurds liked the British people because they built things and showed kindness; whereas the Turk and the Russian destroyed and robbed and ravished. I laughed at this and told him he was just trying to please me with his flattery, but he assured me that for a great part of his life he and his tribe had been obliged to live as fugitives in the mountains. Today there was no fear of molestation and he cultivated his two cornfields and his vineyards in security. In past times the word 'government', as the Turks understood it, meant soldiers waiting to attack him suddenly, to pillage and to burn; today my harmless gangs of coolies busy making the old rocky tracks into graded roads gave him no cause for suspicion or alarm.

With this hopeful opening and its compliments I asked Aziz Agha a question I had long had in my mind. I had heard of great caves in the mountains hereabouts, caves running so far into the bowels of the earth that no man had been to the end of them—did he know of these?

Now caves are used as hiding-places in times of trouble and give protection from the bombs of aeroplanes. The tribesmen will not disclose their whereabouts very willingly, but on this occasion Aziz Agha showed no hesitation. He said he would take me into the great cave of Kospyspee, which he explained lay quite near the line of the road.

Next morning we set out to examine it. The cave entrance lay in the face of a great rock-wall, geologically a fault, which descends the side of the valley from a high ridge, till it disappears under the foaming river. The wall all but closed the valley to caravans, and the old track had to cross it in a narrow winding staircase overhung by a ponderous 'shakh' or projecting cliff which, when the road-head came so far, took us a month of blasting to remove, for no less than six thousand tons of rock had to be displaced to obtain a gradient suitable for motor cars.

Aziz Agha led the way up a steep footpath above the caravan track till we reached the mouth of the cave. He was followed by one of his men, and with me was a Persian coolie and the Assyrian overseer, Benyamin Yonin. The old Agha carried his rifle and a dagger, as there was every chance of such a place being inhabited by wolves or bears or even by a leopard.

The cave began as a low tunnel along which we had to crawl, shoving the lantern before us. Suddenly it widened and we found ourselves in the cave proper. It had a great vaulted roof from which the bats descended in swarms and flashed past our heads menacingly with

The Cave of Kospyspee

swift dives as if they resented our intrusion into their dark sanctuary. When we spoke our voices echoed strangely. We saw before us a glistening white dome, which proved to be a mound of bones, possibly human ones, bedded in a stalagmite. By the dim light of the lanterns we could see a passage ahead with alcoves and secondary tunnels leading to either side; we walked forward to explore the main passage and found that the floor gradually became deep in sticky mud. This did not deter us from going forward, indeed a strange fascination seemed to lure us on and on. After turning several corners the mud was almost up to our knees and we could no longer feel solid rock under our feet; then only did we realize that we were caught in a kind of quagmire which might prove to be bottomless!

The air had become warm and fetid—or was it the heat of a quickening pulse that made me break into a cold sweat? A few yards in front of us a rock platform or dais rose out of the mud. We were wondering whether we could reach it when the lantern I held, which had already flickered once or twice, suddenly went out completely. Was this some sorcery, and were we doomed to perish here as others had done? We remembered the mound of bones which we had passed. The second lantern carried by the coolie at the rear of the party gave a final dying flare and there was complete darkness! We stood knee-deep in a mire that had a horrid stench, doubtless of bat-dung of which it seemed mainly composed, and we felt we were sinking deeper as we stood. We must keep moving. Yet now we could not see where we were to go.

There are scenes in one's life which leave so vivid an impression on the imagination that they can never be forgotten. By the last gleam of the second lantern I had looked round for a way of escape from the subterranean morass. I had seen the grisled old tribesman just behind me holding his long Turkish rifle at the ready, for they fear neither man nor beast, shooting with equal readiness at either. He, like me, was held in the mire. Behind him I had caught a glimpse of the pallid startled faces of the followers. Why were the lights going out of their own accord? The true explanation at once rose to my mind—that the air must be so impure it would not support combustion—but to these superstitious and simple people it could be nothing but the work of a 'jin' or fiend of the mountains. So in a loud voice and with composure that I little felt I tried to reassure them, telling them that there was no danger; I ordered them to strike matches and retreat while the match-heads flared. I asked the old Agha his whereabouts and wallowed through the mud towards his voice and grasped his hand in the darkness.

In truth there was much danger. Even if we got out of the mud could we follow the many turnings aright, for we had come a long way from the entrance? Since the lanterns had gone out I knew there must also be a risk of asphyxiation; and might not the air, so foul from the rotting bat-dung, conceivably be explosive owing to marsh-gas, and ignite from the flaring match-heads like the deadly fire-damp of coal mines?

Aziz Agha was alarmed, though with Kurdish pride he tried not to show his agitation. He told me no one had ever come in so far and returned, and he himself remembered one man at least who had ventured alone within this cave and was never heard of again. To hide his feelings and make an excuse for not going farther he said there was no end to the cave anyway, everyone knew it went on for ever! So we struggled through the mire to the rough wall of the passage where the mud was shallower, and feeling our way along it, helped by the periodical flare of the matches, we at last regained the drier ground. There was a faint shout of joy from the darkness far ahead where my coolie had spotted the dim light of the entrance round a turning. It is difficult to give any adequate idea of our feelings as we crawled back to the fresh air and the blinding light of day.

In the course of the actual road-making I had to keep in store large quantities of explosives and the most suitable places for this purpose were caves. As the cave of Kospyspee was near the road-line it was ideal, and I ordered the entrance to be enlarged so that men could enter standing, in order to pack the boxes of gelignite. The wider opening cleared the bad air in the course of a few weeks and a lantern would burn brightly at least as far as the edge of the mud within. When I told my friend and fellow adventurer, Captain Alf York of the Levies, about our previous experience he was at once all keenness to explore the place thoroughly with a larger party.

We decided to take with us the 'Rab Trema' Yacu Ismail, the chief Assyrian officer of the Levies, who was equally eager to explore the cave. On hunting expeditions and official tours together he had told us many weird stories of caves in the Hakkiari mountains—his old Assyrian homeland in Turkey from which his race had migrated during the war. It was to the caves that the Christian Assyrians retreated before the invading Turks and defended themselves with desperate bravery. They took with them stores of food and water and such powder and lead bullets as they possessed, and they shot from the ledges with their old muzzle-loading rifles, the men holding the entrance while the women reloaded the firearms within the cave mouth. The gunpowder, which the Assyrians made themselves, was said to be as good as that used in the Turkish Mauser rifles. It had to comply with severe tests, one of the most curious of which was that when it was lit on the palm of the hand it must burn so suddenly that the skin was not even blistered—so carefully were the ingredients purified and mixed to explode completely and leave no ash. The 'Rab Trema' remembered the caves of the Hakkiari mountains from the days of his youth. His eyes brightened as he told of the battles of his tribe, the Upper Tiyari, fought and won in spite of the inequality of firearms. He recounted how they would attack from the heights of the hill-passes after they were believed to be scattered and vanquished, and how, like the cunning hillmen they were, they would lie in ambush in the unmapped valleys and capture military stores and transport from the often bewildered enemy.

As we jogged along on mules on the journey from Battalion Head-quarters at Diana to the cave in the Berserini Gorge he spoke also of the hardships the Assyrian people had endured in pushing their way through the heart of Kurdistan to join the Russian forces which in 1915 were attempting to wrest Mesopotamia from the Turks. When they met the Russians at Urmia they were given modern rifles and adequate ammunition; but, later, when Russia became Bolshevik and her army retreated, the Assyrians were left to their fate. They held their own as long as their ammunition lasted and launched many an attack on the enemies who surrounded them.

'Then', said the Assyrian, 'began the tragic march to join the British forces at Hamadan, nearly three hundred miles to the south. Thousands of men, women and children died by the wayside from hunger and disease and the bullets of the enemy.'

Thence they marched through the Persian passes to Khaniqin and were established in a great refugee camp at Baquba. But this is quite another story that has no bearing on the cave of Kospyspee.

We reached the cave-mouth, which was now masked by an enclos-ing stone wall behind which two tons of gelignite were stored. A Kurdish sentry stood guard over these explosives—for local tribesmen were latterly used to protect all my stores and even my own camps—and the man saluted as we passed into the cave. Arrangements for this exploration were better planned and more scientific than on my pre-vious visit. An electric signal lamp was to serve as the main light, and we each carried an electric torch and a pistol. Moreover, the party was sufficiently large to enable us to place men at intervals along the passages to show us the way back to the entrance if need be, or to carry a man out should he succumb in some unventilated corner. To avoid such a danger we carried one lantern with us to test the air as we went forward.

Before we left Battalion Headquarters, Colonel MacDonald had given us much information about the question of human endurance in bad air. As a prisoner in Germany towards the end of the war he had shared in the construction of a secret tunnel leading from within the prison camp to beyond the barbed-wire enclosure for the purpose of escape. The Colonel assured us that men could live for a time in air too impure to keep a lantern alight, though he said it was then found

The Cave of Kospyspee

to be difficult to work with any great exertion. Acting on this assurance we were prepared to explore the cave as far at least as the presence of bats indicated sufficient oxygen to support life.

We pressed forward to the edge of the evil-smelling mire and discovered that with the warmer weather and the freer ventilation it had partially dried, so that we were able to wade through it with much less danger than before. We climbed forward to the dais. Myriads of bats whirled madly overhead. From the platform ramifications of passages led off just as from behind the stage of a theatre. In an alcove we discovered a second mass of calcified bones which we were able to lift out, and they were eventually sent to Baghdad to be examined by anthropologists who were always glad of such material.

Eagerly we entered what seemed to be the deepest passage running directly into the heart of the mountain. It ended finally in a tunnel scarcely large enough for a man's body. We flashed our torches down the narrow opening, but could see no end to it. The 'Rab Trema', who was the smallest man of our party, volunteered to crawl along it—for Assyrians are plucky enough for anything—and he started off, worming his way, pistol in one hand, torch in the other. In a few minutes his voice came to us from some distance saying there was a larger chamber beyond. I was so intrigued by this that I too began to squeeze myself down the little tunnel. I am tall but fairly slim and though the passage was tight at my hips it was down-hill to begin with and so presented less difficulty than if it had been level. After wriggling about twelve feet or more and crawling a little farther on hands and knees, I came out into a small room that might have been the inner chamber in a monastery of an ancient order of priests, so neatly were the sides cut into shelves and benches of solid rock. Neither human nor animal remains were visible, though what may have lain beneath the earthy floor we could not tell.

We could hear the inquiring voice of Captain York, who was rather alarmed at our complete disappearance into the living rock, and already our electric torches were beginning to grow dim with constant use, so after all too brief a search of this interesting place I advised the Assyrian to return. To this day it is scarcely probable that any other human beings have penetrated so far into the cave of Kospyspee, and such remains as there may be still lie there undisturbed, for our visit was not repeated. There may also have been several other openings of the same kind for all we knew, for both my visits to this cave seemed beset with troubles of one sort or another which interfered with the making of a proper search. My most alarming experience of all was now about to occur.

The 'Rab Trema' crawled back ahead of me and I could see that he was having some difficulty in getting up through the narrowest place. I gave him a shove and he managed it. When it came to my turn my shoulders went through the slimy constriction without much difficulty but not so my hips; they stuck fast, and wriggle as I would I could not make further headway. There was a feeling of absolute helplessness as I squeezed and strained in that narrow rat-hole. The earth seemed to tighten about me. My situation brought to my mind the stories of Edgar Allan Poe, a writer whose graphic powers I had always admired till that moment when I wished his gruesome tales of men buried alive had never been written. I thought, too, of the Persian torture in which a man is buried up to his neck in an upright position and left with only his head above ground until the flies, the dogs and the ants devour him. All this while I was wriggling desperately. In front of me at the mouth of the tunnel were my friends, and I shouted to them that I was unable to move any farther. Captain York, always an imperturbable wag, comforted me by replying, 'Cheer up, Ham, remember that the copy-book says "it's a long worm that has no turning!" '

The Assyrian crawled back to help me and pulled my arms while the rest of the party dragged at his feet. In this way I was tugged out like a pull-through from a rifle-barrel. With no little relief I stood up once again beside my friends.

Alf, carefully holding his nose with his fingers, surveyed me with his torch.

'Old boy,' he said, 'don't you ever wash or do you *prefer* to smell like that?'

Only then did I realize that in my struggles in the dirty passage my clothes had become literally saturated with bat-dung, ripe and scented with the ages. Phew, how I smelt! I had certainly had enough of cave-hunting in those clothes, so I led the way back to the entrance.

As we mounted our mules Alf was at his so-called wit again.

'Keep down wind, old chap, if you don't mind,' he said. 'Now I know your tastes in perfumery I'll indent on Headquarters for smelling salts and a gas mask in case we go cave-hunting another time!'

In spite of Alf's impolite badinage I returned to camp well pleased with our holiday, cheerfully anticipating the delights of the hot bath that awaited me.

Check Out Receipt

Englewood Public Library
201-568-2215
http://www.englewoodlibrary.org/

Thursday, January 31, 2019 4:24:46 PM
62832
SCHWARTZ, ROBERT A

Item: 39119051006305
Title: Road through Kurdistan : travels in
 Northern Iraq
Call no.: 915.672 HAM
Material: Hardcover
Due: 02/28/2019

Total items: 1

You just saved $30.00 by using your librar
y. You have saved $30.00 this past year an
d $143.99 since you began using the librar
y!

THANK YOU COME AGAIN!

CHAPTER XV

The Treasure-Vault of the Ancient Kings

It was Sayed Heusni Effendi, the Kurdish historian, who first told me about a cave even greater than Kospyspee, the great cave of the Baradost mountain. He had not seen it himself, he said, but had read about it in his ancient Kurdish books which told of so many interesting things little less wonderful than the stories of the *Arabian Nights* themselves—of the famous Kor Pasha, blind ruler of Rowanduz, who created a Kurdish Commonwealth; of the Princess Zad whose dominions stretched from Persia to the plains of Arbil and whose palace was the castle I had seen, its ruins still standing on the rocky eminence in the Harir mountains; even of the great Kurd Saladin who repelled the Crusaders. Sayed Heusni will read you many a story as you sit with him sipping coffee in his Persian garden under the pomegranate and mulberry trees.

At one edge of the garden there falls away the sheer precipice that bounds the rocky citadel of Rowanduz and renders it well-nigh impregnable. Far below can be heard the dull roar of the river in the gorge; and there is a story that, when the Russians occupied Rowanduz, a squadron of their cavalry charged unwittingly over the brink at this very spot.

Sayed Heusni is not merely an historian, he is also the local journalist and newspaper proprietor. There is a brass notice on his door which reads, *Zari Kermanji* (*The Cry of the Kurdish*) which is the name of his paper. The editor writes his fiery leaders on the decline of the Kurdish people. His type is set by hand. From the oak of the mountain-side he cuts small blocks of wood. He planes them smooth and true and upon them he etches the illustrations for his paper. He inks his plates, turns the primitive printing press, then sets and binds his sheets together to form the monthly magazine. A copy goes to the High Commissioner and another to the League of Nations at Geneva. *The Cry of the Kurdish* is called a 'monthly' magazine, but often enough the little paper is suppressed on account of its Kurdish sentiments which are not always approved of by the Government at Baghdad.

Sayed Heusni, in his picturesque Kurdish clothes with the green waist-band which denotes him a descendant of the Prophet, is not, however, the subject of this tale. He told me all he knew of the legends of the caves thereabouts and spoke of the cave at Jindian (the Wizard's Spring) where the waters for ever rise and fall at irregular intervals, which I had seen myself when I was a guest of Sheikh Sayed Taha. He said that when it is dry in the summer the fissures from which this spring issues can be traversed for miles underground.

As to the Baradost cave, the most famous of them all, Sayed Heusni said that the secret of its whereabouts was closely guarded by the tribesmen, if indeed any were alive today who knew exactly where it was. In it were said to be streams of water, statues and bas-reliefs of ancient kings and rulers cut in the living rock, and the tombs of priests of a religious cult forgotten these thousands of years in Kurdistan. Yet only a short time ago an Armenian had come seeking to know whether Sayed Heusni could tell him the way to the cave. The man was a stranger and the historian had gathered that he possessed some book that told of buried secrets. As to what these were the Armenian would say nothing. Whether or not he ever found the cave Sayed Heusni did not know, for the mysterious stranger had never returned to Rowanduz.

With this information I went off to my companions of the Levies at Diana. In the snug thatched buildings that served as the Battalion mess, I told Captain Alf York my tale while the Arab servant, Khalif, stood by gaping as he held a tray of drinks, more attentive to the story than to his duties.

The Assyrian officer, Yacu Ismail, was sent for. He arrived with a smart salute and his usual polite phrase to his officer, 'You called for me, sir?'

'Well, Rab Trema, what do you know about the great cave of the Baradost?'

At once the Assyrian was all interest.

'I know of it, sir,' he said eagerly. 'You must mean the cave over the high pass from the village of Havdian.'

So I told my tale once again, and Yacu Ismail's eyes flashed with the hope of new adventure and the pride of race.

'You have heard a little of what is said to be within the Baradost cave, sir, but evidently you have not heard of the mill that grinds flour for ever and never stops, yet with no man or woman to feed it; you have not heard of the fire than burns eternally, nor of the secret vault that holds the treasure of the ancient kings of Assyria, looted from enemies when ours was the mightiest nation on earth—thousands of years ago, when men in Europe and in England were mere savages in the forests.

'I am a descendant of those ancient kings! The remnant of our nation that survived the war is now wandering homeless in Iraq. Some

The Treasure-Vault of the Ancient Kings

of us serve you as British soldiers. Yet once all these lands were ours, as the carvings at Batas, at Amadiyah and Nineveh must prove to you. The shape of the heads in those carvings is Assyrian, as you must admit; not like that of Kurdish or Arab heads. By our tradition the treasure buried within the Baradost cave once adorned the temples of a neighbouring town—now only a ruin. The name of that town means "the city of cruel people", for my ancestors were savage fighters. When the town was in danger of conquest the treasure was hidden away. It is still ours by right and I am the one entitled to seek it and to use it for our ancient nation which is in danger of extinction and so sorely needs help today.'

'I heard a strange tale recently,' he continued, 'from my cousin at Havdian, that an Armenian came and bought a donkey in the village and asked about this cave; and that he had with him some old book, mouldy and discoloured, written in the Armenian language. Armenian writing is from left to right like your English, not from right to left like Assyriac and Kurdish. In Havdian no one could read the writing, but on some of the pages were pictures of priests worshipping at altars of fire; and drawings that might have been plans of rooms or underground chambers. These things my cousin saw in the book when he strapped the pack on the donkey, while the Armenian ate food in the chaikhanah. The stranger left by the track that leads up over the high pass on the Havdian Dagh on the way to the valley of the wild tribes, the Surchi and the Barzan, to the south side of the Baradost mountain. The Armenian has never come back. The tribesmen may have accounted for him, or the cave perhaps swallowed him up, but my cousin says that he has disappeared completely.'

'Well, that adds a lot of interest,' said Captain York. 'Let us pack food and kit for a week-end of exploration. We must take ropes and portable electric lamps and examine this mysterious cave thoroughly, if we can find it. And don't forget some beer packed in ice, Khalif, and be sure of an extra mule to carry the treasure,' he added jocularly, turning again to the Arab servant. (The ice, by the way, is snow, stored by the Kurds in caves on the mountain-tops in winter, and brought down in the summer.)

August is one of the hottest months in Kurdistan, and in that country means a temperature of 110 degrees in the shade. The very marrow of one's bones seems to dry up, and there are no springs of water on the steep track that winds up from Havdian through a narrow gorge, hot and still as an oven. As we picked our way warily up one of those narrow ledges which in Kurdistan may be called a road, we watched the shimmering tops of the ravine carefully for any warning of tribal huntsmen or shepherds who might be hostile, for there had been a whisper of trouble hereabouts and some Assyrians had recently been killed. Each of us carried a rifle, and all were well

The Treasure-Vault of the Ancient Kings

accustomed to watch for enemies and were quite as good shots as the hillmen themselves should we be attacked.

In scraping past a projecting rock the box containing our provisions fell from the baggage-mule's back and crashed over the precipice, hurtling clear through the air far down to the tops of the scrub oak-trees in the bottom of the ravine. As always in the East it was nobody's fault! The servants blamed the muleteer and the muleteer blamed the servants. Fortunately, the animal itself had managed to keep its balance on the narrow track and also we had enough food left to feed the party sparingly for one day at least. All who live and work in the Kurdish mountains have to learn to stand privations often enough. But, alas, the beer was gone!

'Perhaps the spirits of the mountains don't approve our journey,' said the superstitious Assyrian.

'More likely they are after our beer,' growled Captain York. 'Speaking of drinks, what are we going to do for water?'

'We have a long journey ahead of us before we come to the watering place,' was the reply—and so it proved to be. The Rab Trema set off at a brisk pace up the track, and at last we reached the saddle of the main dividing ridge at a height of 4,500 feet. Ahead of us in the far distance were more mountains, with here and there little dark specks upon them which were tribal villages. Some thousands of feet below us lay a long straight valley containing the meeting-place of the Rowanduz River and the Zab. The track we had followed evidently led down to the Rowanduz and crossed it where the banks closed and almost met above the torrent. So far off was it we could scarcely see the rude native bridge built of tree trunks covered with brushwood and mud and stones, by which men and animals could cross.

The Rab Trema said we must now leave the main track and ascend the southern face of the Baradost, which rose on our right. He had brought from Havdian an Assyrian hunter noted for his hill-craft and knowledge of the caves in various parts of the mountains; but even this man could give us no help as to which would be the one spoken of in the legend or which the Armenian might have visited. None was easy of access. We obeyed his curt command to follow, for this silent and taciturn mountain man was now our guide and leader. Our first requirement was water and he promised that he could find it in small quantities for us farther on.

The track along which he led us was the worst I have ever taken animals over, winding through rocks and undergrowth on the steep hillside. Eventually, however, we came to a little gully in which was a small cave rather like a well. Somewhere out of sight in the darkness below was a spring. We climbed down an old tree-trunk put there to serve as a ladder and in a side tunnel found enough clear cold water to quench our burning thirst, and to raise in buckets for the

160

21. Coolies taking their Midday Rest, asleep on the Rock

22. Trewhella Winch Operators controlling Bridge Erection

animals which were to be left here in charge of the muleteer till we returned.

With water-bottles replenished, we pushed on round the mountain. By nightfall we had reached the place our guide was seeking, apparently only a wide-open cave used for the shelter of animals; but at the back we could see a narrow opening, black as ink. Beyond was total darkness!

After a frugal meal of native bread we arranged guard duty and then lay and slept on the hard ground. In the dim light of early morning we were awakened by the loud report of a rifle followed by a strange blood-curdling cry, almost human, from the direction of the cave mouth. Our guide had seen some object moving in the faint moonlight, and believing it to be a snow-leopard or a bear, either of which might attack us, he had fired at it to frighten it off. In the bad light he had evidently missed as dawn revealed no dead or wounded creature, neither man nor beast. Yet it was impossible to forget that shriek of anguish that none could explain.

Before we entered the cave one man was posted outside to report our whereabouts should we fail to return, and we passed through the gloom of the larger cave, the walls of which were deeply blackened apparently by great fires of some past time. With a farewell to the growing light of day we crept into the narrow passage beyond. At first the floor fell steeply, and we lowered ourselves by means of ropes which we attached to projecting rocks. After proceeding about twenty yards our powerful electric light suddenly revealed an immense chamber, like some great cathedral, with pillars evidently of stalagmite formation, as large as those of St. Paul's. At the far end there seemed to be myriads of tubes like organ-pipes, but this natural temple was silent as the grave save for the faint sound of dripping waters coming with resonant echo from some deep, obscure recess. We explored more carefully, moving warily. The cavern was so large that the party spread out, and with our torches flashing here and there we seemed to move forward like a procession of the long-dead cult of fire-worshippers at their pagan rites once more.

There was a shout from the man on the right. He had discovered another great cavern below him. We eagerly collected and our lights flashed on a strange scene. Some twenty-five feet below us was a vault of imposing grandeur hung with stalactites of beautiful and variegated colours all dripping with water. In the light of our torches they blazed like pendants of fire. On the floor beneath were pools of water, limpid clear, glittering round their edges with fluorescent crystals of salts of lime. And this crypt was full of stalagmites of the strangest shapes. They might once have been upright human statues, but now glistened with the white sheen of crystalline limestone. Whatever carven figures there might have been in this weird place, nature and the centuries had encrusted and petrified them beyond recognition. Yet we felt that here if anywhere must be the place of hidden treasure and the tombs of kings.

We gave our attention to discovering ways and means of descending to examine the pit more carefully. To our astonishment and disappointment we now perceived that the trunk of a small tree with projecting stumps of branches like rungs of a ladder, had been lowered against the wall. By its green condition and scarred bark we realized that it had been placed there and used very recently.

'The Armenian!' said everyone in a breath. 'The Armenian has forestalled us!'

We were too late! Nevertheless, we determined not to leave the place without a thorough search. The 'ladder' by itself was too short to reach the brink where we stood, so we tied a rope firmly round a convenient pillar and slid one by one down into the vault.

The natural beauty of the spot was of a rare order. Here was a fairyland within a mountain. Strange objects lay around, every one encrusted thickly and stuck to the floor with growing limestone. In the enchantment of this Aladdin's cave all fear left us. We sipped the cool waters of the crystal pools, and hunted about with the joy of children. The air was clean and pure from some hidden source of ventilation. But we could find no sign of treasure nor see where it might have lain.

I was intent on probing into every corner, and with the Assyrian Rab Trema as my helper, I gave little attention to the rest of the party. Our industry was at length rewarded when, in a part of the cave not likely to have attracted previous attention, we came suddenly upon an opening. It was merely a hole a few inches across in the solid floor, but when we shone our torches through it we saw to our surprise a further huge cavern beneath. With great excitement we attempted to widen the opening so that one of us might be lowered on the rope, but the rock was too firm and an entrance could only have been forced with crowbars and explosives. This chamber would have to be left for a later occasion and most reluctantly we decided to rejoin the main party and search elsewhere. To our surprise and alarm we found that none of our companions remained in the vault. We walked rapidly to the place of entry. There was the short tree-ladder quite inadequate in length by itself, but the rope. Where was the rope? To our utter consternation it had disappeared! Intent on our discovery we had not realized that the others had gone, possibly in the belief that we had preceded them. They were evidently far away or perhaps they had met with some evil fate in our absence. Our loudest shouts brought no response, only mocking echoes of our own voices. In direst apprehension we debated what misfortune could have annihilated our companions. We made a desperate search but found neither trace of them nor any way of escape. We were entombed and lost in the bowels of the earth!

We were startled by an awful sound from the main cave above us that made our hair rise on end. There was a choking gurgle as of a dying man which was drowned by a rising shriek that curdled the blood in our veins! It was surely the same sound we had heard at the cave mouth in the early dawn when we were wakened by the sentry's shot, but different now, elated with a fiendish triumph that seemed to betoken our doom.

Suddenly a light flashed out on us from above and in it could be seen the barrel of a rifle covering us.

'Put your hands up,' said a harsh, sinister voice—but not so disguised that I could not recognize (with some relief) the accent of Captain York, who loved to keep dull care away with a daily joke of some sort or other; he chuckled hugely and lowered the rope to us.

The rest of our search in that great cave proved fruitless as far as the finding of the treasure was concerned, yet we were overawed by the grandeur and romance of the subterranean pantheon, so vast and mysterious, so enthroned in strange legend. In the few hours available we could search no more, and it was impossible to explore any of the other caves in the neighbourhood since we had to make the long journey back to headquarters that day to be in readiness for the routine work of the morrow.

The Baradost cave and the strange Armenian remain to this day a mystery to which the silent mountains have given no answer. Were we really in the legendary cave—the Great Cave itself? That the Armenian or another explorer had been there before us was quite certain; but we knew that he, too, was ignorant of the exact whereabouts of the cave, and doubtless would have searched all he knew of till he was successful. On the other hand, we had no knowledge of what was in the secret book or what was the nature of the prize he had sought at such risk.

We had failed, yet had the Armenian succeeded? Or was he entombed and dead in another of the caves, his body being slowly encrusted in limestone? If he had left the district there was one track he might have taken other than that through Havdian and Rowanduz —the track which led down to the river and along the valley of the Barzan tribes. The ultimate head of this valley runs up to a high mountain range which forms the frontier of Turkey. Many weeks' journey to the north lies the Black Sea and the land of Armenia. Off the valley of the Barzan tribes are the ruins of the ancient 'city of cruel people', and had we gone forward to make inquiries there it is possible that we might have gleaned further information. But even had there been time for this, the tribespeople were unlikely to have volunteered information to officials such as we were, especially as it might have brought them under suspicion. In general they would not attack a traveller and it was not they who had been responsible for the deaths of the Assyrians already mentioned—as far as could be ascertained. Robbery might occur, but that was usually just in the nature of a levy for transit through their territory. Though they were sometimes militant against the Baghdad administration, I had always found them a simple and trustworthy people when my work took me into their lands.

Later on, several battalions of the local army of Iraq were sent to occupy this Barzan country, but found it impossible to defeat the determined hillmen until the R.A.F. was called on to bring them to submission. Sheikh Ahmad, their leader, was deeply embittered by our interference and gave himself up to his old enemies, the Turks, with whom he is today a prisoner. It is highly to his credit, however, that two British officers of a bombing aeroplane brought down in his territory were treated with kindness and courtesy by the Sheikh himself, just as was the case in Sulaimaniyah, and were allowed to go free when the curious promise had been given that these particular officers should not be called upon to operate against his tribesmen or his villages in the future.

One part at least of the mystery of the cave was laid bare by a party of Air Force officers who, when they heard the story that has here been narrated, felt the lure of adventure and determined to explore the lowest cavern that I had seen through the small opening in the floor. They took tools and explosives and this cavern was opened up and examined thoroughly; but it is not surprising that nothing was found, for the elusive Armenian who had come so far to make his search could, after all, easily have obtained the wherewithal to open this chamber had his book indicated it to be the treasure vault that he was seeking.

Some day perhaps another cave will be discovered which will be found to be the true cave, with the treasure yet within it, and the disappearance of the Armenian may be solved: but the East is veritably a land of shadows which no man understands, and the truth about the lost searcher and the Great Cave of the Baradost may remain for ever a mystery.

CHAPTER XVI

Ibex Hunting[1]

The old male ibex of the Kurdish highlands with his knobbed horns curving over his grey-white back is perhaps the most agile animal in the world. He lives among the towering walls of rock that form the almost perpendicular faces of the Zagros mountains—inaccessible except to the fittest and surest-footed of men.

It is impossible to catch a glimpse of this noble creature except in the mating season in winter, when snow and ice upon the rocks add greatly to the dangers of climbing. At all other times of the year the large white bucks go into hiding, no one knows where, and only the small brown females and the younger males are to be found. But for a period of about ten days in December the 'old men', with their magnificent spread of horns, reaching back almost to their tails as they stand alertly on guard, will appear mysteriously and lead large herds of females.

The most wary and cunning of creatures, they hear the slightest of human sounds. At the rustle of a garment behind a rock or the stealthiest movement of a huntsman hundreds of yards away the old bull is off over the precipices where he knows crevices for foothold and secret tracks that no man, no snow-leopard or mountain cat can follow, and only the silent hovering eagles can see.

With his enormous rump muscles the ibex can jump twenty feet almost vertically from ledge to ledge, clawing the lichens catlike with his hooves as he ascends; or else he can plunge downwards on to the narrow terraces, taking the shock of his fall on the battered and sometimes broken horns, turning somersaults and racing on round the face of the bluff at full speed.

Once he is alarmed it is hopeless to try to shoot an old ibex. He moves like lightning among the rocks and dashes over the nearest cliff. If he should be hit by a lucky shot he is over and away nevertheless, and even if dying he will rush to some hopelessly inaccessible place hundreds of feet below, finally to become a meal for the vultures or to be swept off in a mountain torrent.

Hunting is as dangerous for the huntsman as for the animal, and I

[1] Reprinted by courtesy of John Murray Ltd. and the *Cornhill Magazine*.

have known tribal mountaineers to slip and fall to eternity from the high cliffs.

Only in the early morning can one get a chance of seeing or bagging an old ibex. To do this one has to climb a thousand feet or more by night up the narrow frost-glazed paths, wearing the soft woven-soled Assyrian shoes which have three great advantages over boots. They are silent, give a good grip except in mud and are such agony to the European foot that the wearer forgets about the dangers of the ascent and the sharp rocks below.

Instead of starting in the early morning one can climb in the afternoon and spend the night in the shelter of an open cave—probably without blankets or camp fire—and wait through the freezing hours until dawn.

In any case one must be in position above the animal before daybreak, with rifle sighted and ready, and remain immovable as the rocks themselves behind a cairn of stones, hardly daring to move an eyelash. As the ground fog lifts a careful search may perhaps reveal some large animal with his flock. If within range of a good flank shot one estimates the distance—always difficult in mountainous country—and, making due allowance, fires. There is usually no time to alter sights. A good shot may mean a kill, but a bad shot means that particular animal will clear off and not be seen again for the season. With a carefully arranged shooting party having an exact knowledge of the mountains it is sometimes possible for several rifles, concealed at different points, to get a chance of a kill as the animal passes through successive defiles, but usually the cunning old beasts will evade the most carefully planned trap and simply vanish amongst the rocks or into some canyon. They seem to have an infallible instinct as to where riflemen are placed.

In Kurdistan a shooting party is one of the most convivial affairs imaginable, in spite of the fact that it is usually composed of the strangest assortment of people.

During my four years in that country while engaged on road construction there was always a standing invitation from the local Kurdish chiefs to join them in their winter ibex shooting.

Each sheikh has his mountain preserves for game as well as his cultivated lands. His position is somewhat that of a country gentleman in England or Scotland, and he takes the greatest possible pride in hospitality and in his shooting grounds.

The invitations to a shoot are written in Kurdish by the Sheikh's 'mullah', and conveyed by the hands of tribesmen armed with the usual rifle and dagger who might walk many miles to deliver them.

An invitation would say that the Sheikh wished 'the Colonel and British Officers, and the Assyrian Officers of his Britannic Majesty's Assyrian Levy Battalion to do him the honour of joining him in his annual winter shooting, and regard themselves as his guests at his village.' He requested that those invited would not fail him because food and arrangements were already being prepared.

A similar invitation would be sent to the engineer at his road-head camp.

It was considered courteous to reply at once, and if the particular Sheikh had behaved well that year his invitation was usually accepted, even though a day and night were normally the most that could be spared from duty at a time. Moreover, the tribesmen are poor people who cannot afford to entertain a large party lavishly for long. With very human pride they won't admit this and would be offended were it suggested. Needless to say, they would be insulted at any offer of payment, and the best that can be done is to give the Sheikh a few boxes of shot-gun cartridges for his old single-barrel, and the tribesmen a few rounds of rifle ammunition to make good the shots they have fired during the winter sport.

They are huntsmen to the core, these highlanders, only rivalled by the Assyrians and by ourselves. To be invited to his shooting is the highest honour a Sheikh can offer. It would be tactless to refuse, because hunting does more to bring diverse peoples to friendship and understanding than anything of which I know. We all looked forward to the outing, practised shooting, and discussed the reports as to where the best animals were likely to be found that season, and so forth.

At last the day would come. The Sheikh (the name of the one of whom I am writing was Amir Mahommed Agha) would have a banquet prepared and some thirty of his best huntsmen mustered. It is curious to think that, before the coming of the British, these people were said to be the wildest tribesmen of the Turkish Empire, and no Turkish official would have dreamed of hunting alone, side by side with them.

In the afternoon Captain York of the Levies, known to that splendid force as 'Alf', goes to the Sheikh to pay his respects and with him are half a dozen Assyrian Levy soldiers picked for their mountain skill, who unload their pack-mules. In charge of the Assyrians is the keenest and cleverest huntsman I know—Yacu Ismail—the senior Levy officer of the British Battalion and generally known as the 'Rab Trema' which, in the Assyrian language, means an officer of two hundred men. Apart from being an excellent soldier his chief business in life seems to be the parrying of the irrepressible and good-natured banter of Captain York, whose light-hearted humour in success or adversity since he first stepped into Iraq in 1916 is so uniquely British. Only such men could have won the trying Mesopotamian Campaign and held Iraq in tranquillity these fifteen years.

Having returned from greeting the Sheikh he says, 'Well, Rab

Trema, the weather is all right, and if it keeps as it is I don't suppose it will alter, will it?'

'I expect not, sir,' says the Rab Trema doubtfully.

'Well, now we are here, have you brought everything? Because if not, someone has got to walk back to camp and fetch it, and he won't be here till we are on our way home tomorrow.'

Captain York pulls out his notebook.

'By the way, what day is it?'

'Friday, twenty-fifth, sir,' says the Rab Trema.

'Of course, yes, it is Friday all day today, isn't it?' and York reads from his diary: 'Iron rations, Mills-bombs, machine-guns; have you got all these, Rab Trema?'

'No, sir, that must be the wrong page, sir; those were for last week's manœuvres.'

'Ah, so they were; well, for the twenty-fifth I've got a note here: rat-traps and flit pumps.'

'Rat-traps? I don't understand, sir,' says the Rab Trema suspiciously.

'The idea was to catch the size of ibex you Assyrians call big-enough-to-shoot and thus save ammunition.'

The Rab Trema smiles broadly. 'As you wish, sir; we poor mountain people shoot ibex for food, you shoot them to show their heads to your friends. If you insist we will shoot no ibex under six years of age.'

'Well, see that you stick to that. Now, here are your orders: Everything must be ready tonight, and we start at 4 a.m. That means tea and biscuits at three-thirty. Have a look through your glasses at the mountains,' and York sweeps his hand to the glorious panorama of snow-clad peaks. 'You will take Corporal Yokhana and three of 'Mir Mahommed's men and work up that central spur and be on the west ridge above the snow-line before dawn. You must not fire till you are signalled, even if the ibex come nibbling at your putties. Understand? 'Mir Mahommed says that some of his men are coming over the saddle from Dergala Valley at daybreak, so even when it is time to fire, don't shoot at any of them in mistake for bears, or the old Sheikh, who will be sitting in his cairn on a lower ridge watching operations through his field-glasses, will get peevish. The Sheikh will open proceedings with two shots. Until you hear his rifle you mustn't fire. After that you can shoot at any big animal you see within easy range of a kill. Officer Baijan will go up the mountain now and spend the night in that cave under the summit to the left, proceeding from the Chombarok Valley so as not to disturb the main ground. Private Bellew had better go now also and sleep on the ridge beyond, where he will probably find a cave to shelter in. His business is to stop animals migrating southward if he can. Is that clear, and have you any suggestions?'

Ibex Hunting

'Quite clear, sir,' says the Rab Trema; 'but you would do better to let me accompany you as I know the mountain——'

'Perhaps,' says York, 'but I am going with 'Mir Mahommed's best "rauchi" (huntsman), who knows it better than you do, though I expect that Assyrian trick of yours of making a trumpeting noise like an ibex will attract the animals and get you a better bag.' (The Assyrians have a wonderful way of calling an ibex if not actually scented or seen by the animal. The curious sound from their pursed lips takes years to practise.)

So having made the arrangements for our early start in the morning, we go to the Sheikh's 'diwankhana', where we are handed cigarettes, tea and coffee and sit round the glowing stove in the centre of the room while our host takes his prayer mat, removes his shoes, kneels towards Mecca and mumbles his evening prayers all oblivious of our presence.

Sometimes from the very midst of his devotions I have known him chip into the gossip going on round him, though usually the earnest cadences of the old man's voice still the room to a respectful silence.

Shortly after sunset the evening meal is served on large circular copper trays some three feet across. In the middle of one tray is a high mound of the most tasty and most expensive of Persian rice and round it large sheets of bread, thin as wafers, in which one wraps the rice to convey it to the mouth. On another tray are many dishes of deliciously seasoned stews of vegetables and fruits and the choicest flesh of game-birds and lamb—the latter having been specially killed for us. The cooking would satisfy the most exacting epicure. The food has been prepared by the Sheikh's wives, but they, of course, do not appear. There are dishes of sweet pastry and mince-pies that melt in the mouth; also wild honey, and 'manna' from Sulaimaniyah, and a kind of curds and whey called 'mast' which, with water, makes a most refreshing drink. Finally we eat large bunches of mountain grapes which grow even under the snow; all topped off with coffee and cigarettes. Unlike many Mohammedans of today the tribal people do not drink wine or spirits.

Knives and forks are not used, so, before and after the meal, a manservant presents water, soap and towel, with which to wash our hands. When the Sheikh and his guests have dined the remaining food (of which there is a vast quantity) is taken away to be consumed by the rest of the household.

We then recline on the divans round the stove and smoke and chat on a hundred diverse topics—from malaria to astronomy, ships to sealing-wax, and the Sheikh shows an extraordinary general knowledge considering his isolation.

With his own quaint humour and ready smile he even tells us all his troubles, including domestic worries. He loves to tell jokes, even against himself, and says with evident truth that he likes to swap stories and ideas with visitors now and again, because his own men and even his wives get a bit boring at times!

So human nature is just the same the world over.

With the good fellowship of well-fed men we watch the embers die in the stove till the retainers bring our beds and bedding. We are rather glad to sleep tonight in the warm room and not on the mountain-tops like Baijan and Bellew, though they will have the best of it in the morning.

The old Sheikh sees that everything is in order and that our rifles are by our sides (a polite formality in case we should be doubting of his goodwill), and then he bids us a Mohammedan 'Good night', shakes hands and leaves us.

With the confidence bred from many years of friendship with our host—an understanding which we feel is a matter more personal than concerning our very different races or religions, Alf and I turn into our little camp-beds and almost before we realize that we have slept soundly for hours, we are being called by the servants and all is bustle and preparation for the strenuous day ahead.

The climb up the mountain in the starlight is the most fascinating of all experiences. Everything is dim and unreal like a wild dream. The seemingly inaccessible peaks stand out black against the faintly luminous sky and the stars themselves seem larger and nearer as one ascends.

Suddenly, out of the darkness looms the trunk of a shattered oak or a fantastic profile of rock like a spectral monster: frost crystals gleam like eyes. Yet all is silent as the grave but for the soft pad, pad of native shoes, the heavy breathing of the men behind and the occasional clink of rifles against rocks.

When he thinks it necessary, the guide stops for a brief rest and I feel his hand upon my arm as he whispers the single word 'rawasta' (stop), and the straggling little party draw up one by one and wait silently for the guide's next orders as he observes our climbing fitness critically. 'Warrin' (Come), he says with equal brevity, for these professional huntsmen rarely speak, even amongst themselves. In this they are very like the Highland shepherds in Scotland. There are indeed many other points of resemblance between the Assyrians and Kurds and the Scottish Highlanders.

It is a lung-bursting work this night-climbing, as it is impossible to conserve effort by placing one's steps and seeing ahead. Yet the British soldier or engineer who has lived in Kurdistan is necessarily no mean performer on mountains and keeps as fit as an athlete. A rifle is an encumbrance as one climbs monkey-like at the difficult places, and if it crashes upon the man below the brass butt may injure or kill him.

Ibex Hunting

Yet somehow or other, up we go, till at last we reach the snowy ridge where the light is better but the foothold a thousand times worse!

A little farther and we reach the natural cairn where Alf is to take up his position with the chief huntsman—overlooking a yawning chasm where dim blotches of rock can be seen in the snowy depths. With a whispered 'Cheerio and good shooting', and a pull at a brandy flask 'to ward off frost-bite', I push on with my two stalwarts for a somewhat higher position which will command the head of this chasm and another valley on the right, for the ridge narrows razor-like.

But what a climb! Suddenly a crash! The Kurdish lad, S'leyman Beg, who is one of my men and has ginger hair and a schoolboy grin in all adversity, descends upon me in an avalanche of powdered snow, ice-axe and rifle, but we sort ourselves out and begin again. The other Kurdish lad is Hamid, my personal servant.

We scramble on with wet and chilled feet and legs until at last we reach our commanding position. Fortunately it is now almost dawn and we shall not have long to wait; but there are no rocks here to give cover, so we must lie deep in the snow, digging a depression in which we shall not be seen.

As soon as we rest it feels cold, bitterly cold, and our feet feel like ice—as they will be if we stay here long.

I dig a peephole through the snow to give me a field of view where ibex are likely to be seen, and Hamid scans the valley on the opposite side.

Slowly the Eastern sky lights up with a pale-blue glow. The stars twinkle fainter, and it is dawn. Daybreak in a clear sky is one of the most beautiful sights in any wild country. Seen from snowy mountain-tops it can be like the birth of a universe—a supreme and overpowering sight. As the shafts of light strike upwards and silhouette the peaks in an azure setting, cold, fatigue and the hunt are forgotten, and like three primitive savages we gaze spell-bound, lost in the beauty of it all. Ibex or no ibex, the climb is worth the toil and hardship for that one great moment.

'Wallah!' say the Kurdish lads, and their single word is full of meaning.

At last we look round upon the valleys far beneath us and, behold! night is gone, and crisp and clear as far as the eye can see lies the desolation of rocks and snow, and in the far distance, to the east and to the north, tower the great mountains of Persia and Turkey—for we are almost at the meeting-place of three frontiers.

The scene is so grand one feels at that moment it would be almost sacrilege to kill any creature that lives in this sanctuary of nature. At the moment there is no animal in view except a fox, far off.

171

Ibex Hunting

Suddenly in the perfect stillness a faint rifle-shot is heard, followed almost at once by another. The Sheikh has fired and the day has begun!

There is a pull at my ankle and an excited voice tells me that a fine ibex has been spotted in the west valley. I turn stealthily round and crawl to a new field of view. Head and rifle are raised slowly above the snow and there, sure enough, is a great ibex with his flock a little over three hundred yards away. I commence to take aim when, alas! I find the foresight and barrel are thick with snow from the changing of my position.

Silently the rifle is lowered and wiped clean, but not before the ibex has become suspicious, his splendid head raised and turned in my direction. This is my moment. With the greatest precision I take aim upon his heart, hold my breath for a second and gently press the trigger.

Click! Cursed be the weaknesses of human inventions! My rifle has misfired, and in a moment the alert animal is gone, with his following straggling behind. Only then did I remember the Colonel's warning, 'Keep your breech-block warm when in snow or the oil gums and lessens the percussion and may cause a misfire.' Yet never had my rifle let me down before.

Depressed at my bad luck I got up and looked for some new station. On the skyline above there was a rocky crag, and behind that possibly there would be ibex. So I sent Hamid down to explain my movements and on and up I went to the new objective, which seemed the highest point of the range.

I waited at the likelier spots for what might appear, but nothing happened, so we struggled on in the deepening snow, which concealed many pitfalls, into which we fell at times as we made our way to the higher peaks, only to find one of the Sheikh's men sitting thoughtfully smoking. This lonely man was the farthest outpost of the hunt and had been out overnight like the two Assyrians. He had seen no ibex as yet, and said they would be below this deep snow, nearer to Alf and the Sheikh, from where, as he spoke, we heard shots far off. I judged then, and confirmed later when I saw the results, that they had much the best of the shooting.

The man was astonished that we should have reached this eminence in an early morning climb; it was unheard of, he said, and we had come much too far.

I pointed below to the south side: what about that valley? It was out of the region of our shoot, but I knew it from my survey work and guessed that it had not been disturbed that season. It would be a difficult climb down, and at first the outpost would not hear of such an attempt; but my Kurdish boy reassured him that if it were humanly possible we would manage it safely—otherwise how had we reached this pinnacle an hour after sunrise? So he agreed and went off with a message giving our movements.

One cannot be too careful to keep in touch with the main party. A broken leg is easily come by on the Kurdish mountains. Moreover, the Sheikh holds himself responsible for the safety of his guests, and if his man had refused me permission to penetrate southward I should not have gone; but evidently he trusted me.

Far down we could see precipices and terraces dropping to the river valley, and we made for these. Yet only a few small ibex did we see, till at last we reached a sloping slab of rock cracked with deep clefts most difficult to jump across.

Suddenly, from one of these, a fine ibex appeared for an instant, dived down again and seemed to make off in a direction where the rock gave place to woodland in a valley. I sat on the steep slab and took a sitting aim as best I could at the spot where I thought the ibex might appear.

'Look!' said the Kurd suddenly, and pointed. Over five hundred yards away the ibex was standing for a second tantalizingly looking back at us before disappearing over a spur.

'Too far,' I said sadly, toying with the trigger. 'It's our only chance,' said the Kurd, and even as he spoke I aimed high on the beast's shoulder and fired.

I had time to hear the bullet travelling before the ibex fell in a heap and then, rising, struggled off with a stumbling gait.

'Wallah, that was a great shot,' said the excited lad, and like a chamois he was leaping over the rocks in mad pursuit, and I was after him.

When we reached the ibex he was making for the spur, but we headed him off and lost him in some low rocks.

Suddenly, with a yell of exultation the Kurd saw the wounded beast, leaped upon it and grabbed the powerful head which tossed him about. I rushed up, seized the long dagger from the plucky boy's belt and plunged it into the creature's throat and the deadly horns fell still.

Covering the beast with a pocket handkerchief to keep the wolves off, for they won't approach a human smell, we returned to camp and sent a donkey by a lower track to bring in our prize. Later on the Assyrians reached camp with some fine 'old men' ibex they had dragged down the slopes.

CHAPTER XVII

The Conquest of Gali Ali Beg

By the summer of 1929 I knew that at last we had the means to drive the roadway through the Rowanduz Gorge. Explosives, machinery, tools, tents and some of the necessary bridges were either on the way to us or already beginning to arrive. The staff and the labour gangs were as eager and keen as men could be. The Kurdish nomads and villagers had apparently decided that not only would they tolerate us, but that they almost approved of our hewing broad roads through their mountains. Our one-time enemies, such as Hamada Chin and his followers, were now giving their unqualified allegiance and help.

It is true that this all-important goodwill of the tribesmen might suddenly turn into active resistance; an error of justice, or lack of tact towards their chiefs might do it. Should they come to feel that the commercial explanation of the road was mere trickery and that their liberty as free hillmen was in jeopardy, there might be short shrift for the whole road party.

I expect that probably they laughed at our prospects of ever conquering the great gorge. That we could build roads across the plains and through the open valleys they knew. The gorge was another thing. It had been a barrier since the world began, would it not remain so? Ali Beg himself and others had in past times made tracks; all but the high caravan path that was still used had vanished. So let this mad foreigner attack the rocks of Gali Ali Beg if he wished, he would give up when he realized the gorge was stronger than he. Those rocks had stood there since before the birth of the first Kurdishman, would they not stay yet another thousand years? 'The Muhendis (engineer) is just a little mad,' they said, 'but otherwise harmless; let him alone and see what happens.'

It was thus the Kurds, grazing their sheep on the hilltops, jested to one another as they peered curiously down into the deep shadows of the gulf where we worked so far below them.

Yet I knew that the stage was well set for the drama, and that the show *must* go on. Raw were the actors, uncertain the temper of our tribal audience, but the time of thought, preparation and exploratory surveying was behind us. There must now follow days of action and ceaseless effort.

Tons of gunpowder, gelignite and ammonal (the last a powerful military explosive), wound their way from the rail-head at Kirkuk across the plains and over the passes to Gali Ali Beg. Some of it came in boxes stacked high on lorries, a couple of policemen perched on the top of each load, contentedly smoking and dropping sparks and cigarette butts among the cases while the whole vehicle swayed dangerously at every bend of the road. The rest came laden on camels, long lines of the ugly brutes filing with deep-voiced grumbling resentment into this strange rocky land, each beast carrying enough explosive on his back to shatter him into fragments.

Tractors, air-compressors, steam-rollers lumbered along the new highway up to the road-head, following the camels like pursuing prehistoric monsters, grunting and puffing as they came. Among them was that house-on-wheels, the workshop-lorry, moving up to the front-line trenches of the attacking army in the gorge, ready to render very necessary surgical treatment to the maimed machinery from the battle-front; and of course many were the breakdowns that occurred, due to our unskilled operators—breakdowns which, but for this repair depot, might have stopped the work altogether.

The lorries unloaded their cargoes of explosives and went back for the hundreds of tons of steel bridge parts, winches, wire ropes, timber-planks, steel shedding, cement, drums of petrol, kerosene and crude oil for the machinery; bitumen for the road surface; bolts, tools of all descriptions, and the countless variety of other things that are necessary for the execution of so large an engineering undertaking—many thousands of pounds worth of stores altogether. (The whole road project was estimated to cost a quarter of a million.)

In addition to our own tractor-trailer transport, several lorries owned by free-lance drivers who contracted for our work, were continuously employed. They were American vehicles and gave amazing service. Ramshackle as they became under the severe loads and the tender mercies of their Armenian drivers, they continued to work for years until the road was finished and we needed them no more. Doubtless some of them are still trundling about northern Iraq.

Though the drivers were sometimes robbed on their way from Kirkuk of such of their valuable loads as the thieves could carry off, and though two of them were callously murdered, never did anything of the kind happen in the land of the nearby Kurdish tribes east of Arbil. Robbery, when it occurred, was always out in the low country near Altun Keupri. For the tribesmen I was friendly with never robbed our stores.

On the hills, however, the heavily-laden lorries often came to grief and many a time I have helped the drivers repair their broken vehicles. In spite of all difficulties the stores had to be hurried through to serve the vast organization of labour at the road-head that depended on them. Should a lorry fall into the ravine, as sometimes happened when the crazy steering gear gave out or the driver grew careless, then after I had dressed his injuries (these men seemed always miraculously to escape death), we collected the debris of the load into another car and sent it on its way. We then dragged the broken lorry up to the road again, using a curious little machine called the Trewhella winch. These winches were, I believe, of an Australian type, and we had originally ordered them for uprooting trees. They proved to be among our most useful appliances. Small and light enough to be carried on a strong man's back even up the mountains, they were made to perform every kind of duty. They erected bridges, they pulled steam-rollers out of the mud, they tugged giant boulders out of the roadway, and were put to many tasks for which they were never intended. There was no use grumbling about lack of ideal equipment on the Rowanduz road, we made the most of what gear we had.

I took a pride in those winches and the many purposes they could be made to serve. Major Perry had been rather ridiculed at head-quarters when he had ordered them for serious engineering work, and I determined to show them off when next we had official visitors who were apt good-humouredly to deride our cherished labour-saving devices, calling them by that most ignominious of soubriquets— 'Heath Robinson contraptions'. Naturally I claim that I am always right when it comes to an engineering matter, nevertheless, I confess that some of my bright ideas don't work out as well as others. On one of the occasions when the Director of our Department came to the road-head on a tour of inspection I was boasting of those winches, their many uses and the ease with which they could be operated. Shortly afterwards we happened to be passing a place where a gang had been using one of them and, while they went away to help unload a lorry, had left it with its load (in the form of a huge rock they were pulling from the hillside) still attached by the steel cable, which was therefore under considerable tension.

'Now, how many men would it take to do that job?' asked the Director.

'Oh,' said I airily, 'with these winches one man can easily pull a rock that size.'

It admittedly looked rather a heavy weight for the single cable, which was so taut that it twanged like a fiddle-string when I kicked it, but this was not the time to miss showing off our plant, so, foolhardily, I said, 'Like to see it pulled? Quite simple, you know.'

Now the winches are worked by a long steel lever that one pulls back and forth and this winch stood on the steep hillside with very

23. The Road near Rayat

24. The Town of Rowanduz

25. The Main Bridge over the Rowanduz River

26. The Main Bridge—Assembly Begins

little foothold beside it. I clambered up and stood as best I could to get a pull at the lever and began. With my first effort the ratchet disengaged and the weight came suddenly on the lever. It lashed back at me with terrific violence. I was literally flung into the air and head over heels down the hill. As I crawled uncomfortably to my feet again the Director sympathized, and then as he saw I was really uninjured, he laughed heartily.

'Oh, it really is quite easy,' I persisted, 'one man can do it once he gets the knack of it. I'm not so practised at it as the men are. Here's the gang coming back. Just watch how easily they operate it.'

They did too. But they let me down before visitors as usual. It took *four* of them tugging on that lever to pull the rock from its resting-place!

The gorge was now a hive of ceaseless activity and the road-line under attack an ever-lengthening one. Each day saw a thousand men in some measure nearer to their goal.

We began by forcing a small footway down the Alanu Su valley till it joined the main gorge. A track was hewn round the great bluff and the narrow ledge round which we had crawled at such peril was widened to give an easy walking path. Across the Rowanduz River we slung out a timber footbridge, lowering it drawbridge fashion, where the stream was narrowest, till it touched the other side. As soon as the bridge was secure the men scampered across like children to explore the newly-accessible territory upon which we had never before set foot; they pitched their tents by the score on the smooth grassy slope beside the river, and with a new zest they forged ahead with the footway.

On they sped to the Balkian junction. Here, across the tributary lay the scene of my harrowing experience with Perry months before. The gorge, now dry and brown in the heat of these sweltering depths, in no way resembled the storm-swept valley I had first entered in the winter. But the same precipices rose sheer before us on the opposite bank and barred our way. Nothing daunted us, however. Those great buttresses would add but a few more thousand tons to the vast amount of rock that had to be blasted away.

Again we threw over a temporary bridge to a point from which one could clamber to the tracks I had followed those months ago. A great rock was now showing above the water and this we used as a central pier for the footbridge.

That bridge was a slender affair, but the coolies crossed and recrossed the swiftly rushing river by it with no apparent fear. Indeed, I had always thought that a nervousness of high places and unstable bridges must be a product of our civilized life, but one day I discovered that even primitive people share this weakness.

A bunch of Kurdish women were making use of this fragile bridge over the Balkian. There were half a dozen or so of them, wearing their dark blue gowns with the baggy, rolled-up trousers and each carrying on her back a bundle of produce she was taking to the market at Rowanduz. Three of them walked silently across without turning a hair. The fourth no sooner got to the centre of the span and saw the swiftly-flowing water beneath her than her nerve deserted her. She went down on hands and knees in an effort to crawl, but she was incapable of movement and clung desperately to the beams, crying pathetically for help. Her heartless companions, who had been watching her with much amusement burst into roars of laughter and made no effort to do anything. A young Arab of the bridge-building party went quickly to the rescue of the damsel in distress and brought her to firm land. She went on her way showering the blessings of Allah upon him, and well-justified abuse upon her callous sisters.

Of course these little low footbridges would be washed away in the winter floods, but by then we hoped we should have no further need of them, for the main bridges should be in place. These would have done their job and enabled us to extend our attack through the whole length of the gorge. By the pioneer footway we could now walk the ten miles from end to end of the valley without the long climbs up the steep zigzags of the high caravan track which made that route so impracticable for motors. This almost level path through the bottom of the ravine, with its very few gradients (not exceeding 1 in 20 as a maximum), would make the way an easy one once the wide road was built.

We did not waste those precious months of low water while the footbridges were still safe, terrible though the oppressive heat was when working in that moist canyon. Even while the footway lengthened, our main attack on the Alanu Su valley had begun.

We were now able to master the vertical faces of the precipices, for with the new rock-drilling plant we could half-tunnel our road wherever necessary. This was a process almost impracticable with the jumping-bar—useful though these tools were for the simpler work that still formed the bulk of our rock-cutting. Alongside the vertical faces the air-compressors roared through the long summer day, their hoses leading off to the 'jack-hammers' held by the drillers perched precariously wherever they could find enough foothold, some squatting on a kind of window-cleaner's cradle suspended by long ropes from above, some even roped singly dangling like spiders against the cliff-face. Their noisy tools clattered like machine-guns, and white rock dust blew everywhere as the holes went deeper and deeper.

Let me try to picture the scene for the reader.

Near the air-compressors is 'Osta' Ahad Rahim, the smith, hard at work at his charcoal hand-forge. His title designates him a wizard of his craft, for in Kurdistan 'Osta' is applied only to master-tradesmen of exceptional merit. Ahad Rahim is sharpening up the blunted steels of the jack-hammers in a powerful pneumatic machine that showers sparks round him as he deftly manipulates the levers that grip and strike the long tubular steels. It forges them to proper shape and to an exact size for their duty. He knows that more than half the battle of rock-drilling lies in keeping the steels properly sharpened and tempered, and he lives for his work. The red-hot tips frizzle and steam as he dips them skilfully into water, watching for the blue and yellow tempering colours that run along the metal. Finally the straw colour comes, he is satisfied and immerses the whole bar suddenly. Long rows of steels, cold and ready for use once more, stand against the rocky roadside.

'Gali Ali Beg sa fabricana—Gali Ali Beg has become a workshop—' says the Osta proudly as he invites inspection of the fifty steels he has sharpened that day.

Near by is an Indian blacksmith, Osta Boota, hardly less skilful at the forging of the jumping-bars that lie in heaps beside his anvil. The jumpers and the pneumatic drills go hand in hand in cutting the roadway, the one method taking up the work where the other leaves off.

So wherever the cliffs are of stepped formation the jumping-bar or 'barie' men, as they call themselves, pound away at the rock. Beyond the air-compressors we come upon such numerous batches that the road-line seems a bristling forest of tall steel rods with half-clad, dust-smeared figures working them up and down like a company of robot automatons, so mechanically similar are all their arm and body movements.

Yet they are human enough, these fellows, and I knew every one of them by this time. An old man stops work and is about to kneel and pray.

'How deep is the hole you have drilled today, Mohammed Ismail?' I ask him.

'Five feet,' he answers. 'I shall drill two feet deeper as the overseer has ordered. Then I shall have enough money for my food and tobacco. I am an old man now, sahib, and I cannot work like the younger ones who drill ten.' (The men are paid according to the depth of hole they drill.)

'True. I'm afraid we must all become old some day,' I reply. 'Has your bar been well sharpened?'

'It has been done by Osta Boota, the Indian, and it drills well,' he says. He then turns to kneel on the hard sharp rock to say his prayers, quite unmindful of the clangour and bustle around him.

Another man is perched high on a jutting slab that projects several feet beyond the rocks below it; he is maybe some thirty feet above the half-formed roadway, steadily striking with his bar. I have warned the coolies of the danger of drilling into overhanging rocks but workmen are notoriously careless the world over. There is a sudden cracking sound followed by a sharp cry—the foothold gives way beneath him, man and rock falling together through the air. The rock bursts in fragments with a loud crash as it strikes the ledge beneath, the man lies a crumpled, motionless thing. We rush to his side. By some miracle the falling rock has not struck him and as we lift what we expect to be a corpse he groans and moves slightly. He opens his eyes and sees me.

'Sorry to cause any trouble,' he says faintly in Persian. 'The rock looked solid enough when I began.'

'Neptullah Feraj, only by the grace of Allah have you escaped,' sternly replies the brusque, capable little Chaldean overseer, George Mikhael, as he orders the injured man to be taken to the hospital tent where I shall see him again shortly.

Actually he recovered, but all were not so fortunate as Neptullah Feraj. Some met with disablement, others with death in the course of the work. We might have lost more men from their injuries but for the help given us by Colonel MacDonald. Thanks to him, as soon as there was even a reasonable track through the gorge, we were permitted to take our casualties to the Battalion's Indian medical officer, Jemedar Gul Akbar Shah. To the capable ministrations of the Jemedar I feel, too, that I owe my own life. When I lay ill for days and nights, sometimes delirious, with the unknown fever that often swept through our camps in the autumn, his medicines brought me peace and sleep at last in a world that had become a mad nightmare of shadows and scenes dancing before my eyes through hours that seemed eternity.

Like the drilling, the blasting had, as a result of our experience, become a much more effective and scientific business. We had determined by this time exactly the kind and quantity of explosive to be used for various purposes. We even made up a special one of our own in a way that doubtless contravened legal regulations in Europe, but produced surprisingly effective results in Iraq. The blasting itself was on a much bigger scale than it had yet been. The holes made by the pneumatic drills were up to twenty-four feet in depth and required huge charges. Lines of men toiled down from the explosive stores in the caves with fifty-pound boxes upon their backs which went to fill the groups of these deep holes that were finally to be wired together in electrical connection.

Electrical ignition merely needs the whirling of the handle of a small generator to set the charges off. It is less arduous and less thrilling than the old method of lighting the dozens of fuses with a glowing torch and then racing for life to get away in time, yet the electrical method can be even more startling in its results. Just press the button as it were and the whole hill seems to lean out with a sullen rumble that swells to an interminable roar as the mighty avalanche of rocks slides and bounces and cartwheels down to the river. Boulders whirl themselves to fragments in mid-air, while bits fly off like comets, trailing dust behind them.

Especially when the 'shot' is high up a precipice-face, such heavy blasting can be a most spectacular sight. The 'old-men' rocks fairly leap out of the mountain-side! When visitors came to Gali Ali Beg, blasting was always the star item on their day's programme. My difficulty was to find safe cover that yet gave a good view of the proceedings. Seldom, I noticed, did they ask for the privilege of the front seats more than once!

As a matter of fact this electrical blasting is apt to encourage carelessness. In three shots out of four the rock just falls straight out and down. So for the fourth I would sit quite unconcernedly out on some ledge merely because it would take time to carry the wiring to a safer position. I turn the handle of the generator. Instead of one of those stately downward avalanches of rock I am expecting, there is a mighty upward *whoof*! At such times the earth suddenly vomits rock fragments that fly in every possible direction. Some come straight as bullets, zipping into the hillside, others soar in parabolas high into the air to burst against the cliffs overhead or to descend again and bury themselves deep in the ground with the terrific force of their fall. They seem to hail everywhere and it is impossible to dodge; one must just sit tight and hope for the best till it is all over. After such an experience I would be very careful—till the next time.

So the half-tunnels lengthened, and the ancient barriers melted before us.

That summer and autumn this hitherto inviolate fastness of nature rang unceasingly with the clash of steel on rock, the roar of engines, the shouts of men and the thunder of explosives; and the Kurdish spectators who smoked their pipes on the hilltops could see little but dust in the valley beneath them. When the veil cleared for a brief space and they spotted the short footbridges they still ventured to prophesy failure. 'The river will win,' they said; 'wait till the rains of winter come. Do we not know that the longest tree-trunk from Shaqlawah cannot span that stream in flood?'

Our bridging was certainly a problem that soon began to hold up the work. Five bridges in all were needed. The Alanu Su was an easy stream to cross and recross, as we had most of the material we needed for these short bridges on hand in the country, but the Rowanduz and Balkian crossings were of considerable span, and the bridge we needed most, over the Rowanduz, was, of course, the last to arrive from England. This bridge was vital for our progress, as its absence excluded our rock-cutting machinery from the whole of the eastern half of the gorge, nor could we transfer the heavy steel sections for the

Balkian bridge to their site until the completion of the key bridge of the scheme—or so it appeared at first.

The road work was almost at a standstill, completed to the river's edge, a clear gap of 135 feet in front of us; soon the floods would be upon us, our footbridges swept away—and the key bridge was not yet shipped. We racked our brains for a solution. There lay around a number of coils of steel-wire rope and some of the despised winches of the type that had hurled me down the hillside, a pulley-block or so, and a few score of jumping-bars.

Thus did the idea of the aerial cable-way come into being.

We levelled out ledges high up on the cliffs, one on either side the river, and at the back of each ledge we cemented jumping-bars deep in their holes as hold-fasts for the winches and the lengths of wire rope to span the ravine. We arranged that the ropes could be lowered to road-level and tightened to lift heavy weights into the air at will. In effect it was a bridge far above the highest flood-level, of a strength and utility out of all proportion to its rudimentary components. Not such a Heath Robinson contraption either! One by one we lifted motor-cars, tractors, air-compressors into the air and hauled them across the gorge on travelling pulley-blocks.

The Persian winch-operators revelled in their job. They loved to see the heavy machines rise inch by inch off the ground, right up into the air above the chasm, and swing across to the far bank drawn in by the opposite winchmen. There were always lots of applicants to work the winches. Personally, I considered the winchmen's job over-rated; I had tried it once, and was now content to look on!

After the tractor was over, the Balkian bridge sections—two tons each part—were 'flown over' likewise and lowered into the trailer, which carted them along the little isolated section of roadway to their place of erection, the Balkian tributary, where the abutments and piers were being built ready to receive them. Another and similar cable-way was established here, and by its means the bridge parts were assembled and slung into position. By the middle of the winter the Balkian bridge was complete and the air-compressors moved on to still new fields of conquest—the Balkian Gorge itself.

Bridge-erection and rock-excavation alike were cold jobs in the middle of winter, there in the heart of the mountains where the sun never shone. I had moved up to a little mud hut nearer this important work of bridge-building, and remained there through the winter watching every step of the vital technical operation of getting the spans safely into position.

That winter was colder, if drier, than the previous one. An icy wind out of Turkestan swept through the bleak gorge and froze everything it could find to freeze, including myself and the workmen. The gelignite froze and became deadly dangerous to handle, causing one or two gruesome injuries before I found a safe method of dealing with it. A tractor and a steam-roller froze internally because, in spite of all my efforts and my strict regulations, water had not been run out of these machines at night. They froze only a few hours after they had been stopped, so bitter was the wind. Both machines thus suffered serious damage that we could not repair locally. There was no ordinary breakage I could not mend in the workshop lorry, but we could hardly make new engines or cast new cylinders.

The air-compressors, fortunately, went merrily on. They broke, too, in minor ways, but we managed to repair them somehow. By day I worked as a bridge-erector, by night as a mechanic. Often enough out on the roadside by the light of a hurricane lantern we laboured into the small hours of the morning fixing pistons, bearings, valves, radiators (which were often hit by flying rock), and all the other parts of such machines that can and do go wrong. As the blinding snowflakes crusted in ice upon the dismantled engine, a man would come with tins of boiling water to pour over the parts and the tools we were using, to prevent our numbed fingers getting frost-bitten.

When the repairs are at length completed and the machine once more ready for its daily task of attacking the rocks, I say a word or two of appreciation to the men who have been helping me (they always like that), and go 'home' to the cheerful fire the night-sentry has thoughtfully kept burning in my hut. The servants rouse themselves from sleep to bring me a cup of tea, Ghunnie, the Kurdish sheep-dog, who has waked to bid me welcome, lies down again just inside the door, his ears cocked even in sleep, and outside can be heard the steady tread of the sentry on his beat. At long last I am ready to turn into bed.

There was a curious feeling of pleasure and satisfaction at the end of those infinitely laborious days in such fantastic surroundings, a feeling that is impossible to describe. There seems no reason why I should not have hated the isolation and loneliness of it all, were it not that I felt some indefinable sense of kinship with the men, even with the animals and with the very mountains themselves, which made those days of our greatest efforts amongst the happiest of my life.

The work progressed as fast as the bitter weather would allow. The men were hardy fellows and willing for anything. Though soaked to the skin they would work night and day during the critical periods of bridge-erection, when the steel trusses swung in the air and had to be launched into position, lowered to their bearings and adequately secured before the work could possibly be allowed to stop; or again when days of rain and storm brought the rivers up and temporary timber-work had to be lifted clear of the rising flood. The men never objected, never refused to come. They got no overtime pay. Most of them had no overcoats, no change of clothes, sometimes no fires to dry and warm themselves by. Some had not even blankets or quilts. Yet I cannot remember that any man became ill from exposure, they were so remarkably healthy, though epidemics took their toll.

The end of the winter found us still battling in the gorge. Neither the road nor the bridges were finished, as we had hoped they might be. The road still terminated in the solid rock of the Balkian ravine, amidst the noise and confusion of air-compressors, jack-hammers and blasting. The bridge for the Rowanduz crossing had not arrived. Yet during that winter we had given the gorge its death thrust.

It was in the springtime of 1930 that we actually won right through. Then the gangs, like hounds unleashed, fairly bounded ahead with the easy construction across the plain of Diana to meet the Rowanduz River again at Jindian. Soon there was even a Ford taxi—a good old model T, quite as dilapidated as its Armenian driver—running from the missing bridge in the gorge all the way to Lower Rowanduz, bumping over the plains and hills of shale with the utmost unconcern. This bus had been slung across the ravine on our aerial cable-way and dumped on the isolated section of the road. Once there the driver did a rare trade while his monopoly lasted—the one-and-only taxi of Rowanduz and Diana.

Then at last in the early summer came the bridge we had so long been waiting for.

It was well that we had by this time trained a gang in steelwork erection, for this long span was a 'teaser' to get into position. To throw such a long bridge (containing some eighty tons of steel) across a ravine at a level far above any possible support from the river-bed, is a job the like of which does not often come the way of the average road-engineer. Even in Europe with skilled erectors and plenty of gear it would be considered a proceeding requiring some little care. With only unskilled coolies in the heart of Asia, I confess that for the first time since I came to Iraq, the responsibility rattled me, for I did not want to see the structure collapse and crumple up into a tangled mass of bent and twisted girders in the bed of the deep ravine. To carry our heavy bridge out over the gorge, to get it seated on its concrete abutments on either side of the river was really no small problem. Nevertheless, we had learnt that the walls of the gorge had their uses. Once again we resorted to our highly successful device, the aerial ropeway—this time setting in whole clusters of U-shaped steel anchor-rods, the legs cemented deep in the solid rock. To these we attached so many steel cables running back and forth across the gorge that I called the winch-operators' platforms high on the precipice-faces the 'telephone exchanges'.

As the next operation we began assembling the bridge, slowly pushing its nose out over the ravine suspended from pulley-blocks on the wire cables, while the fitters working from the roadway continued bolting up the ever-growing structure. It was a Hopkins military bridge of standardized parts, not unlike a huge Meccano set, and it lent itself admirably to rapid erection. I felt it could be made one of those speedy, spectacular jobs which all engineers love to be engaged upon.

I never had seen my men work more keenly than on that bridge, in the face of difficulties that had to be experienced to be realized. Heartily as we had cursed the piercing cold when in the depths of winter we had laboured at the Balkian bridge, using charcoal braziers upon the steelwork to prevent frost-bite, we now execrated the blazing heat of summer with even more emphasis. The steel grew so hot it had to be cooled with buckets of water before it could be touched by hand, and even then it was just as hot again in no time. I feared that the men as they crawled along the girders out over the ravine holding on to the burning metal, might grow faint and fall into the abyss, but their enthusiasm knew no pain, no danger. Nevertheless, their carefree bustle was nearly our undoing.

Hour by hour the orderly stacks of bridge members and boxes of bolts piled by the roadside grew less. Day by day the ever-lengthening structure hung farther out along the aerial rope-way. But as the bridge grew, so did the strain on the tackle and the consequent dangers.

The men, some far out on the suspended girders, worked away happily in a blind faith in my engineering skill. Perhaps I alone realized the critical risks of this class of work. In truth I had checked and doubly rechecked my calculations of stresses, and I had studied every sort of human error I could think of. Nevertheless, I knew that there was danger. Calculate as you will, in this world there is always the human factor that is not amenable to any computation. In the realm of physics and inanimate things one may, from certain premises, predict, but in the greater world of human creatures one can at best but speculate—be wise and yet be wrong. Well was it said:

'The best laid schemes o' mice and men gang aft a-gley.'

For a week the work on the bridge had been going on. It was nearly completed. We had only to draw the structure a few yards farther and it would touch down between the 'goal-posts'—in this case the steel roller-bearings that were waiting to receive the bridge.

All was ready for the last short pull. On the day of days, I examined the winches and the anchorages with an eagle eye. I drilled the operators once again. Every man was at his post, tense to fulfil his duty. It was like an army at zero hour. I descended to the fateful spot where the gap still separated the great hulk of steel from its prepared resting-place. All eyes waited for my signal. I waved my arm and immediately the winches clicked into action. The elaborate system of wire ropes over my head tightened and twanged under the additional tonnage, like a great 'cello. Steadily, inch by inch, the ship we were launching came towards me.

As it was thus pulled forward it had to be controlled in height. Another set of winches saw to this. When I lifted my hand it rose slowly to clear the concrete edge of the abutment.

The gap grew narrower, it was now but a yard, now but a foot. All was going perfectly until——

Quite unwittingly, in their excitement at this great moment, the winchmen accelerated. Suddenly, to my horror, the nose of the bridge now only three inches from its abutment began to fall downwards! Slowly, then faster, faster, ever gaining momentum! Desperately the winchmen worked but the bridge fell a foot for every inch they could lift it. And this at the very moment when victory seemed certain.

No rope had broken, no anchorage pulled out, no winch failed. Instinctively I knew what must have happened. It must be a slipping of certain joined ropes, clip-bolted together. Such joints depended entirely on the tightness with which they had been bolted and one of these had somehow been insufficiently screwed up. Now it was slipping, started off in all probability by the extra jerking of the winchmen in their great eagerness. Just a fractional tightening of those connector-clips and we should have been the victors, instead of the vanquished.

I shut my eyes on the horrid scene, awaiting the crash of the structure in the bottom of the ravine. It never came. To my amazement, when I looked again, I saw that the bridge was held. It had fallen little more than a yard when for some weird reason the joint had gripped once more. The defect was far out in mid-air, impossible to get at; we must pray now that it would continue to hold. So when we had recovered from the surprise of it and realized that our invaluable freight of steel had not gone into the abyss after all, we lifted once more, slowly and gently. Up she came to the vital level. Then with my heart still in my mouth, I waved the pulling winches into action. In came our ship of adventure and was lowered to her bearings. I looked and was satisfied that all was as it should be, and signalled to the men that it was done.

And up from the depths of the canyon there arose the exultant roar of men's voices that reached almost to the mountain-tops.

As a manifestation of Eastern feelings, the enthusiasm of the men was genuine as it was rare. Perhaps it was not entirely disinterested. They knew that that night, in view of our success, I must stand them a banquet. No light matter to feast a thousand men, but well worth it. For we had conquered Gali Ali Beg!

CHAPTER XVIII

The Blood-Feud of Rowanduz

Three years had gone by since I pitched my first camp on Spilik, near the village of Kala Chin. Our work now lay far beyond the Rowanduz Gorge on the final lap to Persia. At long last our labours and hopes were about to bear fruit. We knew that the road would be completed by the time the Mandate terminated.

'Ismail Beg of Rowanduz sends word that he will come next Friday to see the road and visit you if he may,' said Hamid, my servant, standing in the doorway of my hut waiting for the reply.

'Send answer that I shall be pleased indeed to see Ismail Beg. He is welcome as always.'

Ismail Beg was quite the most influential man in Rowanduz. For several years he had been the local deputy to the Iraq Parliament, and he was the hereditary squire of most of the lands around. From him the British rented the site occupied by the Levy Battalion and the important R.A.F. landing ground at Diana. No man was more honourable in his dealings or more esteemed by Kurdish and Assyrian tenants alike.

Ismail Beg had always supported the side of law and order and restrained the tribes when they would have disobeyed the edicts of the Mandatory Administration. He, more than any Kurd, had used his great influence to convince his people of the benefit to them of this road that was to penetrate their land. He said that until roads were built throughout the mountains, Kurdistan would never prosper, and he believed that this hoped-for prosperity could be best achieved through the help of Great Britain. So he was one of the many Kurds who were greatly disappointed that our Mandate was not to be continued for the twenty-five-year period we had originally suggested.

Now Ismail Beg came to see me often at the road-camp and I was often guest of his at Rowanduz. I had noticed that he always travelled accompanied by a strong bodyguard of armed followers. The man was too modest to go about thus merely for the sake of display, and he was so popular and beloved that it seemed wholly unnecessary. I felt there must be some hidden danger that hung over the young nobleman and I asked Hamid, who knew everything about the affairs of Rowanduz, what this might be.

'It is', he answered, 'that Ismail Beg is under sentence of death from his enemy, Nuri, son of Bawil Agha of Rowanduz.'

'Yes,' put in S'leyman Beg, my ginger-haired camp sentry, who was standing by, oiling his long Turkish rifle, 'Nuri would kill Ismail Beg if he ever got the chance—but his own death would follow,' he added grimly as he finally shut the bolt and snapped the magazine of bullets into place.

'What, are you one of Ismail Beg's men?' I asked.

'Yes, I and the men of Dergala who patrol your camp by night. Though you knew it not when you engaged us, we have his special orders to guard you and your work. This is Kurdistan and there are more dangers lurking in these mountains than you are aware of,' he concluded sententiously.

There were certainly risks that I did know about and I had proved the loyalty of these tribal guards on many occasions. They had gone with me on dark nights to arrest armed malefactors among the coolies; they had kept the camps calm when the country was alarmed by a sequence of mysterious murders on the Bazian Pass to Persia, and they had stood by me when the Kurds spoke bitterly of oppression at the hands of the Baghdad Administration and of the indifference of the British to their welfare—even though I was the representative of those powers.

At that time there was much unrest in the land. In 1930 and again in 1931 Sulaimaniyah had risen under Sheikh Mahmud. In 1932 there had been fighting between Sheikh Ahmad, chief of the tribes of Barzan, and a certain Sheikh Raschid, a religious fanatic who, it was said, fought against Sheikh Ahmad because of the latter's leanings towards Christianity. It is true to say that both the combatants were equally fanatical though of very divergent views. Sheikh Raschid had recently made his headquarters in a village not far from my camp. He was a man whom no one trusted. Perhaps it was only because some of his wounded men attended my 'hospital' for treatment that he made no demonstration against me, though doubtless he hated me as an unbeliever. His men came often enough for their dressings, but the chief himself never visited me as most others did.

In these times of disturbance the workmen in the camps were apt to get excited and even my most trusted men would occasionally run amok. A certain 'tindal' of a road gang one day drank more than was good for him in Diana village and a fierce quarrel arose between him and an Arab soldier with whom he was gambling. The workman produced an automatic from the folds of his garments (though it was strictly against rules for anyone except an overseer to carry such weapons). He fired and the Arab soldier fell dead. Perhaps it was accidental, perhaps not. He loudly refused to give up his pistol when called upon, but stood there brandishing it at the excited crowd. An old Assyrian charged empty-handed straight for the drunken murderer, who was so taken aback by this unexpected onslaught that, though he fired twice and wounded the Assyrian, others were able to rush in and disarm him. The miscreant was then handed over to the police and at his trial was sentenced to a long term of imprisonment.

On another occasion a Christian overseer went completely off his head and ran wildly about shooting with a pistol in all directions. I had discovered by this time that an insubordinate man would often obey a sharp word of command almost automatically, no matter what he was up to; but this time the overseer flatly refused to give me his pistol. It looked as though I might have to order the police to shoot to disable the crazy fellow. First, however, I tried another plan. I talked quietly to him of irrelevant matters, and though he seemed to be taking little interest in what I was saying I was able, while I talked, to get close to him. Suddenly I caught his arm with a ju-jitsu grip I had learned in my schooldays. It was no half-measure and the agonizing pain of its application made him drop the pistol. Fortunately I was able to hold him helpless till he was secured.

Though we had frequent minor troubles of this kind in the camp there was never a general disturbance. Nor did the warlike tribesmen around us once in all those years threaten our work. To the south, north and west there were clashes between the tribes, and operations by the Iraq Army and the R.A.F.; yet our work remained inviolate. Relatively speaking, the road seemed to be a sanctuary of peace in a land of turmoil.

For this security I depended in large measure on the goodwill of such influential men as Sheikh Sayed Taha and Ismail Beg. Of course we were by no means unprepared for attack, and could have put up quite a reasonable defence in an emergency, that might have served till help arrived. I had implicit faith in the loyalty of my guards and I could rely upon my staff and even on the majority of the coolies in the event of an outside attack upon us.

In order to seek every safeguard that I reasonably could I took especial pains to discover what risks surrounded us and what tribal feuds might affect us. So, following the significant words of S'leyman Beg concerning Ismail Beg and the enemy who sought his life, I asked Hamid to tell me everything he knew of the sinister danger that hung over the young man. This was the story told me by Hamid and the sentry, and checked as best I could from such written historical accounts of post-war events in Rowanduz as exist.[1]

It all began no doubt long ago when the families of Rowanduz first gave way to hatred and revenge, and that must have been, I think,

[1] See also *Two Years in Kurdistan*, by Captain W. R. Hay.

when the first two Kurdishmen lived there together. As far as the present story goes, however, the earliest scene of importance was played on the old caravan road somewhere near Batas. There, in 1918, Suayid Beg, father of Ismail Beg and strongest man in all that region, was murdered. No one knew for certain who the assassins were, but later events seemed to point a finger at the family of the rival townsman, Bawil Agha. Ismail Beg, at least, believed that this man was implicated in the affair; his father's assassination planted in him a deep hatred of Bawil Agha and all his clan. Ismail Beg himself was little more than a boy, but the flames of vengeance were kept burning by his mother and his near relatives as is the Kurdish way.

About this time (that is in 1918, shortly after our army had occupied Baghdad), a few British officers were sent to Rowanduz to take control there. They found that for three years the townsmen had been almost starving after the Russians had robbed and deserted the place. Hamid told me how eagerly the new administrators were welcomed when it was found that they molested no one, distributed food, and did their best to alleviate distress.

A local force of gendarmes was formed to keep peace between the tribes of the district, and among its young Kurdish officers was Nuri, a son of Bawil Agha.

'Nuri was always headstrong; he takes orders from no man,' said Hamid.

Certain it is that the British officer in command of the small police force found him a difficult youth from the very beginning. One day he refused to obey his company commander. There seemed to be no reason for his insubordination until it was discovered that the Kurds of Rowanduz were divided into two camps, a small one headed by Nuri, the other, far larger, by Ismail Beg who by his boyish friendliness had completely won the approval of the British. Bitterly were the two camps already opposed.

The position became so unpleasant that it was decided to evacuate the town and leave it to settle its own local disputes. Nuri was arrested and was to have been taken to Batas, but just as the party was starting on its journey through the gorge, he made a violent effort and freed himself from his captors. Shouting his defiance, he made good his escape into the hills.

The British had been so popular and had acted so differently from any power that had previously occupied the town, that the people of Rowanduz met together and sent a petition for their return. Following upon this it was decided to give them a second chance and Rowanduz was included within the administrative district of Captain Hay.

When an administrator tours his district it is the universal Eastern custom for all the headmen to come to pay their respects and offer their allegiance. Yet when Captain Hay visited Rowanduz it soon became evident that the faction supporting Bawil Agha and his son, Nuri, was still dangerous, though the majority of the townsmen wholeheartedly favoured the British Administration. It is true that Bawil Agha came forward and pleaded pardon for his son. This was granted provided Nuri submitted and apologized for his conduct; but, when the young man appeared, he came fully armed and defiant, and that was no submission. Nevertheless, he was not again arrested, but on a later occasion when he was sent for to report himself he vanished into the mountains and could not be found.

In justice let it be said that it was the bitter family grievances more than any active resentment of the new administration that first dictated the strange actions of this obstinate youth. He resented the friendship that had sprung up between the notables of Rowanduz, many of whom were his hereditary enemies, and the British officers.

A momentous event occurred which fanned this jealousy to flashpoint: Ismail Beg, still a delicate and unassuming boy of eighteen, was appointed Governor of Rowanduz. The appointment was made by Captain Hay acting in accordance with the wishes of the majority of the people. Perhaps it was unwise to place a mere lad in a position of such responsibility, but the notables pointed out that this office was his by right of birth: his claims were indisputable, he must rule. Certainly no one seemed more popular, and from our point of view, as he was a Kurd of the Kurds, a scion of hereditary rulers, no one seemed more likely to be a help to the British in making a self-governing Iraq. He had an intelligence well above the average and was a good linguist. In addition to his native Kurdish he could speak Persian, Turkish, Arabic and English. Yet as a boy he had been so sheltered by his mother and so neglected by his father, the great Suayid Beg, that he knew all too little of the business of dealing with men and judging the merits of his numerous advisers.

It must have been with some misgiving that Captain Hay made the appointment, though he could scarcely have foreseen the troubles that were to follow.

The occasion of the inauguration was historic yet ominous. All the notables of Rowanduz were there, and most of the chieftains of surrounding districts. One by one they swore an oath upon the Koran pledging their allegiance to the young governor. It was a solemn oath these chieftains took with all their fellow-chieftains as witnesses.

'From that time the word of Ismail Beg became law,' said Hamid.

'And so it must always be,' put in S'leyman Beg. 'Ten years ago that oath was sworn, and still is Ismail Beg obeyed. He has said the road must go on, there must be no interference. Has there been any? Is not the road almost finished?' he concluded dramatically. (In the East they love to put their statements in the form of rhetorical questions.)

'Now let us tell you what happened at the end of the ceremony,' said

Hamid. 'After all the chiefs had sworn their holy oath there was one who came forward and spoke differently. Nuri was not there, but his father, Bawil Agha, was. When his turn came he laid his hand upon the book and with marked emphasis uttered these words: "I will play fair by Ismail Beg as long as he plays fair by me!"'

That must have been a tense moment for the officiating officer. All eyes turn questioningly on the man whose reservation nullifies his oath. All men wonder what will be the next incident in this age-old rivalry, for the suspicion and hatred that lie between this Bawil Agha and the young governor are well known. Yet few guess how completely that hatred is to wreck both their lives.

Meanwhile Nuri steadily refused to offer his submission to the government, and for the most part lurked far out of sight in the mountains where he was believed to be intriguing with the powerful and recalcitrant Surchi tribe. He had found a kindred spirit in Khidher Agha of Kala Chin, and together these two plotted rebellion. Nuri one day came into Rowanduz and was promptly arrested and sent for trial to Arbil. He put up a spirited defence, but the evidence was too strong for him; incriminating letters had been found in the house of Bawil Agha and witnesses sent to Arbil by Ismail Beg spoke words that must condemn him. Captain Hay sentenced him to be taken to Baghdad for imprisonment, but on the way the elusive Nuri once again made his escape, having bribed two of the escort to help him by shooting the sergeant in charge.

He fled back to his mountains where his presence now constituted a definite menace, especially as the rebellion of 1920 was just then spreading up to the Mosul division from the south. With Nuri at large once more it was certain to reach the mountains of Kurdistan unless steps were taken to make him hold his hand. So Bawil Agha was seized and imprisoned in Arbil, and a message was sent to Ismail Beg at Rowanduz ordering him to detain Nuri's four brothers.

The reports of what followed are conflicting. Hamid did not seem to know, S'leyman Beg contradicted himself as he tried to explain the affair. In Rowanduz some said that Nuri's brothers resisted arrest and fired on Ismail Beg's men, others maintained that it was a case of deliberate murder in revenge, and in the light of former events quite justifiable. The fact remains that two of the brothers were killed, the other two escaped. Was it the zeal of the young administrator in carrying out his instructions at whatever cost that led to this bloodshed, or was it the urge once again of the old family feud?

To make matters worse, Nuri's infant son died of a fever, and some said the child had been killed during a search of Nuri's house. This evil rumour served to bring still further condemnation on Ismail Beg who now began to be spoken of as the instrument of a ruthless and infidel government.

27. The Balkian Bridge

28. A Daring Air Photograph of the Balkian Gorge

The Blood-Feud of Rowanduz

Nuri, hidden in the inaccessible country of the Surchi, plotted vengeance. He became a Jack-o'-Lantern, seen here and there in the darkness of the Kurdish night patrolling the gorges and ranging the passes, crossing the rivers none knew how, striking swift blows at the government forces and vanishing into the hills again. There seems no doubt that Nuri with his fellow-spirit, Khidher Agha, were the leaders of the mysterious party that attempted to murder Captain Hay in the Rowanduz Gorge, as I have told in a previous chapter.

Rebellion, which had been simmering for months, now finally burst forth in Kurdistan. Nuri and the brigands of Spilik joined the rebel forces of the Aqra district and marched on Batas. Here Captain Lymington with only a hundred men fought a fierce battle against the whole rebel force. He held his own until he was treacherously attacked in the rear by the supposedly loyal tribes of Shaqlawah, when with the remnant of his gendarmes he had to retreat to Arbil.

The isolated position of the small force at Rowanduz was now desperate. A large band of the Surchi advanced on the place, and the terrified townsmen fled. Ismail Beg, who had attempted to organize some sort of a resistance, had at length to evacuate the town. He and the few British officers stationed in Rowanduz were only saved from capture by the action of Sheikh Mohammed Agha, chief of the Balak tribes, who sent an escort to bring them to his headquarters at Walash, near the frontier in the Rayat Valley. Eventually they reached Arbil after a circuitous journey via Rania to the southward.

It was a long and difficult trek but they were not molested on the way. It was said that fifty rifles were stolen from the party one night by Mir Mohammed Amin Agha of Dergala. Doubtless these would be very useful for the ibex-shooting and the theft was, by Kurdish standards, but a fair price to pay for the safe conduct of the party through his lands.

'Besides,' he explained to me years later with a twinkle in his eye, when I sat in his guest-room, 'it was for their own safety. They were much less likely to be attacked if they had no rifles to arouse the cupidity of the tribesmen!'

The formidable Surchi occupied Rowanduz and even threatened Arbil. This was the day of Nuri's triumph. He stood undisputed master of Rowanduz at last. A gallant leader was Nuri, brave, desperate and implacable; yet not even in the height of his success was he able to gain a vestige of that popularity that never wholly deserted Ismail Beg. Bawil Agha and Nuri ruled in Rowanduz, but they were kings without subjects, for the populace had fled.

Meanwhile the rebel tribesmen, leaving Bawil Agha and Nuri to hold Rowanduz if they could, went off to threaten the towns of the plains. But they were unable to hold the ground they had already won even though the British troops had been withdrawn to assist in quelling the grave menace in the south. In their lust for loot the Surchi decided to attack an Assyrian refugee camp near Mosul. It was an evil day for them, and a notable one for the refugees. The Assyrians had suffered years of persecution, both before and after they had left their homeland in Turkey to fight for the Allies, and they were desperate men well armed once more. They came forth and pounced upon the Surchi host with a violence that drove the Kurds back over the Zab. Great was the loss to the rebels, not only in the battle itself, but also in the swift waters of the river. So skilful were the hill tactics and so brilliant the victory of the Assyrians at a time when the British sorely needed help that they were at once enrolled as Levy troops. And they remained so throughout the subsequent administration of the Mandate.

Meanwhile Rowanduz was in the hands of the enemy until, as I have described in an earlier chapter, it was again occupied by the British and the rebellion crushed. Ismail Beg returned, but not as Governor. To reinstate him was considered too dangerous. Thus it came about that Sheikh Sayed Taha of the Turkish provinces to the north, who also held lands near Rowanduz, was appointed in his place. These two influential men were friendly and held the same ideals for Kurdistan, so that this appointment was not likely to stir up any fresh feud.

Nuri capitulated and was pardoned and given a commission in the Iraq police. The authorities, however, dared not post him near Rowanduz where his personal affairs would certainly interfere with his duty. On this account never once during my four years in Kurdistan did I meet this man about whom I heard so many stories. He was evidently a brave and daring character and I should have made his acquaintance had it been possible. I was especially interested in the unruly Kurdish personalities and would willingly have made an attempt to patch up the old quarrel.

In truth, for many years, the storm clouds of the feud had been but a faint mist on the horizon.

'Perhaps', said some, 'the whole affair will be forgotten. Ismail Beg was but a boy when Nuri's brothers were killed. He has since regained all his old influence and is a powerful notable of Rowanduz. His enemy lives far away. The feud is finished.'

I asked Hamid what he thought about it and whether, after so many years of quiescence, the feud might not lapse.

'Ismail Beg might forgive perhaps, but Nuri, never!' replied Hamid in tones of crisp conviction.

Nor is it the Kurdish way to forgive or forget; and that is why Ismail Beg travelled under the protection of his armed bodyguard.

There were known to me other Kurds who would never leave their homes unarmed. Mir Mohammed Amin Agha was one of these. On one occasion I asked him if he would care to come with me to see a new bridge that had just been completed. He accepted eagerly, for it meant much to these Kurds to ride at the thrilling speed of thirty miles an hour along the hewn mountain-side that they had hitherto covered so slowly on foot or on mule-back.

As always, the chieftain came fully armed with pistol, rifle and dagger.

'Why can't you travel unarmed as I do?' I demanded. 'Leave your rifle behind. No one is going to attack you.'

'In my day,' he answered, 'I have killed many men. There are enemies who would take my life.'

'Well, anyway, they won't kill you while you are driving with me.'

'You do not even yet know Kurdistan,' laughed the old scamp, quite proud of the violent ways of his land. 'They will shoot both of us if they want to. But don't take me if you think you'd be unsafe yourself!'

'Oh well, bring a machine-gun if you like,' I said. 'If we have a puncture it might serve as a tyre-lever,' and off we went together, a strangely assorted pair of joy-riders.

Mir Mohammed Amin Agha was a fierce-looking old chap, but friendly by nature and I cannot believe he really had many enemies. Yet he liked me to think he had, and he and his rifle were inseparable. It was always by his side as he slept when he stayed a night occasionally at my rough house—such was the invariable vigilance of the tribal Kurd.

Many of the quarrels between these primitive folk arose out of almost nothing. An imaginary grievance might set a feud alight, at first carried on with much bombast and noise and little else, but sometimes leading ultimately to violent deeds. I found that there was one certain way of making a Kurd forget his less serious quarrels—this was by ridicule. These people have a strong sense of humour and laughter will cure many evils.

Let me recount the tale of the affair between Taufiq Agha and his relative Ghuffar Agha of the next village.

The quarrel concerned the hand of a Kurdish princess, an eligible widow renowned for her beauty and her wealth. Each of the two men fiercely demanded the lady and threatened to kill his rival. The quarrel assumed such proportions that the tribes were on the point of conflict, and a most unpleasant and dangerous situation had arisen which interfered considerably with the administration of the district. Each of the claimants endeavoured to get official sanction for his marriage; the idea being that if the other took up arms he would then be considered a rebel against the government and find himself in extra difficulties. The princess herself seems to have had no choice in the matter; perhaps she was allowed none; perhaps she liked being fought over. Doubtless the whole affair gave her much feminine glory and prestige.

The Blood-Feud of Rowanduz

Each man asserted so vociferously that he would murder the other that something had to be done about the matter.

With the utmost secrecy the Political Officer in charge of the district sent to both parties and asked them to attend at the Serai at Arbil on a certain date at a given time. Neither knew the other had been summoned.

Taufig Agha arrived first as had been arranged and was told he must wait a little before seeing the Officer. Meanwhile Ghuffar Agha turned up and was put in another room. Then by different doors (both now of course disarmed), they were ushered into the presence of the Political Officer. To their consternation, they came face to face.

'You two are just a pair of braggarts,' said the Englishman. 'Because you both happen to want the same woman you go about boasting what you will do if you meet, and upsetting the whole country. Well, now you've met and we'll see what happens. I have here two loaded pistols. You are to be taken to opposite corners of the courtyard outside and each given one of them. You can then shoot away at each other until only one of you is alive to claim the lady.'

He turned to two policemen who were standing at attention by the door. 'Show these gentlemen to the courtyard. I've ordered a mule-driver to be ready to take the dead one back to his village,' he added.

The rivals looked sheepishly at each other and at the pistols. A duel in the Parisian manner was not their idea of the affair at all.

'But *we* can't be expected to fight,' said Taufig Agha.

'Certainly not,' agreed Ghuffar Agha.

'It is our men who must fight. We don't have to fight each other,' they added in unison.

'Will you take these pistols or not?' the Officer demanded. 'No? Well, don't come to me any more wasting my time. If I hear anything further of this affair I shall tell the lady just what sort of cowardly humbugs you both are. I guess she will hear of it in any case.'

The two grinned and then laughed and went off quite happily together to settle the matter in some more amicable fashion.

Thus could such small quarrels be dispersed, but not so the feud of Ismail Beg and Nuri where there were dead men to be avenged on both sides.

CHAPTER XIX

The Fate of a Kurdish Chieftain

$Ismail$ Beg was always a cheery visitor, he was no misanthrope. Nor indeed are the Kurds in general.

If the reader has not already suspected it, let me say here that Iraq was not a land of all hardship and sorrow, neither for the Kurds, the Arabs, nor the British officials who worked there. Far from it. The Arabs from a social point of view are vivacious and accomplished, and the modern townsman, whether as host or guest, is the most entertaining fellow one could wish to meet. He loves a game of cards—for a decent stake—and is by no means as teetotal as the Koran instructs. He may oppose the British in principle (by nature he must always oppose someone) but for all that he is a most trustworthy friend to those whom he likes.

The Kurd, being a hillman, is a little different—more reserved, more of a Scot in disposition. He is less of a *bon viveur* than the Arab, yet he loves a joke, especially if it is against himself or his race. He is something of a mystic, something of a philosopher and fatalist; once a friend, he is even a truer friend than the Arab. He is no fool either. He follows the world with sharp eyes and takes a keen interest in all modern developments of science and industry, backward and primitive though his own land may be.

Hence I was not surprised when, during an evening of his quiet but distinctly intellectual company, Ismail Beg turned the conversation to the progress of wireless telegraphy and broadcasting in recent years.

'I wonder whether, while you are on leave in England,' he said, 'you would look for a wireless set for me? I am told there are now many broadcasts from Europe and from Turkey and Russia. I should like especially to hear those from England. I can speak English and I could listen to the news and to your Western music. It would be a great blessing to me because, as I expect you have heard, I usually sit up most of the night.'

I knew his reason for this; he felt he was more likely to be attacked at night and so must be especially on guard then.

'I shall be only too pleased to bring a wireless set back with me,' I answered, 'though I fear there may be almost insuperable difficulties

197

in getting it to work in a place like Rowanduz. Tell me, though, why must these midnight vigils and this ancient feud of yours go on? Surely you could come to some agreement with Nuri!'

Ismail Beg was silent for a moment, then slowly shook his head.

'I fear that is impossible,' he said with brevity, and I did not question him further.

So it came about that I hunted London for a suitable wireless receiver. No easy problem either. As it was to be used a thousand miles from the nearest broadcast station, the set must be able to receive short waves as well as the long and the medium bands. This should give it every chance of picking up what little was on the air so far from the centre of things. Also it was no use considering a 'mains' set, since Rowanduz had no electrical supply. I knew therefore that it had to be a 'battery' receiver, yet was only too well aware that batteries would run down rapidly in the extremely hot weather. Moreover the set must be portable and strong enough to stand long journeys on mule-back if necessary.

Fortunately I happen to be a wireless enthusiast. I began as a boy of twelve when, using a spark coil and the device known as a coherer (consisting essentially of iron filings in a glass tube), I succeeded in making a bell ring at a distance of fifty yards. Later I used to steal out at night and sit through the midnight hours in a hay-loft with headphones and a crystal detector patiently listening for Morse signals from ships at sea, which were then just beginning to adopt wireless. How little did I dream as I diligently transcribed the dots and dashes that some day I should be demonstrating wireless music to the untamed people of Kurdistan!

At length I made my choice of a receiver for Ismail Beg. It was one of the first of the superheterodyne sets that are now so popular. They called it the 'super-sixty portable' because, used anywhere in England, it was said to receive sixty stations.[1] Whether, in the land to which it was to be taken, it would receive any station at all seemed to me to be very problematical. In deference to my early enthusiasm it was a 'home constructor's set', and before I got the box of components to Kurdistan I found I had to persuade the various customs authorities that none of the parts was a secret receptacle for 'hashish'. To make quite sure of this a zealous official broke open one of the valves. I was furious, but fortunately was able to replace the part in Beyrout.

The upshot of it all was that my box of mysteries in its heavily padded case finally arrived back with me to my headquarters in the Berserini Gorge. As I drove along the last stretch of road on which the men were still working they shook their bars and shovels in the air in welcome. I had been away four months and felt glad to be back among the old faces again. We had worked together so long that I knew

[1] It was a set described in the *Wireless Magazine*.

nearly all the workmen individually and recognized them as I drove past. There was Allah Dad, Indian fitter, grinning as he always did, however unpleasant his job might happen to be—a veritable Gunga Din; there were Kerim and Mahmud working away with the roaring drills just as the street navvies were doing in Kensington when I left England; there was Simoon, the Armenian orphan who had been reared by a Kurdish woman, lolling by his air-compressor quite unmindful of the falling oil-gauge—just as usual. Yes, it was good to be back. Even the air-compressor itself seemed an old friend, no longer a machine but an animal with rudimentary senses and intelligence, so often had I healed its ailments. The Kurdish chiefs and Ismail Beg all came to welcome me, to ask questions about England and tell me the local news.

As for the wireless set, I knew there was going to be some difficulty in getting it to work. To give it every chance I put up three aerials, a short one across the roof of my mud-house, a second stretching over the river to a dar-e-balu (oak) tree high on the opposite bank, and finally one of steel wire, one thousand feet long, which sloped down from the rocks where the eagles perched away up the mountain-side. It was late summer and the high tension batteries were already rapidly deteriorating in the heat as I had expected. But they still had a 'kick' in them so I charged the accumulators from the lighting system of the car—it was the only way I could think of—and connected up. I switched on and twiddled the knobs—while Ismail Beg stood eagerly by.

I had thought till then that I knew the worst about atmospherics, but never have I heard such noises as the 'static' of those Kurdish mountains. I found, after many trials, that short waves were less liable to be blotted out by these disturbances, and for that evening we concentrated on them. At length the first music came through, continuously interrupted by crackles and explosions, but music nevertheless.

Hamid grinned with delight and Ismail Beg came across to see how it was done.

'We must let the tribal chiefs hear this,' he said. 'It will amuse them greatly.'

Night after night I worked away at that radio, trying to improve the reception. In time we heard nearly every station in Europe. I had scarcely hoped to receive the English stations which were two thousand miles off, but when conditions were favourable, late at night after the big transmitters of central Europe had closed down, the English programmes came sailing through serenely. Surprisingly enough, the best station was one whose usefulness was at that time much debated by English listeners—the London National on 261·6 metres.

Big Ben chimed forth loudly, and I set my clocks accordingly, and my ragamuffin crew of Arabs, Kurds, Persians and the rest worked by

English time. If I failed to hear Big Ben, Italy filled in the deficiency and the gangs did not worry. Even had my calculations gone wrong and given them an hour's extra duty by mistake, I doubt if they would have grumbled, so willingly and cheerfully did they always work.

At that time the short-wave broadcasts from England were generally inferior in reliability and strength to those from France, Germany and Holland. That was before the Empire Broadcast system got going properly. Today British listeners in remote parts of the world can, with luck, receive a London programme by day or by night; and when the eccentricities of these waves are finally mastered the isolation of many a wanderer in distant lands will be made more bearable.

From a technical point of view the reception results in that deep mountain valley were very interesting. Through the good offices of a friend in the B.B.C. I was able to contribute an occasional report on the reception of G5SW, at that time the only British short-wave broadcast transmitter, then still in its experimental stages. I was informed that the reports coming from all the widely scattered band of Empire listeners throughout the world were of some help to the B.B.C. authorities in their planning of the present system of Empire transmissions. Speaking for myself and the others in lonely places, on farm, on trawler, on lighthouse, in distant seas, in polar lands or tropical jungle, at least I hope so. We are grateful that in return we, the outposts, have not been neglected.

Sometimes, on ranging the short-wave band all I could get was the London-Sydney telephone service. The Australian run-holder speaking to England would have been surprised to know that his conversation could be heard in the unknown mountains of Asia. (With later systems it is now impossible to hear the actual words of a radio telephone call.) Wireless had certainly gone ahead since the days when the 'coherer' detected electric waves at a distance of fifty yards from the transmitter.

When the Kurds first heard of the mysterious box that brought noises from the air in unknown languages they came from near and far to see and hear for themselves. Hamid had spread the news with much gusto (he always liked to acclaim my doings), though he had to apologize that the box usually produced music of the poor Western variety only. It was not often that I could tune in to the Turkish stations that gave the 'chulgi' which would wreathe these Kurdish faces in smiles of real approbation.

All Eastern peoples are great lovers of music of their own peculiar sort. In order to learn something of Kurdish music I have sat by the roadside while the 'shimshar' or flute-player played me his melodies—the soft tones of the love song, the gay trilling romance, or the martial gallop of battle; and it was all in that mystic, melancholy scale of quarter-tones that the snake charmers use.

The Fate of a Kurdish Chieftain

If the Kurds did not think much of our Western music (and they never will), at least they were entranced with the novelty of hearing the voices from the air.

It was known that the best of the noises were to be heard late at night, so my visitors always came prepared to stay in or about my camp until things were ready to happen. After they had once enjoyed the entertainment they invariably asked if they might go home and bring their little sons to listen too.

Try and imagine the nightly scene in the wild gorge where the crowding rocks far overhead blot out half the starlit sky. A fire blazes in the corner of the room; round it are seated a few of my Kurdish guests, their long rifles piled against the wall, their eyes wide with astonishment as I turn the knobs of the instrument on the table and sometimes music, sometimes words in an unknown language and sometimes ear-splitting atmospherics come forth, as the *jinn* of the mountains decrees.

'How many days' ride has that voice come?' asks one chief (all distances in Kurdistan are reckoned as so many hours' march or so many days' ride).

'Oh, about a hundred days' ride with fast horses,' I reply.

'And how long has the voice taken on the journey?'

'Less time than it takes you to blink your eyes.'

'Wallah!' exclaim the whole company, with that universal all-meaning epithet, and gape with open mouths at this marvel.

Ostensibly to discover what they like best, though secretly, I confess, for my own amusement, I switch the dial from station to station: Berlin, Vienna, Moscow, Madrid, each in turn, scorning to stick to any single programme. This unforgivable sin, so characteristic of the wireless 'fan', is quite overlooked by the Kurds, though a more civilized audience would doubtless have thrown something at me.

At length I turn on the attractive voice of the lady announcer at Rome, clear and melodious.

'Aha!' says Mohammed Amin Agha, 'after all there's nothing like the sound of a young woman's voice.'

'With as many wives as you have I should have thought you would have tired of women's voices,' I reply, for he has half a dozen or so.

'Never,' he answers, 'though I am sorry to say I am getting to be an old man now,' and he shakes his head with a sly grin at the company.

Ismail Beg took the radio to Rowanduz to relieve the monotony of his midnight vigils, and I went and fixed it up for him. Unfortunately it proved most difficult to keep working, and small troubles that threw the set out of order were always arising. Moreover, the problem of keeping the batteries charged was a most serious one. I went to Rowanduz when I could and did all that was possible to keep the thing going, but even so, often enough it refused to work.

The Fate of a Kurdish Chieftain

Yet it was well worth while bringing that box of trouble to Kurdistan. On those evenings when all my efforts failed to bring forth any decent response from the air Ismail Beg said, 'Well, never mind,' and would talk to me of the affairs of his people, as he loved to do. Thus I learned much of the man and of his country.

'Little by little we shall get what we need in Kurdistan if only you British will help,' he would say. 'Since you came we are at last going ahead, but if you go and leave us to our fate what have we to hope for? Not one of our neighbours will help us, they seem rather to wish to hinder our progress. Kurdistan should be to the Middle East as Switzerland is to Europe, a small but inviolable neutral State. Instead we are partitioned among three nations who are not of our race or language and care little for our welfare, and are always laying traps for us as the Persians did for Simco.

'Take Turkey, for instance, and compare their fine words with their actual deeds. In order to gain our support after the Arabs revolted against the old Turkish Empire in 1917, this was the sort of proclamation that was distributed round Mount Ararat and Julamerk to the north. Copies even reached Rowanduz. Translated into English this is what the proclamation says. Excuse my literal translation:

' "COUNTRYMEN,

' "The Turkish Republican Government is of entire and definite agreement as regards the introduction of the necessities of civilization in our beloved country (Turkish Kurdistan).

' "Your roads will be constructed. Your villages and towns will, in a short time, see the railways. Your children will not be left without schools and teachers. Your family will become most glad and happy in a wealthy prosperity. Security and law will increase the wealth of your country.

' "The life, property and honour of our countrymen are under the sincere and real protection of the law of the Republic. Those who commit any offence against it will make themselves liable to serious and continuous pursuit and will be punished without mercy. All attempts at disloyalty will be blotted out at once without having the least chance of success.

' "All officials are charged with the duty of adopting and introducing these proposals for the happiness and prosperity of the people."

'Apart from the threats it sounds well,' said Ismail Beg, 'but does Turkey put such fine principles into practice? Where are the roads and the railways in Turkish Kurdistan? Why are there destitute Kurdish refugees coming from Turkey pleading for help? Why cannot the Assyrians return to their old homes in the Hakkiari mountains if the Turks are as tolerant as they claim to be?

'So much for the Kurdish provinces in Turkey; and the condition of affairs is no better in the Persian part of our land. There the Kurds are forced to wear strange new hats—as if that in itself would make them loyal Persians! There has been a war over those same hats. Yes, you may laugh, but there has actually been a war about hats! Our Kurdish chiefs were ruthlessly killed or imprisoned for failing to wear the official hat. You have met Khorshid Agha, chief of the Hurke. He was a peaceful chief, yet he and many other poor Kurds have been killed by Persian troops in recent months. Sheikh Sayed Taha, who was foolish enough to enter Persia last year, will never come back from his captivity there. Even your British power cannot help him now.'

'Anyway,' I said, 'you must admit that the Kurds get a fair deal from Iraq.'

'Yes, for the last few years we have been better off than ever before, but now that the Mandate is coming to an end, petty injustices and racial hatreds are creeping in again. For instance, strife is being stirred up between the Kurds and the Assyrians to try and make us kill each other. We live pretty peaceably together when we're let alone.'

'Do you mean that Assyrians and Kurds could really live in the same country without destroying each other?' I queried. 'That's not the popular impression.'

'Where else have the Assyrians lived for centuries but in Kurdistan?' was his unanswerable reply. 'We are much like them in many ways and we all speak Kurdish. Have you heard that a petition has been taken through Kurdistan asking all Mohammedans to declare a holy war on the Assyrians? That petition was brought by a man from Mosul. He was the agent of a political party in Baghdad. We of Rowanduz understood its evil purpose and refused to have anything to do with it, but the chiefs of other districts may yet pay heed to such malicious emissaries. You realize, of course, why the Assyrians are so intensely disliked by some official circles in Iraq. It is because they served as Levies during the Arab Rebellion.'

'But', I said, 'Iraq will soon be united into one nation and there will be no racial difficulties to bother about any more. Already your government is freely elected of all races.'

'Is it?' exclaimed Ismail Beg with sudden heat. 'Last year I was the Parliamentary Deputy for Rowanduz; this year I am not, yet practically all Kurds voted for me at the so-called elections. As I am not popular in Baghdad at present, I am not elected—*selected* would be a better word to use.'

'Why are you unpopular in Baghdad just now?'

'I'll explain that later on. In my place there has been chosen a man of whom no one in Rowanduz has ever heard. You know that the 1930 elections in Sulaimaniyah raised such a storm of Kurdish protest that the soldiers of the Iraq Army fired on the crowd. What free people would not resent such false elections? No wonder Sheikh Mahmud rose in protest and rebellion. Why didn't your people investigate things more closely before they consented to take sides with Baghdad against the Kurds? Now at last after two years of warfare the Kurds have been crushed by your air power, yet never has there been any inquiry into the source of the trouble. Surely you can see there must have been some cause for dissatisfaction!'

'We're doing our best for Iraq,' I answered. 'We have taught the principles of free elections. Iraq will learn in time.'

'Not so long as you agree to support injustice with force. Only when Iraq sees that coercion is a failure will she have the least chance of governing Kurdistan. The situation is just as bad as possible and the old Turkish methods are in use once again. In this very district Sheikh Ahmad of Barzan has just been subjugated and the R.A.F. is busy bombing the tribesmen. You have told us often enough that your road would bring trade, and we believed you. But what are the first articles of commerce that we see upon it? A marching army of many battalions of Arab soldiers, an endless string of lorries bringing ammunition and aeroplane bombs, armoured cars with machine-guns. Strange merchandise indeed!'

'Official reports say that Sheikh Ahmad is an obstructionist to the government and that he attacked other tribes. Hence the Iraq Army had to be sent,' I interjected.

'But remember', he replied, 'that for two years there has been no British administrator in this district to report what is happening. Captain Clarke, whom we all respected and trusted, has been transferred out of Kurdistan long since. So how can your people in Baghdad judge? You are here among us, but you are an engineer and care little about tribal affairs. Nevertheless, you should know something of them, and I will tell you.

'Sheikh Ahmad is a young man with strange ideas about our Mohammedan religion. For a time he became half-Christian and invited friendship with the Assyrians. At once propaganda was spread through Kurdistan saying that Sheikh Ahmad was plotting with the Assyrians to suppress all Mohammedans—lies, of course, but his fanatical neighbour, Sheikh Raschid, was encouraged by the mysterious political agent I have referred to to attack the "Kaffar" or unbelievers. He was told that their bullets would turn to water. He was actually silly enough to believe this and attacked Sheikh Ahmad. As you know, he got much the worst of the fight. Thereupon the Iraq Army was brought up "to bring peace to Kurdistan" as they said. The army got into difficulties almost as soon as it arrived and was only saved from destruction by the intensive bombing of your R.A.F.'

'Sheikh Ahmad should have let the army occupy his district peacefully and there would have been no bombing,' I suggested.

'Did he ever resent the peaceful penetration of the Government?'

Ismail Beg rejoined. 'Has he interfered with your road or obstructed your building? Never. No one came to investigate and settle the trouble with Sheikh Raschid peaceably. Instead an army was sent here at enormous cost; that money might have educated and won the allegiance of every boy and girl in Kurdistan and so removed suspicion and distrust for ever. The position is now worse than before, for many have been killed, villages have been destroyed, and there is starvation and misery, and by his nature the Kurd can neither forget nor forgive!'

I had no reason to doubt the truth of Ismail Beg's words, but as an engineer I had to avoid taking sides in politics, and often when I talked with the more important men of the district, I tried to calm them down if they began to get excited about what they considered the wrongs of their people. The most successful plan was to divert the conversation—a laugh did it best of all. So now——

'Have you heard about the hens?' I asked.

'Hens?'

'Yes, hens—dijaj.'

'What hens are you talking about?'

'The hens that flew from Heaven upon the Iraq Army when it was besieged by Sheikh Ahmad and sorely in need of food.'

'Why do you talk nonsense?' asked Ismail Beg suspiciously.

'Not nonsense at all, plain fact,' I said. 'This was how it happened. You know, of course, that Sheikh Ahmad's men pounced on the army's supply column and drove off four hundred mules laden with food and bedding and ammunition?'

'Yes,' said Ismail Beg, 'we know how the Arab army was practically paralysed by some three hundred of Sheikh Ahmad's men. That was just before the British aeroplanes were ordered to take up the combat and bomb the tribesmen at Kani Linja.'

'First they had to relieve the army,' I resumed. 'Blankets, food and other requirements were dropped from the planes and the troops had to run for cover as they fell—except when hens came down, *they* flew to earth quite placidly and then ran about cackling. The R.A.F. had to experiment a bit though to get the birds landed alive. It was not so easy. When the first were flung overboard the terrific wind from the propeller blew their wings out of joint and the poor birds crashed. So the gunners took to shoving them into open paper bags and then throwing them out. By the time the hens flapped themselves free they were out of the air-current and made excellent landings.'

Ismail Beg laughed and returned, with more good humour, to his original theme.

'I read a good deal about other parts of the world and as I read I make notes of all the things that Kurdistan lacks. Here is my list.' (He drew several sheets of paper from his pocket.) 'We need hospitals and schools and schemes of afforestation, and improved breeds of sheep and goats so that we may sell more meat and wool. Electricity should be supplied from our rivers and waterfalls. Improvements are needed in our dyeing and weaving, so that we could compete with the Persians in carpet-making. Then we ought to have freezing works and cool stores for our meat and fruit, for we produce a good deal in the season. A great irrigation scheme would provide work and lands for the Assyrians if they are to remain in these highlands and yet not be a worry to us. If our orchards and vineyards were improved Kurdistan might become a garden from north to south, and we grow excellent tobacco—a valuable product in the world today.

'Kurdistan could be one of the most attractive places in all Asia for tourists.' (He turned another sheet.) 'They'd come from afar for the scenery and the hunting and mountain-climbing and winter sports and they'd love our spring flowers. Why, you can now reach Kurdistan in only two or three days from the Mediterranean.

'Of course, we can't get all this at once, but the large revenue Iraq gets from the oil-fields might be used to help us instead of being spent on waging wars in these mountains and making the Kurds bitter and hostile. Remember the oil-fields *are* in Kurdistan, so we have some right to ask for benefits from the revenue they earn. Yet all we seem to derive from our oil are bullets and bombs.'

I broke in again, 'But first of all there must be peace, and to this end the R.A.F. *must* support the Iraq Government if needs be. Anyway the bombing of Sheikh Ahmad was very humane. His men were told by loudspeakers on the aeroplanes that if they submitted and gave up their chief they would be pardoned, and the villagers were warned by the leaflets that were dropped before the bombing began, so that the women and children should have time to escape.'

'Have you been so long in Kurdistan and yet do not know that Kurdish men and women fight and die side by side—and where are the children but near their parents? Could you think that Kurdish men would give up their leader? Sheikh Ahmad gathered his chiefs round him under a tree and laid a rope on the ground at his feet and said:

' "Choose, every man of you, hang me to this tree and make your peace with those who molest us or die with me for our freedom!"

'Whereupon every man gave his oath that his people would fight till death. Ask your airmen if Sheikh Ahmad's followers ran away before bombs or machine-gun bullets. As for the leaflets, could one single man be found to read them in those illiterate villages? In any case if the crops are all burnt by incendiary bombs it means starvation and famine when winter comes, which is worse than a quick death in a fight.'

'But, Ismail Beg, the official reports that have come through from Baghdad say the Kurdish casualties were almost negligible because it

The Fate of a Kurdish Chieftain

was only necessary to explain by loudspeakers that the mission of the army was one of peace, and the rebels laid down their arms. How fortunate for the tribesmen that the advance of science has enabled such a wonder to be achieved. Our methods are at least kinder than those of the Turks.'

'Do you believe such reports? You surely must have heard from your men what the interpreter who spoke so loudly from the aeroplane loudspeakers really said. This was his message of goodwill. It began with sacred lines from the Koran that are known to all Mohammedans.

' "Bismillahi 'rrhmani 'rrahim", it commenced—"*In the name of God, the compassionate, the merciful, we are going to drop bombs upon you,*" so said the voice from Heaven!

'Is your boasted Western Christianity so much better than the methods of the Turks over the border? Sheikh Ahmad at least does not think so and has preferred to give himself up in Turkey than to become a prisoner in Iraq, even though he knows he can hope for no mercy from the Turks and will probably be hanged. Yet before he went he liberated two R.A.F. prisoners who had fallen into his hands. He had treated them kindly and when he was about to set them free he banqueted them and even served them with his own hands, which is a great honour from any Kurdish Sheikh—though in this case an ironical gibe at your infallible Western justice and chivalry.'

I could not dispute this story. I had heard it from one of the officers concerned and have already mentioned it elsewhere in this book. It certainly spoke well for Sheikh Ahmad. He might quite reasonably have shot those officers in revenge for the men, women and children of his tribe who had been killed.

I pointed out to Ismail Beg that naturally the R.A.F. did not want to bomb the tribespeople. They admired their bravery and spared them when they could.

'Besides,' I added, 'it wasn't all jam for the R.A.F. You may think dropping bombs a one-sided business, but it's very far from it, especially against such fearless and determined men as Sheikh Ahmad's followers. They stood on the ridges and fired straight into the aeroplanes that were swooping towards them. We were lucky that only one British gunner was killed. Many planes were disabled and some crashed in flames. There is the story of the one that reached Diana with a hole right through its main petrol pipe. If the bullet had struck the pipe a fraction of an inch off the dead centre the plane would have been done for. Fortunately enough petrol squirted past the fracture to keep the engine going, though there was not a drop left in the tank when the plane finally glided, with dead engine, on to the very edge of the landing ground. Of course you realize that a forced landing in these mountains means almost certain death to the pilot.'

The Fate of a Kurdish Chieftain

'I know there were risks and that the R.A.F. officers had no ill feeling towards the Kurds; they were under orders,' said Ismail Beg, 'and only carried out those orders as any soldier must; and, believe me, I don't love Sheikh Ahmad; but all Kurds protest that the British know, and at other times use, much better methods than these of securing peace. Why do you act at the beck and call of the Arabs? By encouraging the development of the country wonders might have been achieved without wasting money on warfare that can only bring misery.'

'Then would you have an independent and lawless Kurdistan?' I asked. 'You know that enemies would attack from all sides. Remember the old Turkish saying that there is but one cure for Kurdish troubles—extermination of the Kurds.'

'No, I believe our best plan lies in co-operation with the Arabs and the Assyrians. What we all seek is prosperity, but the present curse of the country is an ever-expanding army that eats up our national resources, and does not bring it. I was asked in the Iraq Parliament whether conscription would be welcomed in Kurdistan. I said, "No, the Kurds do not want or need conscription." That is why I was not elected again this year, and it is the answer to your earlier question.

'To tell the truth, though I was asked my opinion, the Arabs in Baghdad bother very little about Kurdish views. We are their old enemies, so why should they? They also have a proverb that sums the whole matter up:

' "There are three plagues, the rat, the locust, and the Kurd." '

Such were my talks with this young Kurdish nobleman of Rowanduz. His high ideals might have borne rich fruit for his country had they been given time to mature and flourish. Yet, even while he studied the ways of other lands and planned for the development and prosperity of his own, the sword of Damocles hung always over his head, and it was not the vagaries of the Iraq Government he criticized nor the policy of Great Britain in agreeing to the early termination of the Mandate that prevented him from ever realizing his ideals. It was the ancient primitive code of his own Kurdish race.

Nuri bided his time. Only the certain knowledge that he would be caught and hanged kept him from attempting to assassinate Ismail Beg. While the Mandate remained in force the feud lay dormant.

Ismail Beg was often advised to leave the country and live in Europe. His means were quite sufficient; but he said no, he was a Kurd who loved his own mountains beyond all other lands, and to him his own wild people were the best on earth. So he lived always armed, always on guard, always in the shadow of death.

I asked an administrative officer who had known all about the history of the affair whether the quarrel could not be settled.

29. Ismail Beg on the Kurdish Bridge at Rowanduz

30. Sayed Heusni Effendi, Sir Francis Humphrys (H.M. High Commissioner, Iraq) Ismail Beg Rowanduzi, at the Levy Mess, Diana, 1932

The Fate of a Kurdish Chieftain

'No,' he said. 'Ismail Beg is a doomed man unless he will consent to leave Kurdistan. Sooner or later Nuri will seize his chance. He waits only till the Mandate ends, for then he thinks he may be pardoned if he pleads the right of ancient custom and tribal law in the Baghdad courts. He counts too on the fact that, because of his part against the British in the Rebellion, he is more popular with the Nationalists than Ismail Beg.'

In 1932 the Mandate duly terminated. One day soon afterwards, as Ismail Beg was passing through Arbil, a son of Nuri suddenly sprang out, ran towards him and fired a pistol at close range. The Chieftain was seemingly mortally wounded in the head, his jaw smashed, blood streaming. But after some weeks in hospital he recovered. The youth was arrested and sentenced to several years' imprisonment. This abortive assassination and the ignominy of his son's imprisonment only enraged Nuri, who again swore that with his own hand he would end the life of Ismail Beg.

In spite of these reiterated threats Ismail Beg still refused to leave Kurdistan and seek safety in exile. Instead, while he was yet weak from his wound, he left Arbil for Rowanduz.

In his car with him was his invariable escort of armed followers. Perhaps he would have been more cautious had he known that Nuri had thrown aside his official status as an officer of police and that on Spilik Pass he bided his time with what men he could collect of his old and desperate crew. After thirteen years the world was to hear again of Nuri and the brigands of the Surchi tribe. Engineers, roads and radio receivers might come to this land in the interval, but the spirit of Kurdistan and Spilik Pass were as if such things had never been.

How Nuri heard of the coming of Ismail Beg is not known, but that he had word and waited patiently for his enemy is certain. A car taking money to Rowanduz for the wages of the men still employed by the Public Works Department travelled down the far side of Spilik where the road winds through a clump of stunted oak trees beside the dry bed of a stream. A band of some thirty men suddenly barred the way with levelled rifles. The driver pulled up sharply and Nuri came forward and questioned the party; then the car was allowed to pass on untouched. These men, robbers almost by birth, knew that here was money enough to make every one of them rich, but on that day they did not wait on Spilik for loot or riches. Perhaps Nuri's sense of duty as a police officer had not wholly deserted him, for he had served many years with great credit in the police force; perhaps the Surchi of Spilik were not able to forget that they had always been friendly towards me and my staff, and this car belonged to the Department for which I had worked, though I myself had left the district by that time. Anyway, it was with relief that the party found that they were liberated. They drove on, puzzled by their escape and wondering greatly why so large a body of armed men waited in ambush by the roadside.

A short while later came Ismail Beg, little dreaming that he was never to see his home in Rowanduz again. Suddenly, from behind every tree and rock there poured a hail of lead. Bravely those of his escort who were not killed by the first volley returned the fire and fought desperately for their lord. Several of the enemy fell and Nuri himself was wounded before the last of Ismail Beg's men, none other than my one-time faithful sentry S'leyman Beg of the ginger hair and the cheery grin, fell beside his chief. Nuri rushed forward and emptied his pistol into the head of his enemy, already dead from several wounds. Vengeance was satisfied at last.

So fell Ismail Beg, the last of the barons of Rowanduz.

His blood dyed the road that he had so materially helped to build. So at least let that road be the monument to this young ruler who dreamed that some day it might bring prosperity and advancement for his people. May it be a more lasting and a more useful memorial than the crumbling forts and castles of his famous ancestor, the blind Kor Pasha.

Nuri, strangely enough, this time made no attempt to escape, but gave himself up to the police. He was tried and after many hesitations and delays was finally sentenced to death, but following an appeal for a royal pardon on the grounds of tribal law, the sentence was changed to one of life imprisonment.

Thus ends the story of Ismail Beg, a noted Kurdish chieftain. It was his fate to die the violent death of so many of his forefathers, but let us hope that with the sacrifice of his life, there has died also the unforgiving age of these bloody tribal feuds, and that there may come to his country the peace and prosperity for which the young Beg strove so steadfastly.

As for the implacable Nuri, a Kurdishman to whom the quality of mercy was unknown, he too is a character not without some strange attractiveness. Twelve years ago Captain Hay, whose life he had attempted at a spot but a few miles from where Ismail Beg met his death, wrote these words, which it would be an injustice not to record here.

'I made many friends in Kurdistan, and not a few enemies. . . . But foremost in my mind stands the slight elusive figure of Nuri, a man fired with a purpose other than the avarice which is characteristic of his race, a patriot and a hero whom one would far rather see honourably reconciled than brought to the gallows. Without money or tribal influence, solely by his personality he became a force with which the Government found it hard to cope.'

CHAPTER XX

The Assyrians

The year 1932 saw the road completed. By the end of the fast of Ramadhan, which fell that year in the late winter, the road-head parties were through the Berserini Gorge and the last two important bridges were in position. What was left to do we could take in our stride.

Vastly different were we from the crude inexperienced gang of men who had begun work on Spilik four years earlier. We now had the knowledge and assurance of masters of our craft. Moreover, we had all the machinery for road-making and for bridge-erection that we could reasonably need and we had the right men to use it. The coolies handled explosives and rock-drills with the expert cunning of Western quarrymen, and I felt that, if need be, we could go on cutting our way eastward right across Asia to the China Sea, so smoothly did the work swing forward day by day!

Even after the rainy season the road as it wound through the gorges and over the passes to Arbil was no longer the ribbon of mud it had been in previous winters. During those dreadful days of isolation when derelict motor-cars lay abandoned, sunk deep in a miry roadway, we had learned our lesson. More haste, less speed had been proved a true maxim. Those grim years were behind us now. The metalling and the steam-roller parties kept pace with the road-head gangs, and upon the surface of machine-crushed rock that covered the foundation of boulders, a battery of steam-rollers trundled ceaselessly: there emerged a highway, smooth and true to camber and super-elevation,[1] over which a carpet of boiling bitumen was swept, and sanded till it hardened. The coolies called the curved cross-section of the roadway 'marci-pi', which, literally interpreted, means 'fish-back'—an apt description of the cambered surface.

So one could motor now, wet or fine, whither one liked. The rivers might rise in flood as they pleased, our bridges were secure and the tribal menace was a thing of the past. All the chiefs were friendly towards me and no longer a cause for anxiety as far as the road work was concerned.

[1] The slope from outside to inside of a road at curves.

211

One evening about this time I sat in my hut in the Berserini Gorge chatting with Captain Baker, an officer who had motored up from a district farther south to visit our part of the country. We had just come in from a walk along the road. As we passed the men's camp a coolie had pointed out to us in the V of sky between the steep sides of the gorge to the westward, the new moon that proclaimed the end of the Fast of Ramadhan.

'The gangs will be feasting tonight to make up for their month of comparative starvation,' I said to Baker. 'Had they consulted a calendar they would have discovered that the new moon was there behind the clouds two nights ago.'

'Well, that's Iraq for you,' said Baker, 'and yet we are said to have absolutely completed the education of the people—at least so one must infer from our reports to the League of Nations.'

In the sheltered hollows on the mountain-sides there were still broad patches of snow, and the wind blowing from the high ranges to the north was chill, so we drew our chairs up to the blazing logs, and rested our heels on the rough mantelpiece in bachelor comfort as we smoked and talked.

Now Baker was a most interesting character—a man whose knowledge of the people, and the languages and traditions of Iraq was profound. Some might call him a dilettante and a cynic—and so, superficially, he seemed to be—but beneath his vein of evasive sarcasm lay a deep sense of responsibility to those he served, and to the ideal which he believed the British nation ought to strive after in Iraq. Of all the Englishmen I knew there, none more truly loved the East and its people. A gallant leader of lost causes and forlorn hopes was Baker; a man who believed in forming his opinions and making his decisions according to the facts as he found them. A man, therefore, who chafed under any orders he could not reconcile with his own clear-cut principles of justice.

Like most other out-station officials in Iraq, he regarded with apprehension the recently proclaimed termination of the British Mandate, considering that this policy was bound to bring misfortune to many in the country who had trusted us. The reasons for the proposed hasty evacuation of the land were never made clear. We had to obey our orders. Yet we all knew that our work was but half completed and that the future—if we left now—was ominous. We felt that if our statesmen knew as much as we had learnt from our daily contact with the people they would have acted more cautiously. Storms and troubles surely lay ahead. As to the why and wherefore of it all we could but speculate.

The following conversation is presented in some detail to the reader that he may have a clear picture of the Assyrian-Iraq situation as it was then presented to me—before the disastrous events of the following year.

The Assyrians

'Yes, I am afraid that real education, and even toleration are still meaningless words in Iraq,' Baker was saying. 'The people of the country seem affable enough towards us on the surface, of course. In reality I believe that they consider us so many humbugs who always cloak our real aims under a guise of altruism and humanitarianism. They may despise us for this, but, more important, I believe they no longer respect us as a strong power.

'Occasionally, as individuals, we may be popular and even praised by this faction or that—depending on whether we've acted decently towards them or not—but as for talking of Iraq's everlasting gratitude towards Great Britain, that's merely tommy-rot, and we're fools if we let ourselves be led into delusions by such nonsense. Anyway, it's a slipshod policy, this evacuating without fulfilling our obligations. We've made friends with men like Ismail Beg here in Rowanduz for instance, yet we're quite prepared to leave him and many others who've been equally loyal to us to their inevitable doom. We talk glibly enough about the assured security of the minorities when we know that if we leave Iraq they have absolutely none. Such conduct can breed neither respect nor gratitude from any section.

'As for gratitude, the Arab is a most astute judge of motives; he reads character intuitively and his real and lasting gratitude can be won only by the greatest self-sacrifice, and his respect only by pre-eminent qualities of leadership and fidelity to his interests.'

As Baker leant forward to knock out his pipe after delivering himself of this speech, there came a rap at the door and Hamid ushered in my old friend, the Assyrian Rab Trema of the Levies, Yacu Ismail.

Yacu was resplendent in his major's uniform, complete to sword-belt and service revolver. With moustache that turned up and with a slight lisp in his speech, he was a very familiar visitor in my camp. His eyes had a way of lighting up and shining brightly when adventure was afoot, and I well knew his trusted worth as a companion in the mountains; but today he looked serious, even tired.

'I have brought my father, Malik Ismail, the head of our upper Tiyari Assyrians, to see you, sir,' he said.

'Delighted,' I said. 'Bring him in to meet Captain Baker whom he already knows, I believe; come and sit by the fire, and Hamid shall fetch us some supper.'

The old man who entered on the arm of his son was a dignified Assyrian, wearing, as he usually did, the native dress of his people. It was similar in many respects to the Kurdish costume, though more varied and striking in colour, and instead of the grey fringed turban of the Kurd the head was surmounted by a shallow conical cap of thick felt which is peculiar to the Assyrians. White-haired, solemn and silent, with deeply-lined face of stone-grey colour, the old man looked and was one of the patriarchs of his people. He greeted us in Assyriac for he spoke very little English.

'I have just taken my father', Yacu explained, 'over all your new bridges by car and far up the new road quite near to the Persian frontier. He is pleased to think that soon he will be able to motor to Urmia, and that we in Diana will then be but a few hours' journey from those of our people who still live in Persia.'

'Yes,' I replied, 'it will be only a month or two before we reach the Persian plateau. Already my Department has arranged that Prince Ghazi shall open the new road, though I shan't be here to see it. They say that King Faisal is also coming with his ministers to inspect it, and I am sure he will be pleased with the part that the Assyrians have taken in its construction. One way and another you've helped a great deal, and my chief regret is that now my job here is completed I must be transferred from this district, and soon I may be out of the country altogether. I shall not see much of you from now on, Rab Trema, and shall just have to remember the good times we've had in the past.'

'We hear rumours of so many changes,' said Yacu with a trace of some anxiety in his voice. 'Do you think King Faisal will allow the Assyrians to remain at Diana, if, as we hear, the British Mandate is to terminate?'

'Oh, presumably,' I answered. 'You Assyrians have built Diana from a village of a couple of houses into quite a thriving town. It is now the capital of your Assyrian Empire just as Nineveh once was,' I laughed. 'Nobody, I imagine, will want to dispossess you of your little town.'

'So many rumours have reached us in the last few months,' he persisted. 'They have broken in upon the peace and optimism that was beginning to revive in our community. We hope that if the Mandate terminates, we shall still be under the protection of your all-powerful Air Force if we are to remain in this hostile Iraq?'

Baker laughed and said rather cryptically, 'Why, of course, that's the whole idea—as the League of Nations has been told.'

But Yacu just looked puzzled by these words and turned to me for an answer to his question.

'I am merely the road-engineer,' I said, 'and these matters are not within my province at all, but have not the Assyrians been regular British soldiers for the last ten years—to say nothing of their sacrifice for the Allied cause during the war? All necessary protection is always given to those who have served under our flag. And, quite apart from that, what is it you fear? The constitutional law of Iraq says there shall be no discrimination among the people, neither according to race nor religion. Arabs, Kurds, Jews and Christians have now all equal rights as they never had in Turkish days. Britain gave that pledge to the League.'

The Assyrians

'So the law says, but in truth are we Assyrians really a part of Iraq? Have we any lands that are our own as were the wild Hakkiari mountains in Turkey, which we left sixteen long years ago to fight for our freedom? We cannot return to that old homeland, victorious though the Allies have long since been.

'I know I have no right to ask you or Captain Baker any questions as to our future, for that will be arranged by your Government and the League of Nations, but perhaps you could say something to reassure us at this anxious time.

'You who have worked among us may know, but does your nation as a whole realize what we have done since we first joined the Allied Powers in 1914? And now that the Mandate is to terminate will they see to it that our case is treated with that honour and justice for which the British people are noted?

'More than thirty years ago in the Hakkiari mountains there came amongst us an English clergyman and missionary whom we greatly revere. I refer to the Rev. Dr. Wigram, a brave man who devoted his life to the education and betterment of our people. He founded the schools in which all we younger Assyrians have been educated. He taught us that the British nation stands for justice and liberty and that she has always stood by her pledged word. We believed him and that was why we joined the Allies and why we now hope that Britain will not leave us at the mercy of our enemies.'

'You've got a claim right enough, but your losses have branded you with the name of refugees, and the fact that you were an ally may easily be forgotten,' said Baker.

'But', said the Assyrian, 'by our desperate fighting and our slain soldiers did we not, when we fought our way to the side of the Russian Army, help materially to weaken Turkish resistance in Palestine and Mesopotamia, and thus contribute to the Allied victory?'

'Your little nation fought as gallantly here in Asia as Belgium did in Europe,' was Baker's reply.

'Then is it known that though we lost nearly half our people in that struggle yet we have been dispossessed of all our lands and of our very homes ever since? Your British statesmen are well aware that we have served as Levy soldiers for ten long years and fought both Arab and Kurd on your behalf. Yet with what reward? We have not one inch of territory that we can call our own.'

'We all appreciate your loyalty,' I said. 'Could this road have been built without the help of the Assyrians? The Kurds knew very well that they dare not challenge the Diana battalion in mountain warfare.'

'Then', said the Assyrian, 'it is strange that the Arabs have reaped a kingdom while we Assyrians, steadfastly supporting the British, reap nothing but promises—as far as we yet know.

'Hearing that Captain Baker was visiting you, we came to ask for any news of what might be provided for us in the future. It has been said in the past that we might perhaps be given some undeveloped corner of the British Empire. For centuries now we have been poor mountain folk and the Hakkiari lands are so barren that even the Kurds have not used them since we left. The worst of territories would do if only it were a place of safety. If it should be impossible to arrange a migration of our twenty-five thousand people at the present time, we should at least like to feel that we can rely upon British protection here in Iraq.

'Look at our position today. We are scattered here and there in isolated groups, unwanted tenants in a hostile land, guarded only by the Mandate which now we hear is to terminate.

'We believe that this scattering of our people throughout Northern Iraq has been planned by our enemies, who are allowed to suggest which places they think most suitable for us. Invariably they choose spots impossible for us to defend, or else malarial and unhealthy. For that matter it is pretty obvious that all the land in Iraq, which is naturally fertile and habitable is already occupied. What we need is some big irrigation scheme to open up new country. As yet nothing of the kind has been arranged for, and now the Mandate is to terminate.'

'You Assyrians', I said, 'are as bad as the Kurds. You both seem to want a great deal in a very short time. After all, are you not now citizens of Iraq and free to take part in the Government, or at least able to persuade it to develop irrigation schemes or anything else you want?'

'To ensure our protection such a scheme would have to be under British control. As for our share in the Government we have none,' replied Yacu.

'Oh, but there are many Assyrians in the police and other Departments of State,' I exclaimed.

'Yes, there are a few in junior positions,' he admitted. 'But none as senior officials, magistrates, judges, army officers or ministers or even Deputies in Parliament—where our numbers would seem to warrant some representation.

'We would not mind there being no share for us in the government if we could only be assured of our security in this northern territory we have helped to open up. We have assisted with the roads and the buildings and in the police work of the north. We are not unfriendly with the Kurds. Ismail Beg, for example, has always treated us in as generous a way as we could desire. Do you think that perhaps Iraq will agree to keep us here to guard the northern frontier? No other troops could do it better. Then we might stay on at Diana.'

'I'm sure something suitable is being arranged for you,' I said. 'Just you go on trusting us as you have always done.'

'Sorry to disappoint you, Yacu,' said Baker, speaking slowly and standing up as he spoke, 'but there is little hope of your remaining at Diana.[1] Instead you are all to be moved to the lowlands well south of the Zab. Iraq knows all about the Assyrian as a mountain fighter and you have altogether too many friends here in Kurdistan—at least certain people think so.

'Moreover, I am able to give you the hint that you will be "demobbed" and given orders to move from Diana even before we give up the Mandate. You will be told so officially before long, and then it will be "good-bye" to the mountains of Kurdistan.'

'To be moved to the Arab lowlands of Iraq!' said the Assyrian in a low voice. Then after a pause, 'Is that true?'

'It is, I'm afraid,' said Baker. 'Have you not been warned that your battalion is to be disbanded and that the air-landing ground, the barracks, and the town you have built are to be handed over to the Iraq Army?'

'We have heard it rumoured,' he replied. 'Hence my questions to-day. Please allow me to tell my father.'

Yacu spoke a few sentences to the old man, who had sat during our conversation still as some sculptured figure hewn from the rock. He looked round upon us as Yacu ceased speaking and gave his reply in a voice that betrayed deep emotion. A grim, formidable warrior in his time, this head of the Fighting Tiyaris, as they proudly called themselves. Even now as he spoke to his son he was calm and dignified, but no longer was there any trace of hope to give life to his lined face.

'What does he say?' I asked.

'He says', answered Yacu, 'that it was an ill day for his tribe when he led them to fight in a war for the liberty of small nations. Now we have to meet death at long last, so let us prepare to face the enemy whom we know, that we may the more readily forget the desertion of those whom we once thought to be our friends.'

'Very decent of the old chap to say nothing stronger than that about us,' muttered Baker, 'and for God's sake let's change the subject,' he added in my ear.

I pulled hard upon a bell-cord communicating with the kitchen next door, and Hamid promptly appeared with a tray of Kurdish savouries which satisfactorily disposed of the perplexing Assyrian situation for the time being.

Of course Baker proved to be right in the prophecy he had given of the impending demobilization and transfer of the Assyrians from

---

[1] The Levies, of course, were guarding the important Aerodrome at Diana in the interests of the Royal Air Force. With the termination of the Mandate, the activities of the R.A.F. in connection with the internal affairs of Iraq were to cease, and their place at Diana was to be taken by the Iraqi Air Force who would naturally be protected by the Iraqi Army.

Diana. It was announced to them one day when the battalion had been specially paraded, and a bitter day it was for the Assyrians and their officers alike. They were told that these were the final months of their long term as British Levies.

Though every Assyrian knew full well the significance of this parade, they marched and counter-marched across the mountain aerodrome with the precision of guardsmen—the pride of 'Alf' and 'Mac' and the other company commanders who had laboured many a weary year to train their men to so remarkable a pitch of efficiency.

Malik Ismail and the older patriarchs and leaders turned out too, and came forward to salute the man who for years had been their beloved idol, the veteran Scottish colonel whom they knew had the welfare of each one of them at heart, but was now powerless to help them further. To do him honour Malik Ismail and his fellow-patriarchs, arrayed in their best ill-fitting European clothes, tried to step as proudly as they had done in their youth while already knowing the sentence about to be pronounced upon their people.

These old men were the leaders who, sixteen years earlier, had brought their followers from the Hakkiari fastnesses into a great world war, little knowing that it was likely to be the last fatal pilgrimage of their ancient nation. Disappointed, disillusioned, decimated as they had been in those years of war in Persia and Turkey, the period of service in the Levies and life at Diana had been happy enough, and for a time a new optimism had been born; so they came now to honour the British soldiers who had shown understanding and given help, and whose leadership they were now to lose.

One by one the old men bowed with due deference to the Commander. Silently they awaited the fateful words announcing their dismissal from Britain's charge.

The instructions for the future, when read, spoke highly of the past work of the Assyrians and emphasized Britain's continued interest and good intentions towards them. The proclamation said that, in accordance with the policy of terminating the British Mandate, this fine force of Assyrian Levy soldiers must be disbanded.[1] The British Government were fully appreciative of the steadfast loyalty of the Assyrians and, though it was considered advisable that they should evacuate Diana, it had been arranged that lands near Mosul should be put at their disposal. There, and in the other regions already selected, they could live in peace and prosperity under the Government of Iraq. Each Assyrian would be allowed to retain his rifle and be given one hundred rounds of ammunition in return for the Russian or Turkish rifles brought with them when they joined the force. Needless to say the British Government would continue to watch and safeguard

[1] As many as could be accepted were re-enlisted in the new British Aerodrome guards formed on the termination of the Mandate.

their interests through the Iraq Government, which they would find generously disposed towards them and anxious to absorb all the Assyrians into the national life of the kingdom.

Thus was judgment passed on this unfortunate people, the disastrous march of events which was to follow quite unforeseen by those who had formulated this policy, though guessed in some measure by many Englishmen in Iraq.

Alf was silent and grave. He had no shafts of wit for the Rab Trema on such a day.

The Assyrians raised no voice of protest. They looked but once to the Ser-i-Hasan-Beg mountain towering before them, emblematic of the Kurdish fastnesses where, with all its dangers, for centuries they had preserved the integrity of their race and their religion; and at the word of dismissal they saluted smartly and were gone.

With their going was lost a prestige that had been hard won by the untiring effort of a little band of British soldiers and officials during fifteen long years of war and toil in Mesopotamia.

The Assyrians tried to make the best of the new situation, but again their efforts seemed cursed and doomed to failure.

'Doubtless', said Yacu, 'there is something of special importance in the arrangements made between the British and the Iraq Governments to absorb us into the national life of Iraq. With my military experience I shall apply for a commission in the Iraq Army, or, failing that, in the Police.'

'Yes, do,' I said. 'I am certain the Arabs will welcome the chance of making friends with the Assyrians now that the much-criticized British régime has practically come to an end.'

But it turned out that his hopes were unfounded and his plans frustrated at every point.

When I saw him again my job in the Kurdish mountains was almost finished. In a week's time I was to pack my gear into the long-suffering car for the last time and go down to report at Headquarters in Baghdad. We had built a road which, it was hoped, would not only assist trade between Persia and Iraq, but would also carry peaceful administration into this most remote corner of the new Kingdom. Yet as I spoke with Yacu Ismail I almost wondered whether it would not have been better for all the mountain people had road-makers never come their way.

Yacu told me the result of his applications and interviews.

'The senior Iraqi officials say they are not wanting any more Assyrians in Government service, and they will not have me either in the Police or in the Army. In fact, many of those Assyrians who already hold Government positions are now being dismissed. Two of my cousins who were at the new Military College at Baghdad have just been rejected. They were of our fighting tribe and well educated

—ideal men for soldiers one would have thought. I cannot understand it. It can be nothing but an unjust prejudice against us, although considering our role during the last ten years as chief agents of the Mandate, I suppose it is not surprising that the Arabs dislike us.

'Moreover, the Assyrians in the Police are being steadily reduced. Really it seems all very curious in the face of the statement given to us so recently by the British Government. I wonder what is the real truth of the matter?'

I was beginning to wonder this myself, for I was frequently receiving instructions from Baghdad questioning the further employment of this or that Assyrian. There were no orders for their transference to other works of the Department when they were no longer needed for the road.

This surprised me, for I had always told my men, and believed implicitly myself, that Iraq would fulfil its undertaking to absorb the Assyrians and all others of the Minorities into the full life of the country. What did it mean?

CHAPTER XXI

The Goal Attained

It came at length to the day for me to leave my road-head camp and my coolies for the last time. We had achieved our great objective. I therefore handed over to the Iraqi relief and left secretly during the full swing of the day's work, saying no word of farewell to the vast army of workmen whom through stress and travail I had led for so long; even an engineer is human, and frankly I could not have faced them.

Hamid came with me, half-buried under the pile of gear in the car, and only the camp guards saw us go.

As I left, the one-armed, one-eyed watchman of the store (the man whose life we had saved by a desperate midnight drive to Arbil, after he had exploded a stick of gelignite in his hand), showered the blessings of Allah upon me, and his one arm was still waving as I saw him last standing outside my rough hut in the Berserini Gorge; God knows where that poor crippled man is now. Beside him stood the faithful sentries, tribesmen lent by Mohammed Amin Agha of Dergala. They held their rifles above their heads in their last salute.

The bitumened road stretched smooth before me and tempted me to speed. I was always said to be a reckless driver on the hair-pin bends and precipice edges, and today I honestly deserved this reputation, for I 'trod on the gas', the sooner to get away, to think the less. After all, had I not 'banked' the corners for speed, and why drive a car on four wheels when it can be made to run on two? Any excuse was good enough.

So with Hamid hanging tightly to his seat, we whirled down the roadway, past the cave of Kospyspee, past the Zoroastrian burial ground where lay the bones of the ancients, past the rocky outcrop where the coolies had gone crazy over the discovery of 'diamonds' (these proved to be the most perfect double-ended quartz crystals, beautiful but quite valueless), and so out of the Berserini Gorge, the echoes ceasing as though we had emerged from a tunnel. On we went through the woods and fields of Zewa to Jindian. I made no stop at the deserted rest-house that I had built and lived in for a season—incidentally it was the only iron roof I had ever had over my head in

221

Kurdistan. The garden I had made there was not yet lit by the brilliance of spring, and the fountain bubbled coldly in its pool, while over the river on the branch road that led to Upper Rowanduz the magic waters of Jindian poured forth tempestuously from the cave where ages before, as it seemed to me, I had feasted with Sheikh Sayed Taha. We could see the Sheikh's great house where his wives and retainers still lived, now but a 'banquet-hall deserted'—the lord of the manor a prisoner in a far land.

Above, upon that great rib of naked rock, rose the grim grey citadel of Rowanduz, where Death still stalked and slew the Kurdish people. Clearly discernible, stood the house of Ismail Beg where I, a stranger from the uttermost ends of the earth, had supped and found friendship, little knowing how soon the life of my young host was to be cut short. As I last saw it, awe-inspiring was the setting of the town amidst the wilderness of snow-bound peaks, barren as the mountains of the moon; and the picture of it all will live for ever in my memory.

In a moment Rowanduz was lost to sight behind the bare shale hill where stands the ruined castle of Kor Pasha, and we descended into the plain of Diana, now strewn with the tents and munition dumps of the newly-arrived Iraq Army, who had marched up the roadway to replace the Assyrian Levies. The latter were packing such of their goods and chattels as they could remove from Diana, ready for their departure to the plains.

I went to the Orderly Room to ask for Alf but found he was away at Mosul. So, after saying farewell to Colonel MacDonald and the few other officers still at Diana, I was on again and into the Rowanduz Gorge.

Here I was passing the scenes of my greatest labours, where for two years we had struggled to overcome the precipices and chasms. It is the mysteries and the excitements of life that leave their deepest impression, not the daily round of work; so it was Dead Man's Pool where the coolie's murdered body had been found and the great Hopkins bridge that had so nearly crashed 'in the ditch' that I looked especially for as we sped round the ledges and under the half-tunnel where the swallows, quickly approving of new-found security, had come to nest by the thousands beneath the rocky ceiling the drillers had left.

Up the Alana Su, past the waterfall and by the police post, I came at length to the site of my old camp at Gali Ali Beg, all pulled down two years back. Even the eagles had deserted it.

Gali Ali Beg once more, and for the last time! A few of the eucalyptus trees I had planted still grew, perhaps they grow there yet for aught I know, in spite of the fierce winters; though they are never likely to rise to the majestic grandeur they attain in their native Australia. I had thought often enough that Gali Ali Beg would be my grave as it so nearly was the grave of Hay and of Lymington before me. The bones of many a Briton lie in the soil of Mesopotamia; but my lot seems to have been otherwise decreed.

On and out of Gali Ali Beg, winding up through the scrub oak where Ismail Beg was soon to meet his doom, and so past my first camp on Spilik, where mosquitoes and bullets had sung merrily together in the night-time.

There were no labourers to be paid on this section of the road today, nor should I ever direct them again if there were, so I stepped hard on the throttle once more and raced through to Shaqlawah and Arbil without further delay.

Some time after my arrival in Baghdad I ran into Baker, who happened to be in on one of his rare visits to the city. In the course of conversation I mentioned the Assyrians, referring especially to those of my late staff who were now looking for work.

'Oh, that's all right,' he said. 'Tell them to apply to the oil companies for jobs. Those with engineering experience will be needed on the pipe-line that is being built from Kirkuk to the Mediterranean. When it's finished they'll just have to join up with their pals of the demobilized Levies who are wandering like bands of lost souls with your friend Yacu in the Dohuk district. Some say the Assyrians may move across the Tigris into Syria, the idea being that the French may offer the protection we've refused to give.

'Whether it is fortunate or unfortunate for Iraq that we have armed the country—both the Assyrians and the Arabs—with British rifles, it is not for me to say. But it seems strange considering that only a few years ago we were confiscating every rifle we could lay our hands on in order to keep the peace. You know as well as I do that despite all our efforts we have not eradicated racial and religious hatreds in this land. Sooner or later someone is going to get excited, those guns will go off bang, and a whole lot of people will be killed.

'Frankly and in confidence,' he added seriously, 'I don't like the look of it. Time and again I have reported what I believe to be the dangers in the present situation, and others have done so too, but we are not popular at Headquarters, we out-station men with doleful forebodings. They just reply from H.Q. that we take our jobs too seriously or words to that effect.'

A year later.

I was back in England. Like many hundreds of others of my profession I was busy searching Victoria Street, that Mecca of engineers, for new worlds to conquer; in other words, looking for a job. Anything but a cheery business. Kurdish road-makers were not at a premium in Victoria Street in 1933, that year of economic depression.

In the daily fatigue and worry and in the roar and bustle of London's traffic, Iraq and its problems became but a faint memory of a past life; Kurdistan a romantic dream of places that surely never existed and characters which never really lived—Ismail Beg, Sheikh Sayed Taha, Sayed Heusni Effendi, Yacu and the others. And the Assyrians, who were they?

I elbowed my way towards Victoria Station.

'Assyrians!'

The name seemed to come.out of the crowd around me. I stopped dead and was instantly assailed on all sides.

'Taxi? No, thanks, I'll walk. Oh, so sorry, I'll get out of the way. I didn't notice you were running for a train. No, I don't want any balloons.'

Surely I had been dreaming. This was London, not Kurdistan. A newspaper vendor, his boards tied to the railings, shouted lustily:

' 'Ere y'are—all the results. Latest edi-shun. Full account of the races. All the results. Assyrians——'

There was the word again, and it was even on his bill-boards! I bought his papers and scanned the headlines:

ASSYRIANS MASSACRED
IN IRAQ
315 VICTIMS FOUND
PRISONERS SHOT

There has been a massacre of Assyrians near the small town of Simel, forty miles north of Mosul . . . villages full of panic-stricken women and children . . . 14 Assyrian prisoners shot in cold blood . . .

That is a past and unhappy history. The Assyrians have emerged from the fiery furnace into which they were hurled, scorched but still alive, still a racial entity. They are, however, still in Iraq, largely in refugee camps. An attempt indeed, full of promise, was made to provide them, on the banks of the Orontes, with an area suitable for settlement, to whose development the British and French Governments were generously to contribute. Unfortunately, when the French decided to abandon their Mandate over Syria, the tribes in the neighbourhood of the chosen area declared themselves hostile to the scheme, and, consequently, it had to be dropped.

A benefit may, however, yet be wrung from this disappointment. For Britain has again the opportunity to right, within her Empire, a great injustice for which she is largely responsible. British Guiana—a country suggested for settlement by the Assyrians and investigated to that end by the League some two years ago—may perhaps be regarded

31. The Author at the Main Bridge Construction, Rowanduz Gorge, 1929

32. The Lali Callender-Hamilton Bridge, Karun River, Iran, 1951

33. The Mandrare Callender-Hamilton-Paindavoine Bridge,
Madagascar, 1957

as a land neither well-developed, nor wholly suitable for a mountain people; but it is better by far than a refugee camp in Iraq, and it offers a splendid opportunity for opening up a little known and potentially wealthy corner of the Empire, to the joint advantage of Great Britain and her ancient allies.

It remains my fervent hope yet to see my Assyrian friends settled in a peaceful land far from the 'fret and fever' of past tribulations.

Index

226

Index

Index

Index

snakes, 144-5
Soane, Major E. B., 48, 56, 136
Spilik Pass, 57, 59-73, 74-5, 79, 93, 95, 130-2, 187, 209, 211, 223
    military operations at, 62-4
Suayid Beg, 190-1
Suez Canal, 8
Sujan Singh, 110, 121
Sulaimaniyah, 60, 91, 135-8, 164, 188, 203
Surchi tribes, 65, 67-8, 148, 159, 193-4, 209

Tabriz, 54
Taufiq Agha, 195-6
Taylor, Col. G. B. O., R.E., 230
Teheran, 54-5
Tigris, 33, 77
transport of raw materials to Kurdistan, 175
Turkey, 25, 30-2, 48, 62, 112, 151, 153-4, 164, 202, 207, 215

Two Years in Kurdistan (Hay), 189

Ushnu, 111

White-Parsons, Douglas, 230
Wigram, Rev. Dr., 129, 215
Willcocks, Sir William, 57
winch, Trewhella, 176

Yacu Ismail, 92, 153, 155-6, 158, 160, 162, 167-9, 213-17, 219
Yonin, Benjamin, 60, 66, 95, 151, 237
York, Capt. A., 91-2, 108-9, 153, 155-6, 158-60, 163, 167-9, 171-2, 219, 222, 235
Young, Lt.-Col. H. P., *see* York
Younis Effendi, 112-15, 135

Zad, Princess, 52, 58, 157
Zagros mountains, 54, 165

NOTE—With those characters in the book marked (*) in this index I have lost touch, and so have not their permission to give their real names in this edition.

229

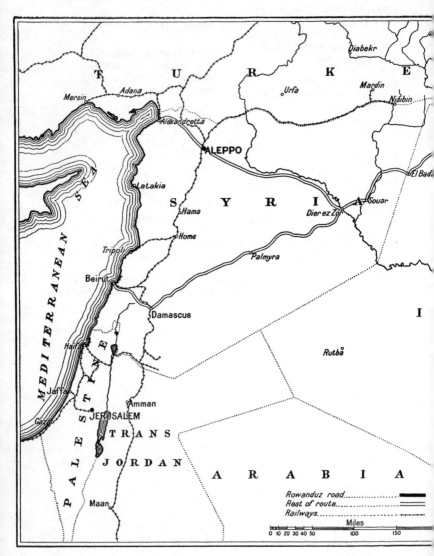

IRAQ AND THE RO

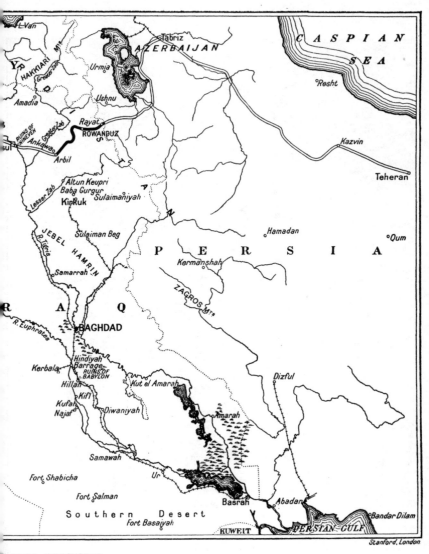

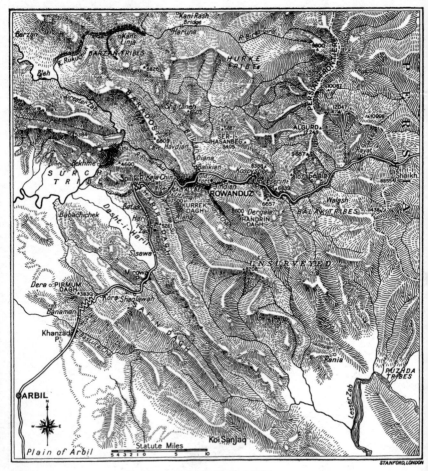

THE ROWANDUZ ROAD